Northwestern

JAY PRIDMORE

NORTHWESTERN
UNIVERSITY

CELEBRATING 150 YEARS

 NORTHWESTERN
UNIVERSITY PRESS 2000

CONTENTS

Library of Congress
Cataloging-in-
Publication Data

Pridmore, Jay.
Northwestern University:
celebrating 150 years/Jay
Pridmore.—1st ed.
p. cm.
Includes index.
ISBN 0-8101-1829-7
1. Northwestern University
(Evanston, Ill.)—History. I.
Title.
LD4048 .P75 2000
378.773'1—dc21
00-008901

First printing
First edition

Produced by Kim Coventry,
Chicago

Designed by studio blue.
Typeset in Bell Gothic, HTF
Acropolis, HTF Leviathan,
and HTF Ziggurat.

Digital captures and color
separations by Professional
Graphics, Rockford, Illinois

Printed on Furioso and case-
bound by Snoeck-Ducaju &
Zoon, Belgium

Jacket front: (Background)
University Hall; (foreground)
students on the steps of Old
College in the 1920s.

Half title: Professor Robert
McLean Cumnock, founder of
the School of Oratory.

Title page: Members of Omega
Upsilon in the 1890s.

Page 6: Members of the class
of 1880 at the Old Oak.

Jacket back: The tower of
Wieboldt Hall.

FOREWORD

The vision of Northwestern University's founders preceded renowned Chicago architect Daniel Burnham by nearly a half-century. Yet his famous advice, *"Make no little plans; they have no magic to stir men's blood,"* exemplifies the ideals on which Northwestern was founded and that continue to this day.

Despite the prosaic location of its origin – a meeting in 1850 of nine men in an unpretentious law office above a hardware store in Chicago – the vision of Northwestern's founders reached far beyond what was then a rough frontier town. Rather than create an institution simply for their city or state, they decreed that the new university should be named for and serve the entire Northwest Territory, a vast region of the still-young country that now includes the states of Ohio, Illinois, Indiana, Michigan, Wisconsin, and a portion of Minnesota. In addition, although firmly grounded in the Methodist faith that united them, the founders created an institution that would welcome students of all faiths in a variety of academic disciplines. Indeed, the resolution passed at one of the earliest board meetings, *"...to make it a University of the highest order of excellence, complete in all of its parts...,"* was startling in its ambition, in part because the University at that time had no students, no faculty, and no money.

What Northwestern University had then, however, and continues to have today, is a willingness and determination to strive for greatness. Northwestern occupies a relatively unusual position in the landscape of American higher education. It is a private university with a strong emphasis on undergraduate teaching coupled with a dedication to research; it offers a broad array of programs across several colleges and schools centered on an education that remains grounded in the liberal arts; and it retains a firmly held belief, just like that of its founders, that Northwestern's ambition and influence should extend beyond its immediate geographical area.

Published on the occasion of Northwestern's 150th anniversary – its sesquicentennial – this history details the vision of Northwestern's founders and many others who have contributed to the University's rise to national prominence. By its very nature, a book such as this cannot be a complete, scholarly examination of the historical record of Northwestern's 150 years. That task remains for another academic colleague – perhaps one who is today helping create Northwestern's continuing history. What this volume can do, however, is recount the rare combination of vision, good fortune, and sheer determination that has made Northwestern the special place it is today.

As important, this history tells some of the many wonderful stories of Northwestern's students, faculty, and others who have contributed to its history. *From the early visionaries who established an institution of "sanctified learning,"* to the stellar faculty who have gained national renown, to the thousands of bright, eager students who have succeeded here and after graduation, Northwestern's history is rich with their stories. Some of these are inspiring, such as that of the drive and determination of Northwestern's 17th president, Walter Dill Scott, who led the University for nearly 20 years through the Great Depression while establishing its Chicago campus. Other tales, such as those of the late 19th-century students who engaged in fierce debates in literary societies, may now seem merely amusing. In their variety, however, the stories exemplify the diverse fabric that makes Northwestern's history so interesting.

As we celebrate our sesquicentennial, we also enter a new millennium, the third century in which Northwestern has been in existence. In the 19th century, Northwestern's founders began the work of creating the University. During the 20th century, that work continued, and a firm financial foundation was laid so the University's academic mission could be pursued vigorously. As we reflect upon Northwestern's remarkable heritage, we now enter the 21st century renewed in the purpose of making Northwestern an institution of the highest order of excellence.

HENRY S. BIENEN
PRESIDENT
NORTHWESTERN UNIVERSITY

EVANSTON, ILLINOIS
SEPTEMBER 2000

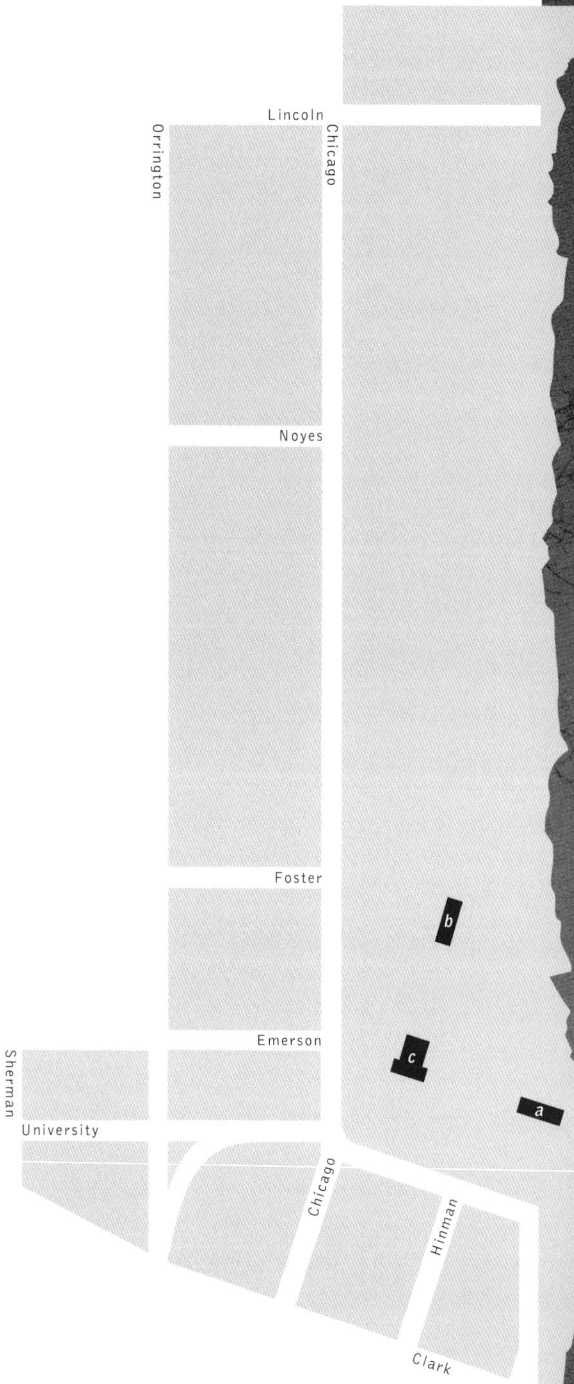

Orrington

Lincoln

Chicago

Noyes

Foster

Emerson

Sherman

University

Chicago

Hinman

Clark

a **Old College** (1855)
Originally located
at the northwest corner
of Davis and Hinman;
moved to campus in 1871
and moved again in
1897. Razed in 1973.

b **Heck Hall** (1867)
Dormitory for Garrett and
later Northwestern
students. Burned in 1914.

c **University Hall** (1869)
Pictured.

b

c

a

NORTHWESTERN'S EVANSTON CAMPUS 1850–1871

*BUILT DURING
THIS PERIOD*

*AT THE START OF
EACH CHAPTER
IS A SCHEMATIC
MAP SHOWING THE
DEVELOPMENT
OF NORTHWESTERN'S
CAMPUSES. THE MAPS
SHOW ONLY THE
MAJOR BUILDINGS
AND STREETS.*

A PLACE FOR SANCTIFIED LEARNING

The idea for Northwestern University came to life on May 31, 1850, when nine good citizens of Chicago met one morning in a simple law office on the second floor of a downtown hardware store. Their aim was to establish an institution of higher education to serve America's vast northwest. Their hope was that Chicago, already a center of commerce for the region, could become a center of learning as well.

The business of founding a university would require patience and organization. But before beginning their work that morning, the men knelt and prayed. This, at least, was how Northwestern's founding was remembered decades later, after the school had achieved a measure of greatness, and after the town that grew around the University was lined with wide-spreading elms and grand oaks. Indeed, a prayer was very much in order, because the founders were all Methodists, and three of them were ministers.

After the invocation, the men got down to business. Attorney Grant Goodrich, who had opened his office for the group, picked up a prepared document and read: "Whereas, the interests of

When the artist J. T. Palmatary created this bird's-eye view of Chicago in 1857, he rendered the city in astonishing detail and with a sense of rectilinear order that was not apparent at street level. Palmatary did capture the character of Lake Michigan, which featured an active harbor and a windward stretch of the lakeshore just north of the river called "the Sands."

Built in 1845, when the congregation moved from a log cabin, the First Methodist Episcopal Church in Chicago at Washington and Clark Streets had the simple look of restrained Protestantism. By 1873, however, the elders noted the Loop's rising land values and replaced the old church with a new one that was combined with a commercial structure.

The life of John Evans (1814–97) was cast in the pioneer's mold. He was born in Ohio and ended his career as an entrepreneur in Colorado, where he also served as territorial governor. He lived in Illinois for fewer than 15 years, but in that time he helped found a university, gave his name to a town, and made a mark on a variety of other fields from medicine to the railroad industry.

sanctified learning require the immediate establishment of a University in the northwest under the patronage of the Methodist Episcopal Church...." Goodrich finished his relatively short statement, which concluded with a resolution to organize such a university, whereupon those present agreed and divided themselves into committees to accomplish that end.

It must have appeared a tall order. Chicago was not then a place of campus-like charm. The streets could turn into a quagmire when it rained and could swallow, it was said, a horse and a man in a single gulp. Nor were its citizens of scholarly stripe. Chicagoans, declared an English traveler not too many years before, were "sharpers of every degree; pedlars [sic], grog-sellers, horse dealers, horse stealers...rogues of every description." Money was being made in Chicago — and was being lost.

But things were improving. By 1850 the town was just 17 years old and had 28,000 residents. Chicago was a crude outpost, to be sure, but already the world knew that it was no geographical accident. The central hub of America's Northwest Territory, a vast region of great future wealth, Chicago had attracted pioneers of ambition and intelligence who were now leading citizens of this celebrated if rough-hewn boomtown.

Dr. John Evans

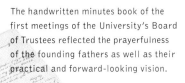

The handwritten minutes book of the first meetings of the University's Board of Trustees reflected the prayerfulness of the founding fathers as well as their practical and forward-looking vision.

Northwestern's founders included several of Chicago's young and ambitious newcomers, some of whom were educated in their professions, but only one of whom had the benefit of what could properly qualify as higher education. That was Dr. John Evans, whose considerable skills as a physician were matched by his gifts as a visionary. Chicago's promise resided in the character of individuals such as Evans, a leader all his career. His influence began with his graduation from Lynn Medical College in Cincinnati in 1839 and his successful medical practice in Attica, Indiana. While there he saw the need for a state mental hospital and developed plans to create one. It required considerable political work to convince the legislature to back this idea. It also occupied several years of Evans's life to direct construction and then run the asylum. But the project was successful and clearly broadened the doctor's ambitions.

As a young man, Evans became a deeply religious Methodist, falling under the influence of revivalist minister (and later Methodist bishop) Matthew Simpson, president of Asbury College, which became DePauw University. Simultaneously, Evans decided that his future was in Chicago, and in 1848 he accepted the chair of the Department of Obstetrics at Rush Medical College. Here he showed himself to be a medical man of distinction, inventing obstetrical instruments (such as forceps with woven silk parts) and understanding before most that the origin of cholera was bacteria and not, as was previously thought, something in limestone bedrock.

Evans's private practice in Chicago quickly prospered, and success enabled him to invest in Chicago's most active commodity, real estate. His first project, the

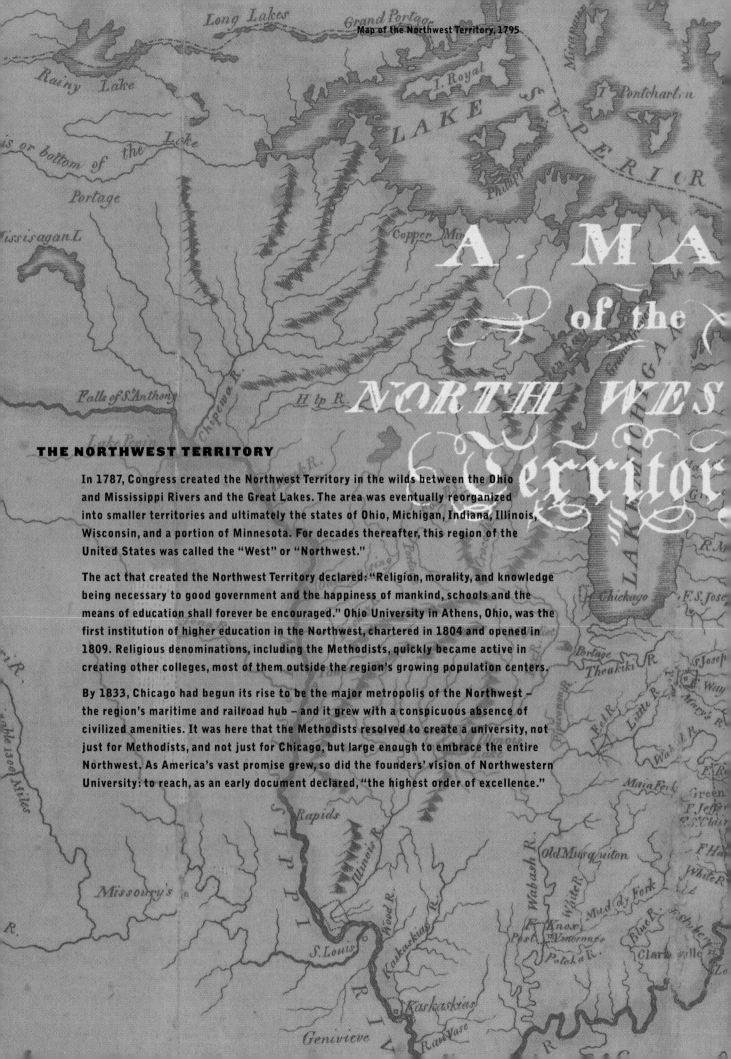

THE NORTHWEST TERRITORY

In 1787, Congress created the Northwest Territory in the wilds between the Ohio and Mississippi Rivers and the Great Lakes. The area was eventually reorganized into smaller territories and ultimately the states of Ohio, Michigan, Indiana, Illinois, Wisconsin, and a portion of Minnesota. For decades thereafter, this region of the United States was called the "West" or "Northwest."

The act that created the Northwest Territory declared: "Religion, morality, and knowledge being necessary to good government and the happiness of mankind, schools and the means of education shall forever be encouraged." Ohio University in Athens, Ohio, was the first institution of higher education in the Northwest, chartered in 1804 and opened in 1809. Religious denominations, including the Methodists, quickly became active in creating other colleges, most of them outside the region's growing population centers.

By 1833, Chicago had begun its rise to be the major metropolis of the Northwest – the region's maritime and railroad hub – and it grew with a conspicuous absence of civilized amenities. It was here that the Methodists resolved to create a university, not just for Methodists, and not just for Chicago, but large enough to embrace the entire Northwest. As America's vast promise grew, so did the founders' vision of Northwestern University: to reach, as an early document declared, "the highest order of excellence."

Evans Block at Clark and Lake Streets near the Chicago River, housed medical offices as well as tenants such as the Chicago post office and the fledgling *Chicago Tribune*. Evans initially had a partner, but he quickly bought him out, acquired more property, built additional buildings, and found that land interests were taking him away from the practice of medicine.

Capitalism did not divert Evans from the work of the Lord, though in Methodism the two were regarded harmoniously. Indeed, Evans's organizational skills made him a central figure in the establishment of the Illinois Hospital of the Lakes, for example. As a one-term alderman, he also pushed for the establishment of public education in Chicago. Later in his career, he worked hard to consolidate the railroads, which secured Chicago's greatness and also earned the doctor a respectable return on his investment.

Thus, Evans was a logical man to involve in plans for a Methodist university. He not only possessed the abundant cash that would be needed for such a cause, but he was also drawn to idealistic and sometimes even quixotic schemes. Evans also could articulate with clarity why others might support a project like Northwestern University. A family living in Chicago, he stated, would save $1,000 by sending a student to a local university instead of shipping him off to Harvard or Yale. That had the ring of a convincing argument – and also an optimistic one, since few Chicagoans were troubled at that moment with the extravagance of trundling children east to college.

The founders' vision

Other founders of Northwestern were likewise conspicuously ambitious and farsighted. Grant Goodrich had become a leading attorney in Chicago since arriving in 1835 from upstate New York, acquiring his skills of persuasion as a circuit-riding lawyer in courthouses throughout northern Illinois. Goodrich exemplified not just the business side of Methodism but the political side as well. He was known as a "violent antislavery man," a sentiment shared not just by fellow churchmen but by Free-Soil Democrats and Whigs in Illinois, among whom was another circuit-riding lawyer named Abraham Lincoln.

Orrington Lunt frequently opened his personal cash box for the University that he loved.

Among the founders of Northwestern, none cut a figure quite so impressive as Orrington Lunt (1815–97), pictured here with his daughter, Cornelia Gray Lunt. He was credited with the "discovery" of Evanston but was too modest to have the town named for him. Lunt was a prosperous Methodist, but after a serious reversal in the grain market, his capitalistic drive was slowed. He remained an institution builder, however, donating funds for Lunt Library and toward the end of his life helping to fill that library with books from his own collection and those of others.

The third of the three principal founders, and the one often noted as the University's most devoted and faithful servant, was Orrington Lunt. Lunt came west from Maine in 1842 and entered the grain market in its formative years. In a trade noted for sharp practices, Lunt was a man farmers could trust. A founder of the Chicago Board of Trade, he quickly made a fortune, although by midcareer he suffered the sobering blow of a speculation gone bad, which inspired him to retire from the increasing rigors of the commodities business. As a result, Northwestern benefited as much from Lunt's time and attention as from his money.

These founders, who were primarily men of worldly affairs, were joined by others like them, such as hardware merchant Jabez Botsford (over whose store Goodrich kept his office); lawyer Andrew Brown, whose family dated back to the time of the *Mayflower* but who endured the hard life of a pioneer before achieving great success in Chicago; and lawyer Henry W. Clark, twice city attorney of Chicago and later secretary of the Illinois Humane Society. Substantial power in this time also resided in the hands of the church, and the founders made sure their ranks included three leading pastors from local Methodist congregations: Richard Blanchard, Richard Haney, and Zadoc Hall.

While the founders' vision of Northwestern was taking form, they found practical strength and direction in their churchly roots. Within weeks of their first meeting they made contact with six regional divisions of the church, or "conferences," and convinced each to send representatives to serve on the Northwestern board — from Michigan, Northern Indiana, Wisconsin, Iowa, and Illinois, as well as from their own newer Rock River Conference in northern Illinois. As these men met and discussed prospects for a major university, they reminded each other of the Methodists' commitment to worldly education. This would hardly be a church school (though some of them were imagining a new seminary as well).

"If our schools were originated only for our own people," said one early Methodist educator, "and afforded little more than instruction in our peculiar views, they would contribute to make us a bigoted sect."

Still, church-related colleges stirred resentment in the state legislature, where an official university charter would have to be passed. Goodrich was fortunately a

Jabez Botsford was a good churchman and prosperous dealer in the hardware business, which was essential to building a new town such as Chicago.

The Methodists had many practical virtues, and being active in publishing was one. Methodists communicated with regularity and at length throughout the United States using denominational newspapers, circulars, and other printed matter. After the idea for Northwestern came from the church's Rock River Conference in northern Illinois, it garnered support in other Methodist conferences and their publications, especially in the Northwest.

Dempster Hall, the first building of the Garrett Biblical Institute, was built in 1854 near the site of the present-day seminary on Sheridan Road. The building was sold to Northwestern when Garrett's Heck Hall was completed in 1867. Dempster Hall burned to the ground in 1879.

GRANT GOODRICH (1812–89)

Making good in early Chicago required an ardent will as well as a practical sense of doing business, and Northwestern founder Grant Goodrich made very good indeed. He arrived in Chicago in 1834 after studying law near Buffalo, New York. Goodrich became a devout Methodist in his early years, and while upstate New York was a hotbed of the religious revival movement, Chicago and the West represented a place where individuals could make a career and leave a spiritual mark.

Goodrich became Chicago's "Methodist lawyer," with his religion aiding his legal practice and his legal knowledge aiding his church. Goodrich was a founder of the First Methodist Episcopal Church in Chicago, a strong temperance crusader, and an organizer of the Chicago Bible Society, which collected money and purchased Bibles to put in the hands of people who might not otherwise have them.

He moved naturally into secular politics as well, becoming a Chicago alderman and a party organizer, first for the Whigs and later the Republicans. He had violent antislavery sentiments, which he shared with a friend and downstate lawyer, Abraham Lincoln.

Thus, Goodrich became the natural person to put forward the idea of Northwestern University. He called the first meeting of the founders in his office. He framed the charter and engineered its passage in the state legislature.

No one could bring a plan or even fond hope to fruition quite like Goodrich. After Northwestern was created, he persuaded Mrs. Eliza Garrett to fund a new Methodist seminary, Garrett Biblical Institute, which was named for her late husband, Augustus Garrett, a former mayor of Chicago. Religious belief and political skill also brought to completion the amendment to Northwestern's charter prohibiting the sale of alcohol within four miles of the University and exempting the University from property tax forever.

Grant Goodrich

familiar figure in Springfield, where the lawyer pressed the cause by pointing out that Chicago's closest institution of higher education was Knox College in faraway Galesburg. Goodrich also called on his political allies in the legislature, many of whom shared his ardor on the slavery question. All of that resulted in a charter for "The North Western University," passed in the first session of the new year's General Assembly and signed by Governor Augustus French on January 28, 1851.

News of the Methodists' plans drew considerable interest in the Chicago community, naturally enough; a favorable report in the *Chicago Tribune* brought an important visitor to Evans's office one morning. Ferdinand W. Peck, Chicago's leading real estate dealer, had a proposition – that Northwestern buy land at the northeast corner of LaSalle and Jackson Streets. Evans listened politely to Peck but pointed out that talk of property seemed premature.

"We haven't a red cent," Evans said. "We have been doing the wind work." This was the doctor's way of saying that Northwestern consisted mostly of talk and good intentions.

"I'll sell you cheap and give you time to pay," Peck countered. And Evans, who knew a bargain when it came to real estate, nodded and went out to find the money: $2,000 for a down payment on 16 lots; $6,000 to be paid off in the next three years. Whether or not the new university would be located there – rumors of a red-light district nearby created doubts – the transaction was one that a true Chicagoan could only love. Land values had appreciated in downtown Chicago for nearly 20 years and promised to rise for a long time to come.

The first president

With both a charter and a mortgage in hand, the next challenge was to select a full-time president. A detailed job description was lacking, but a forceful and decisive figure soon presented himself. The Reverend Clark T. Hinman, then president of Albion Female College, first joined Northwestern as a trustee representing the Michigan Conference. When the founders met him, Hinman seemed well suited to the organizational work of a school that waxed ambitious but still needed to somehow attract teachers, develop courses, and find students.

Hinman, a graduate of the nation's largest Methodist institution of higher education, Wesleyan University in Connecticut, matched and in some ways surpassed the boldness of the founders. Legend has it that he settled the question of

The Reverend Clark Titus Hinman (1819–54), first president of Northwestern University, had a great impact on the institution, although he died before a single student was enrolled. He is credited with insisting that the new University be located not in Chicago but well outside so that it could grow unencumbered. He promoted Northwestern tirelessly in his short tenure, selling perpetual scholarships and advancing the cause. He died of exhaustion and "complication of diseases" in service to the institution that lived and flourished after his death.

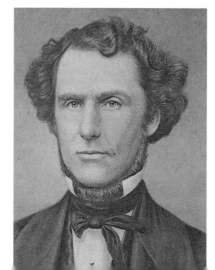

Northwestern's location before he even accepted the post, bridling when informed that the board was inclined to build on the Chicago lots and begin the University with a prep school. "But our idea was that you were going to build a university for the Northwest," Hinman told Evans. Go outside the city, he said. Keep the lots in Chicago, but find land with space to grow. Evans agreed, and Hinman was hired.

There can be little doubt that Evans had similar thoughts all along. He certainly knew, for example, that the railroads were opening great tracts of previously remote real estate. Evans later recalled, too, that he discussed the Northwestern plan with his friend Walter S. Gurnee, president of the as-yet-unbuilt Chicago & Milwaukee Railway. Evans inquired if the new line might pass through a settlement known as Ridgeville, and Gurnee indicated that it would. Ridgeville was the outpost that became Evanston, and Evans's farsightedness turned out to be crucial for the future of Northwestern.

The "discovery" of Evanston

As the years passed and Evanston grew, another version of the "discovery" of Northwestern's location took hold. The story involved a trip to the north made by Orrington Lunt just as the University's trustees were close to purchasing land in Jefferson Park, nearer to the city and on an existing northwest rail line. Perhaps Lunt was unsure about Jefferson Park. Perhaps he was on a pleasure trip. But what he noticed on a stretch of Lake Michigan shore 12 miles from the city enchanted him. Here, close to the remote settlement of Ridgeville, the marshes to the south changed to the high bluffs and hardwoods of the North Shore.

"The thought first struck me that this is where the high and dry ground began," Lunt said. "It continued in my dreams that night and I could not rid myself of the fairy visions constantly presenting themselves in fanciful beauties – of the gentle waving lake – its pebbly shore – the beautiful oak openings and bluffs beyond."

Lunt returned to the committee responsible for selecting a site. "We drove into what is the present campus, and it was just as beautiful as now in its natural condition. We were delighted – some of the brethren threw up their hats – we had found the place."

Although Lunt's story has the ring of fancy, it is one of many turns in early Northwestern history that combine the conduct of practical commerce – specifically real estate – with revels born of deep conviction. In fact, the acquisition of valuable and seemingly enchanted property was fundamental to Northwestern's future, though before land could be purchased, another capitalist, Dr. John Foster, entered the story.

Foster owned the 360 acres that Lunt, Evans, and the other founders desired, but he made it clear that he would not sell it "for any human price." A physician as well as a land speculator, Foster had plans, he said, to establish a female academy on the land. Only when Evans described their educational idea in great and sometimes passionate detail did Foster relent, though he set a high price for the undeveloped land: $25,000. Foster offered the terms of $1,000 down and 10 years to pay the rest. "We took it," said Evans, who made the down payment in October 1853 and provided his personal guarantee for the balance.

North-Western University (as it would be called for the remainder of the 1850s) now possessed a president, a location, and soon-to-be valuable assets. As a next step, the trustees hired a business manager to direct the finances of the new institution in a suitable manner. And in the Methodist tradition, they found someone who had one foot in the church and the other in the everyday conduct of commerce. The person they chose was the Reverend Philo Judson, who helped survey Evanston and promote the sale of lots to businessmen and professionals from Chicago who might commute by train.

This was the beginning of Evanston, which was named, according to tradition, when the modest Orrington Lunt declined to have the town named for him and deferred to his brother-in-law, John Evans. Others referred to it as the "sanctified town," created by Methodists who were tolerant of other denominations but also distinctly frosty toward behavior less than Christian in nature.

Evanston's pious dignity was not only bred in the bone but was legislated by the University's trustees, who in 1855 sent an amendment to their original charter to Springfield, which with legislative passage would prohibit the manufacture or sale of "spirituous, vinous or fermented liquors within four miles of the location of the said University."

In fact, this required some of Grant Goodrich's old political magic, as the "wets" and "drys" had been doing battle in Springfield for years. He engineered a compromise that the act "may be repealed by the general assembly whenever they think proper."

Far less debate was expended on another section of the 1855 amendment to Northwestern's charter: a sentence that stipulated that "all property of what ever kind or description, belonging to or owned by said corporation, shall be forever free from taxation for any kind and all purposes."

While Northwestern appeared to have the makings of a great university, with wealthy and sincere trustees and a scholarly president trained in the East, a dreadful setback took place in 1854 with the death of Clark Hinman. He died while doing precisely what the University needed – traveling the region,

The golden-tongued Randolph Sinks Foster (1820–1903) assumed the presidency of Northwestern in 1856. A fervent Methodist preacher, he maintained the spiritual tone of Northwestern when the trustees were convinced that spiritual guidance would enable the institution to overcome all obstacles. Foster was an indifferent businessman, however, and Northwestern continued to be seriously in the red. In 1860 he returned to the pulpit.

John Foster inherited his Ridgeville farm from his late brother, a veteran who had received the land as a bounty payment for services rendered in the Black Hawk War. Foster agreed to sell because he deemed the University's cause a worthy one, but he sold at a price that suggested he knew the value of North Shore property.

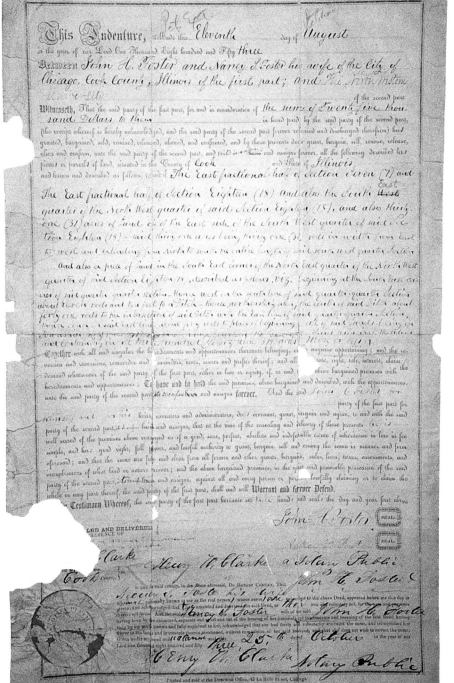

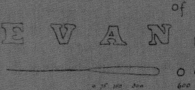

This map of Evanston, created by Philo Judson in 1853–54, platted the land that Northwestern had purchased from Dr. John Foster. It is the first map to use the name Evanston.

THE REVEREND PHILO JUDSON (1807-76)

The Methodist Church valued individuals of both piety and managerial prowess, and Philo Judson, the University's first business manager, stood as a Methodist of the highest stature. A native of upstate New York, Judson came to the pastorate at the age of 30, then migrated to Illinois where he served various churches of the Rock River Conference, including Chicago's First Methodist Episcopal. In 1852 Judson was called to perform the duties of business agent for the fledgling Northwestern University.

It fell to Judson to supervise the survey and platting of the Foster farm, which had been purchased by the University. Judson then undertook the dual responsibility of raising money for Northwestern through land sales and of creating a town that fulfilled the Methodists' dreams. He opened the first dry goods store in Evanston; he also executed deeds and leases, many with the permanent stipulation that consumption (in addition to the manufacture or sale) of alcohol on said property would return its control to the University.

Judson's career continued to be active and colorful. He was involved in the establishment of the village of Glencoe and helped incorporate Rosehill Cemetery (where he now rests). During the Civil War, Judson joined his son-in-law, Captain (and later General) John Beveridge, in Company F of the 8th Illinois Cavalry, one of the few Illinois units to fight at Gettysburg. With the aging Judson as chaplain, the 8th Illinois distinguished itself as one of the first Union units to repulse the Rebels' initial attack on Gettysburg's Seminary Ridge.

Philo Judson

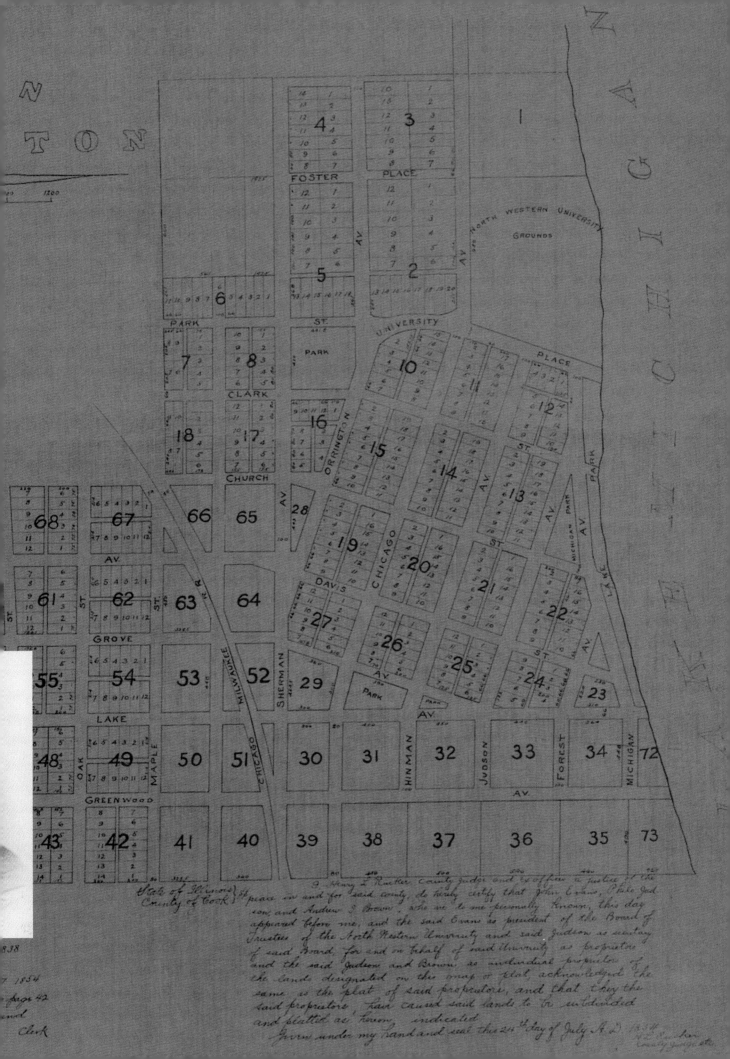

talking up the new institution, and selling what would be Northwestern's first substantial source of revenue, "perpetual scholarships," or contracts to enroll lineal descendants of purchasers free of tuition, in perpetuity.

Northwestern's modest beginnings

Without a president but marching bravely forth, the new university had but one more prerequisite before it could accept students. That was a building, and to build one Northwestern hired Chicago's most experienced architect, John Mills Van Osdel.

Van Osdel later designed elaborate hotels such as the first Palmer House and the Tremont Hotel in Chicago. At this stage in his career, however, his style was not one of grandeur; it was getting sturdy buildings built with boomtown speed. Van Osdel was an expert in the new technology of balloon-frame structures – using light studs and joists, not heavy posts and beams – that some architectural historians believe was invented in Chicago precisely because it was sturdy and fast.

With plans to open the school in the fall of 1855, Northwestern scheduled its cornerstone ceremony for June 15 of that year. In fact, scheduling the fete was premature, as the foundation was not ready for the cornerstone. But the founders kept the date because it was also the day of Garrett Biblical Institute's formal inaugural ceremonies. Garrett was the Methodist seminary founded the year before when lawyer Goodrich had induced the widow of former Chicago Mayor Augustus Garrett to fund it and Dr. John Dempster, a well-known Methodist theologian, to serve as its first president.

Garrett had a frame building on the north edge of the Northwestern property, and for the ceremony, "the elite and literary cream of Chicago society came out by train and carriage," according to one newspaper that covered the festivities.

"Festivities" might be a misnomer, because the day began with a two-hour address by a Methodist dignitary, followed by more of the same. So when attendees walked from Garrett to Northwestern's building site at Davis and Hinman Streets, it must have been a pleasant diversion. There was no cornerstone, but Bishop Matthew Simpson, Evans's fiery Methodist mentor, joined several trustees who spoke about the future of this soon-to-be-great university.

Later that summer, the foundation was completed, and carpenters set to work cutting and nailing a boatload of pinewood shipped in to Evanston from Michigan. Frugal as ever, the Methodists found this to be the most economical way to purchase building materials, but it was hardly the easiest method, as Evanston had no dock at that time. To get the cargo ashore, deckhands tossed the lumber overboard, and local farmers hauled it up to the beach board by board.

That fall the University Building was complete, but the cream of society did not rush back to Evanston for the opening of Northwestern, which went relatively uncelebrated on November 5, 1855. Convocation exercises remained modest, beginning naturally with a prayer. Events were remembered as "quite colorless." Evans,

THE UNIVERSITY'S FIRST CHICAGO PROPERTY

Northwestern's first property acquisition was arguably its best in terms of appreciation on the investment. The University's 16 downtown lots at the corner of LaSalle and Jackson Streets, purchased for $8,000 in 1852, were never used for educational purposes. Rents from the Grand Pacific Hotel, which leased the land, had risen to $53,000 yearly by 1896, when the hotel went out of business and was razed.

LaSalle and Jackson was still prime real estate, fortunately, and when the Illinois Trust Safety Deposit Company leased the property to build a grand neoclassical bank building in 1897, rent for the land was $70,000 yearly, and escalators were built in for the first 30 years of the 99-year lease. Upon expiration of the contract in 1996, the land was sold outright to Bank of America, which had succeeded Continental Bank and Trust as the building's occupant a few years before.

The Grand Pacific Hotel, built in 1870.

CIRCULAR.

NORTH-WESTERN UNIVERSITY,

EVANSTON, COOK COUNTY, ILLINOIS.

JOHN EVANS, M. D.,   *President Board of Trustees.*
REV. P. JUDSON,   *Financial Agent.*

FACULTY.

REV. R. S. FOSTER, D. D.,   *Pres. and Prof. of Mor. Phil. and Logic.*
REV. ABEL STEVENS, LL. D.,   *Prof. Rhetoric and English Literature.*
J. V. Z. BLANEY, M. D.,   *Prof. Natural Sciences.*
HENRY S. NOYES, A. M.,   *Prof. of Mathematics.*
REV. W. D. GODMAN, A. M.,   *Prof. of Greek,—Secretary.*
DANIEL BONBRIGHT, A. M.,   *Prof. of Latin,—(in Europe.)*
ROBERT KENNICOTT,   *Curator of Museum, (now engaged in collecting specimens.)*

THE NEW BUILDING.

The Trustees, at their late session, resolved to proceed to the erection of a new and permanent building as soon as plans are adopted.

GENERAL INFORMATION.

The University has had, during the last Academic year, two classes, Freshman and Sophomore, total number nineteen. No preparatory department. For the next year, 1857-8, we shall have *three* Collegiate classes. The fourth, or *senior*, class will be organized if applications are made and satisfactory examinations passed. An *Academic School*, or *Grammar School*, will be opened by a competent person, *on his own responsibility*, in the present College building, which is but temporary, for the University. In this Academic School all the preparatory branches of study will be taught, and those who are *prepared in part* for the Collegiate course will be allowed *to recite with the University classes.*

There are two courses of study, each embracing *four* years, viz.: The *Classical*, or Regular Course, and the *Scientific* Course. *The majority of young men who have attended the higher Common Schools will be prepared to enter the Scientific Department.* The entire courses of study will be published hereafter.

By 1856, "North-Western University" was sufficiently well established to publish its first circular. Admission was limited to students 14 and older, and knowledge of Greek and Latin was required. Students could choose either a scientific or a classical course. Tuition was $45 per year, and living expenses were $2.50 to $3 per week.

Henry Sanborn Noyes (1822–72) came to Northwestern to teach, not administer, but when he arrived in 1855 the Northwestern presidency was vacant, and he was made acting head of the school. Noyes held up well, though he was definitely overworked. He helped survey the land, engineered drainage ditches, taught mathematics, listened to Greek recitations, and traveled to sell perpetual scholarships to families living a long ride from Evanston.

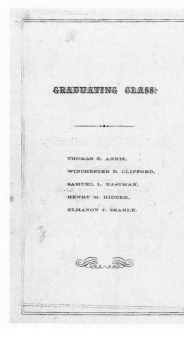

GRADUATING CLASS.

THOMAS E. ANNIS,
WINCHESTER E. CLIFFORD,
SAMUEL L. EASTMAN,
HENRY M. KIDDER,
ELHANON J. SEARLE.

Lunt, and Goodrich were on hand. Some brief remarks were made on the steps of the building and were heard by a few townspeople, including the innkeeper, whose business stood to increase. Also in attendance was an "eccentric man by the name of Wilbur," whose eccentricities were left unstated in a written report of the day.

The faithful faculty

In the absence of a president, Northwestern opened with two professors – William Godman, classics, and Henry Sanborn Noyes, mathematics, who was acting president and who took charge of greeting students and ascertaining their readiness for university work. Although Northwestern was receiving good notices in the church press, just five students arrived on the first day of school.

It may have felt like a poor start to Noyes, who left the principalship of Newbury Seminary in Vermont to teach at Northwestern. Newbury was an established and reputable secondary school where Hinman had served and met Noyes some years earlier.

Noyes, who was in his early 30s, had left Newbury precisely so that he could teach and unburden himself of administrative duties. Now the University had hardly opened, and he was the head man with more problems than students. But it was Northwestern's fortune that Noyes possessed energy and concentration. Besides teaching, he often set out on horseback, traveling the area around Evanston and northern Illinois selling perpetual scholarships. As a mathematician, he helped survey Evanston, preparing parcels for sale or lease, which was the school's primary source of income. He also reported to trustees on University finances, a dismal task that revealed that his own salary, $1,500 yearly, would be paid with less than perfect regularity.

"Loyalty to the University characterized every act and thought" of the acting president, according to **Arthur Herbert Wilde, who edited the University's first history in 1905.**

There was hardly any task that did not fall Noyes's way – and often two or three of them fell at a time. One early student remembered that Noyes could listen to Greek recitations while composing letters related to school administration. He simultaneously maintained classroom decorum, casting a doleful, even wounded glance at any perpetrator of mischief and quickly returning order to the proceedings.

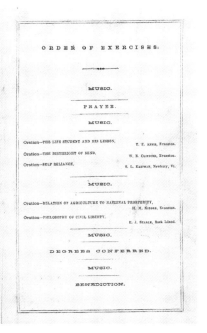

ORDER OF EXERCISES:

MUSIC.

PRAYER.

MUSIC.

Oration—THE LIFE STUDENT AND HIS LESSON.
T. E. Annis, Evanston.
Oration—THE BIRTHRIGHT OF MIND.
W. R. Clifford, Evanston.
Oration—SELF RELIANCE.
S. L. Eastman, Newbury, Vt.

MUSIC.

Oration—RELATION OF AGRICULTURE TO NATIONAL PROSPERITY.
H. M. Kidder, Evanston.
Oration—PHILOSOPHY OF CIVIL LIBERTY.
E. J. Searle, Rock Island.

MUSIC.

DEGREES CONFERRED.

MUSIC.

BENEDICTION.

Northwestern's first class graduated in June 1859. Student orations for the occasion were of an academic nature, but the remarks of Dr. John Evans, president of the Board of Trustees, were more immediate. "Will the foundation of the University, which if wisely managed must yield its magnificent revenue, be held sacred or squandered?" he intoned. "It is also asked: Will those permanent buildings be erected?" With the help of Providence, Evans said, they would.

Before the end of the first year, as many as 20 students enrolled at Northwestern, and within a year or so, additional teachers were hired. Among the newcomers was Professor Daniel Bonbright, who would remain at the University for 58 years. "Dr. Bonbright brought to his teaching a peculiar flavor of intimacy with the Latin authors," wrote a student some years later. "Through him, the Latin authors lived in almost visible presence before his pupils. He used to walk to the window, and, standing with his hands behind him, look out — I verily believe! — over the fields and plains of Italy. At such times I used to have a strange feeling that the spirit of the old poet had become reincarnate in him."

Another early professor was James Blaney, a graduate of Princeton and Jefferson Medical College in Philadelphia, who was teaching at Rush Medical College when he was spied by Evans. Blaney agreed to divide his time between Rush and Northwestern. He moved to Evanston, where he cultivated the town's finest garden. The doctor's approach to "the wondrous ways of God," as pious scholars described scientific theory at the time, was enhanced, according to one student, by his presumably discreet demonstrations of the processes connected with the fermentation and distillation of substances such as good wine brandy.

Progress through hard times

The nation's economic panic of 1857 put the University in fiscal straits for several years, a condition that the trustees aggravated that year when they chose Dr. Randolph S. Foster, previously pastor at Trinity Methodist Episcopal Church in New York City, as the next president. A golden-tongued orator, Foster could sell the splendors of salvation peerlessly. He could not, however, sell perpetual scholarships with zeal, nor did he have an aptitude for closing real estate deals.

Another obstacle faced by the early University was the paucity of students in and around Chicago who were ready to undertake higher-level academic work. Thus, the faculty formally recommended that the trustees establish a preparatory department, or secondary school, "as the majority of young men, within the limits of our prospective patronage, are not prepared for the college course." While the trustees initially balked at this (their vision was for a university and not a high school), the Preparatory School was established in 1859, and it was a success.

The University Building, as it was called in 1855 when it was built at Hinman and Davis Streets, was moved once in 1871 to the present campus and again in 1897 to the area just north of Fisk Hall. Later called Old College, it housed the Preparatory School and had a variety of uses until it was torn down in 1973.

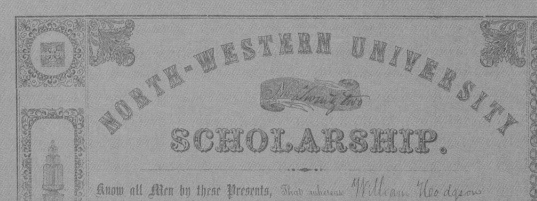

PERPETUAL SCHOLARSHIPS

Perpetual scholarships to Northwestern were sold from 1853 to 1867. In return for the $100 contract, the buyer was entitled to free tuition for sons and all other male direct descendants in perpetuity, limited to one student per generation and to bearers inheriting the contract by specific provision in a will.

Northwestern has always honored its perpetual scholarships and even replaced a number of scholarship documents that were lost in the Chicago Fire. In fact, Northwestern probably enjoyed a net gain on the contract – selling 1,161 scholarship bonds and issuing only 341 scholarships as of 1959. Since then, a few additional scholarships have appeared for redemption.

The Evanston area was not empty in 1855 when Northwestern arrived. There had been Potawatomi settlements prior to 1833, when the government moved the last Native Americans from the area. For years after the founding of Evanston, rugged pioneer families lived and farmed here and occasionally waved pitchforks and clubs against public works projects, which to them promised little in comfort but assured the payment of taxes.

Methodist theologian Dr. John Dempster bought land in Evanston after accepting the presidency of the Garrett Biblical Institute, and he quickly built several houses near what is now Garrett Place. Dempster lived in this comfortable but simple home until he left Evanston in 1857 to found another Methodist haven, Oreapolis, Nebraska, which failed to attract enough students and residents to survive.

An outing by horse-drawn sleigh in downtown Evanston, circa 1880.

Evanston had several connections to Chicago – rail and steamship being the most comfortable. But wagon transport was still using the slow and less-than-modern road along the old ridge when this photo was taken in 1878.

"Prep" had 50 students in its first class, and its enrollment outpaced that of the rest of the University for several years.

Although most prep students came at the age of 12 or 13 with meager skills, the training was rigorous, particularly in Greek and Latin. Early faculty members were graduates of Northwestern and Garrett, and one of the early principals was a German, Louis Kistler. Classicists, especially German classicists, were rarely noted for humor, but Herr Kistler sometimes allowed his lighter side to show. During roll call one morning, for example, the name of a new student called "Beans" triggered barely muffled laughter among the older boys, to which the principal responded, "It's better to be Beans than not to know beans," which solved the problem at once.

Memories of early Evanston

Life in Evanston in the 1860s, where residents were moderately affluent, religious, and shared a concern for the University, was peaceful and usually dignified. From the time the town was settled and the train ran through, business types from Chicago built homes in a variety of architectural styles. Italianate villas were most popular among the early commuter class even before proper streets were cleared and paved. Early memories were of prosperous lawyers and merchants trudging over beaten paths to the train station, holding lanterns before dawn, and leaving the lanterns at the station to light the way home after work.

Improvements came, but they were sometimes resisted. Tensions brewed in those first years when Evanston's Drainage Commission set pick and shovel to the

Scene 1878. J. J. Lutz one of the group

old road toward Chicago, normally a quagmire. This work agitated the "big woods people," residents who had lived west of Evanston before Northwestern moved in and who opposed anything suggesting a public assessment. This time they marched to the work site with clubs and pitchforks and threatened violence against the engineer in charge, who nevertheless "was firm and held to his purpose," according to a Northwestern official, and Ridge Avenue was made permanently passable.

Mostly, Evanston was peaceful and sober – so much so that Abraham Lincoln wanted to skip a scheduled visit during his presidential campaign in 1860. Perhaps tired, the candidate told a friend he had little desire to socialize with "a lot of college professors and others, all strangers to me."

Lincoln warmed up to Evanston, however. The town had wealth and learning, but its Methodists also had antislavery fever. There were even rumors that Evanston was a stop on the Underground Railroad, and that John Evans himself was a "conductor," helping runaway slaves en route to Canada.

Northwestern and the Civil War

Evanston and Northwestern were prepared for the rigors of the Civil War when it came. The day after the Confederates took Fort Sumter, town fathers called a "war meeting" at the Methodist Church, where the preacher made an impassioned call to arms. In response, a highly motivated group of Northwestern students started for Chicago to enlist. Too late for the evening train, they set out on foot and by horse. Since Chicago's quota was already filled, the students were sent home, but they were quick to form drill teams on campus to prepare for the war they presumed would last a few months.

One of Evanston's earliest structures, the Round House, resembled a Midwestern round barn, a masterpiece of efficiency and wind resistance in its day. It was built near present-day Garrett Place with boards recovered from a wrecked lumber schooner. It served as a dormitory for Garrett students and later as a wayside inn. From the beginning, it was said to be haunted by the ghosts of lost sailors. The Round House was torn down in 1899.

Of the 59 Northwestern students and faculty members who eventually
went to war, at least two fought for the Confederacy, hardly a popular position in
Evanston or at the University. Before the war, campus literary societies had
conducted polite debates on secession and slavery. But as the war brewed, ardor
replaced measured discourse on the University campus. When a student from
Baltimore interrupted an otherwise patriotic discussion by yelling, "Down with the
Stars and Stripes," he was taking his safety into his own hands. "To the lake
with him!" cried a loyal Union man, and most of the student body seemed willing
to dunk the Rebel when a faculty member intervened, averting violence.

Seven Northwestern men died in the Civil War, including Alphonso Clark
Linn, class of 1860 and a teacher at the Preparatory School. Linn was a captain
in the University Guards, a company of unseasoned undergrads who trained on
campus and then enlisted to man Union garrisons behind battle lines. This was
considered light duty that would release experienced soldiers to fight. But hazards
were everywhere, and Linn became a casualty when he died of typhoid in Kentucky.

Solid purpose and good limestone

The University came through the Civil War with a new sense of purpose, which
was made manifest when the cornerstone for University Hall was laid in 1868.
Trustees assembled $125,000 for the new main school building, mostly through
the continued sale of lots on the old Foster farm and through a bank loan.

Students rarely regard war
with indifference, and in
the Civil War, Northwestern
students were eager to serve.
In 1864, Alphonso Linn,
class of 1860 and then a mathematics and Latin instructor
in the Preparatory School,
raised a company of students
and trained them on campus.
Captain Linn died of typhoid
fever in Kentucky. He was
one of seven Northwestern
men to die in the war.

Veterans of the Civil War were still being
honored decades after the conflict ended.
At Northwestern, the class of 1905
placed this cannon as a monument to the
University students who served in the war
that ended slavery. The cannon remained
on campus until 1942, when it was recycled
in a World War II scrap metal drive.

In 1875 the town of Evanston had grown, but the campus was still largely undeveloped. This stereopticon view from University Hall was made by Chicago's most prominent photographer of the period, Alexander Hesler.

University Hall, initially considered large and ample, was quickly filled with classrooms, laboratories, and the University Museum. Its Victorian Gothic profile impressed the outside world – at least Chicagoans – as one of the finest university structures in the United States at the time.

President Erastus Otis Haven (1820–81) accepted the presidency of Northwestern in 1869, coming from the University of Michigan with the understanding that Northwestern would enroll and educate women as well as men. Coeducation was quickly established, but, almost as quickly, Haven returned to Michigan, which had something Northwestern lacked: a solvent treasury.

The architect of the new building was Chicago's Gurdon P. Randall, although credit for its design went to Professor Bonbright. If University Hall resembles a fortress in any way, this might be attributed to an event during Bonbright's days at Yale. The story is that students and townspeople were embroiled in a violent interlude, and the New Haven citizenry had actually trained a cannon on the college and were ready to fire. Heroically, Bonbright broke through enemy lines and disabled the weapon. At any rate, University Hall's heavily rusticated Victorian Gothic style, with towers and turrets, was in keeping with the fashion of the time. In the spirit of John Ruskin, the nobility of medieval craftsmanship was in high repute, and good limestone, known as Lemont stone, was available southwest of the city.

The completion of University Hall in 1869 was a milestone, affirming the hopes and dreams of Methodists and Evanstonians. The Chicago papers were favorably impressed as well. The site with trees curving down toward the shore was called an "eyebrow of beauty" in the language of Indians who once lived there, according to the *Chicago Republican*. University Hall "compared favorably with any university building in the land," wrote the *Chicago Tribune*.

Students of academic distinction organized the Northwestern Chapter of Phi Beta Kappa in 1889. Qualified members of past graduating classes were initiated at that time, and one of the oldest initiates was James W. Haney, class of 1861. Haney was a Methodist minister in central Illinois and served as a Northwestern trustee from 1878 until his death in 1900.

Quaecumque Sunt Vera is emblazoned on the Northwestern University seal, created for use on letters and documents and approved in its fully evolved form in 1891. Knowing its translation from the Latin and its source – "Whatsoever things are true…" (Philippians 4:8) – separates seasoned Northwesterners from neophytes. Less well known is the Greek quotation on the open book: "The Word…full of grace and truth" (John 1:14).

35

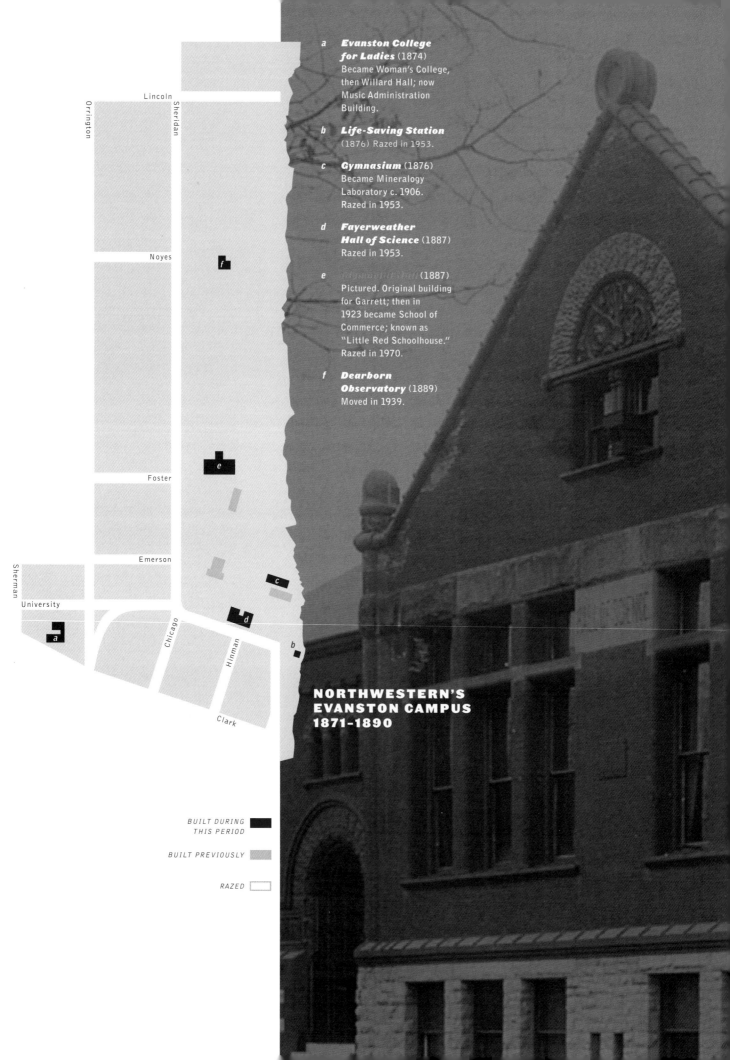

a **Evanston College for Ladies** (1874) Became Woman's College, then Willard Hall; now Music Administration Building.

b **Life-Saving Station** (1876) Razed in 1953.

c **Gymnasium** (1876) Became Mineralogy Laboratory c. 1906. Razed in 1953.

d **Fayerweather Hall of Science** (1887) Razed in 1953.

e **Heck Hall** (1887) Pictured. Original building for Garrett; then in 1923 became School of Commerce; known as "Little Red Schoolhouse." Razed in 1970.

f **Dearborn Observatory** (1889) Moved in 1939.

Lincoln
Orrington
Sheridan
Noyes
Foster
Emerson
Sherman
University
Chicago
Hinman
Clark

NORTHWESTERN'S EVANSTON CAMPUS 1871–1890

BUILT DURING THIS PERIOD

BUILT PREVIOUSLY

RAZED

CONSTRUCTION AND COEDUCATION

In 1871 Evanston witnessed a powerful demonstration that an act of God could alter lives and history. On October 8 of that year, the Great Chicago Fire changed everything. Within two days of the conflagration, it was obvious that Evanston would no longer be a backwater but a place that would grow whether old-timers liked it or not.

The fire was still burning when young Frederick French sat on the roof of his father's house on Hinman Avenue near downtown Evanston and watched "what seemed to be an endless funeral procession.... In many of the carriages all the available space was used for family heirlooms, gold and silver; strapped on top of the vehicles were much-prized family portraits," he wrote in a memoir years later.

Hundreds of Chicagoans left homeless by the fire chose Evanston and were "learning, now, how much cleaner and more quiet and pleasant our village is than the city," according to the inaugural issue of the *Evanston Index*, published in 1872. The mere fact that Evanston could support a daily newspaper was evidence of its tremendous growth.

Some older Evanstonians, of course, preferred the idyllic town as it was, before gas lamps illuminated the houses and streets. But new Evanstonians included Orrington Lunt, hardly an arriviste, who finally left Chicago and purchased a mansion on Judson Avenue. By the summer of 1872, the Evanston pier was unloading lumber by the boatload for the construction of large houses in the Victorian style of the day.

Evanston's educated women

Another sign of the times was the changing role of women. Already, Evanston was a place that valued their contributions; as the town grew in those early years, there was never any question but that the women bore the difficulties of pioneer life – this included faculty wives such as Mrs. Noyes and Mrs. Godman – equally with the men.

It was natural, therefore, that women should seek a college education, though this subject sometimes generated debate focusing on the separate spheres of men and women. The Civil War represented a turning point for the question, largely due to the importance of women in battle hospitals and on the home front. By the end of the war – and once the abolition of slavery was accomplished – there was little doubt that female aspirations for education, among other rights and privileges, would make a deep mark on society at large.

Almost from its founding, Evanston had a college for women, but the situation was not perfect. North-Western Female College had opened in 1855 and quickly flourished, largely because it was a rare civilizing influence for the town.

But the Female College rankled certain members of the community – and particularly the University's founders – since it was unrelated to the true Northwestern except in choice of name.

The Female College founders, William P. and J. Wesley Jones, were wily entrepreneurs; Wesley boasted of a past as an Indian fighter, gold miner, and early photographer. Believing that they could ride along with the success of the men's college, the Joneses certainly understood the growing middle-class fashion for educating women.

The Jones brothers purchased property at Greenwood and Chicago Avenues shortly after Northwestern chose Evanston as the location for the University, and they began raising money (largely by selling Wesley's daguerreotypes of the Western frontier) in order to build. By 1856, the North-Western Female College, which also included a preparatory school for boys, had an enrollment of 84 students. These numbers were a distinct irritation to the founders of the University, who were struggling to keep 20 students on their rolls.

William Jones, president of the college, was not particularly crass, but he was an opportunist. A Methodist in good standing, he convinced Bishop Matthew Simpson to speak at his 1855 cornerstone ceremony on the same day that Simpson was in town to celebrate Garrett Biblical Institute's inaugural (also the day Northwestern's cornerstone was not ready). Jones ignored demands from the University board that he must delete "North-Western" from his school's name. Then a year or two later, Jones took audacity to its limit, appearing before the trustees to request needed space for his school in the University Building.

"It does not require historical or other imagination," wrote early Northwestern historians Sheppard and Hurd, "to picture the promptness with which Professor Jones was shown the door."

Nevertheless, the Female College had resources and even published Evanston's first newspaper in 1858, called the *Casket and Budget*. Its lasting claim to fame was certainly not its name but a poem by Frances Willard, a student who would later become a legendary suffragist figure at the University and in the United States. Her poem was plaintively titled "The Unloved."

Running a school for pecuniary gain eventually took its toll on William Jones, and in 1862 he left the business in the care of his brother and traveled to China, partially for his health but also to assume the post of consul general in Macao. The Female College continued to grow for a few years after that but then found itself in financial straits.

This caused the Northwestern trustees no distress; the turn of events even benefited them, though in a circuitous way. Loans to help the Joneses avoid embarrassment came from families with close ties to the University. In 1869 many of these same families assembled to charter an entirely new school, the Evanston College for Ladies. The families then prevailed upon Jones to cede his charter to them in exchange, presumably, for erasing his debt. Finally the University was rid of its irritating neighbor.

Coeducation at Northwestern became inevitable in 1869, when the trustees offered the presidency to Erastus O. Haven, a progressive Methodist minister who had been president of the University of Michigan. Forty-nine years old, Haven was blunt about one condition for moving to Evanston: coeducation. At the same board meeting at which Haven was elected president, the trustees also voted to admit women. Shortly thereafter, a local girl, Rebecca Hoag, became the first female to enroll.

It was somewhat strange that Evanston College for Ladies, with founders in sympathy with Northwestern, should establish itself that same year and operate separately. Nevertheless, the new college had an active life of its own. Its most enduring decision, perhaps, was the appointment of Frances Willard as president. By now a seasoned teacher of arts and aesthetics, Willard had just returned from extended study in Europe.

Willard's first major project upon assuming the post was to oversee the construction of a new college building. A full-blown cornerstone ceremony was set for July 4, 1871, the "Women's Fourth of July," as it was called. Happily for everyone, the day's festivities turned into Evanston's biggest public celebration to date, beginning with a magnificent parade.

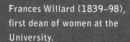

FRANCES WILLARD AND THE EDUCATION OF WOMEN

In 1870 Frances Willard showed her suffragist colors. "The idea that boys of 21 are fit to make laws for their mothers is an insult to everyone," she said. An Evanston woman who knew her share of Northwestern students, Willard spoke on this subject with authority.

As the 19th century proceeded, Willard became one of its most famous women. An educator, temperance leader, and feminist, she built a career and influenced society with a force that seemed unlikely in her time. Willard sought social reform with a progressive zeal that earned her the nickname St. Frances. Yet she seemed so conservative and sometimes inflexible that newspapers lambasted her as a tyrant.

Narrow-minded she was not. Growing up in Evanston in the midst of strong church women, she studied art at North-Western Female College and later traveled to Europe to tour and write with romantic fervor about the art and ruins she saw. In 1871, she returned home to become president of the new Evanston College for Ladies, and she was filled with a sense of her mission. Educated females, she believed, could deeply enhance the tone and nature of society.

She had disappointments in Evanston, but she found a calling on a much larger stage, eventually as president of the Woman's Christian Temperance Union, one of the great voices of independent women in this period. She worked in an inner-city mission, where she saw urban distress, spiritual collapse, and, too often, demon rum. In Chicago, she placed herself among the "dregs of saloon and gambling houses" and preached. "I'd like to go out by myself, looking only to God, and preach the unsearchable riches of Christ," she once said.

Quickly, she acquired fame as an orator and platform speaker. Under the tutelage of Dwight Moody, the great evangelical organizer, she became a woman of renown, though she left her ministry in part because Moody exhibited sexist tendencies. The separation of men and women in revival meetings struck her, she said, as "a relic of an outworn regime."

As leader of the Woman's Christian Temperance Union, with some 200,000 members, Willard was one of two or three leading voices among American women. Her travels, pronouncements, and reform (sometimes socialist) politics were heavily reported in the press. In just a few decades after her death, however, Willard's fame was all but extinguished. Prohibition, largely the result of her temperance work, had been discredited. Her spinsterly image seemed anathema to the freedom of expression valued after World War II.

But historical interest in Frances Willard remains strong. Her powerful career expanded the women's sphere as powerfully and as permanently as any feminist endeavor since. She believed that true womanliness – "Mother-love," as she said – could enhance public life. Today Willard's voice remains poignant in the continuing fight for gender equality.

Chicago's leading classical sculptor, Lorado Taft, created a marble bust of Frances Willard that is now in the University Archives. Another Taft sculpture of Willard was later placed in the rotunda of the United States Capitol. Willard was the first woman so honored.

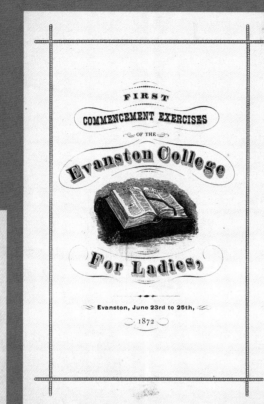

Coeducation at Northwestern
had a complex history, voted
in by the trustees in 1869 and
taking hold after Evanston
College for Ladies merged
with the University in 1873.

The inaugural issue of
the *Casket and Budget*,
published by North-Western
Female College and thought
to be Evanston's earliest
newspaper, carried a poem
of lamentation entitled
"The Unloved" by student
Frances Willard.

At North-Western Female College, music was a prominent part of the curriculum and also a part of student life that included the community.

Construction of the stately Evanston College for Ladies building began in 1871, but work was suspended later that year after the economic chaos caused by the Great Chicago Fire. The architect was Chicago's Gurdon P. Randall, whose previous work included University Hall. A proposed tower atop what is now the Music Administration Building was never built.

General John Beveridge, a local Civil War hero, performed duties as grand marshal, a brass band filled the air with music, and a famed drill team called the Ellsworth Zouaves marched and performed. Orations were delivered, one by President Haven, others by college supporters appealing for subscriptions. Ultimately they laid the cornerstone for what would be a large French-style building designed by Gurdon P. Randall, who had also designed University Hall.

Naturally, Erastus Haven and Frances Willard were discussing an association between their two schools from the beginning. Whatever their plans were, however, fate intervened. The new college's solvency depended on its investments, which were impacted by the Chicago Fire; thus construction of its building was suspended. Although the Chicago Fire led to a remarkable period of building growth for Evanston, it also presented the opportunity, or necessity, for the two institutions to consolidate, which they did in 1873. Coeducation would be Haven's major legacy in Evanston. He returned to the University of Michigan later in 1873.

But the new situation of coeducation did not evolve without difficulty. Haven was succeeded by Charles Henry Fowler, a pastor and orator without equal, it was said, in the Northwest. Fowler had been pastor of the Centenary Church in Chicago and had shown skill in raising funds to rebuild his and other Methodist churches after the fire. He was also the former fiancé of Frances Willard, who had broken off the engagement, evidently, rather than surrender her independence. A sharp division quickly opened between Fowler and Willard, now dean of the Woman's College of Northwestern University. She insisted that the nearly 200 females enrolled in the University remain under her strict control. Fowler insisted otherwise – that female students should behave according to rules of the University faculty, not the dean of women, and that they might interact as freely as male students, even attending church with male escorts, for example. Willard did not give in, but she was destined to lose this clash.

When one Chicago newspaper received a copy of her detailed and restrictive rules, for example, a reporter judged her to be tyrannical and a "female Bluebeard."

Sensing a weakness in Willard's power, Northwestern men harassed the female dean and at least once put a howling cat in her desk drawer. The Fowler administration provided Willard no support and continued to diminish her authority over the women for whom she felt responsible. With great regret, Frances

As the University came of age, the Reverend Charles Henry Fowler (1837–1908) shepherded the institution through several milestones. Taking the reins of the presidency in 1872, he administered the early days of coeducation with the conviction that men and women should live and study on equal footing. Fowler left Northwestern in 1876.

THE LIFE-SAVING STATION

Lake Michigan revealed its treachery as never before on September 8, 1860. Before dawn, the Milwaukee-bound steamer *Lady Elgin* collided with a lumber-laden schooner, the *Augusta*, a few miles north of Evanston. The death toll of 287 would have been greater had it not been for the heroics of a dozen or so Northwestern and Garrett students. Among them was Edward W. Spencer, class of 1862, credited with the rescue of 17 people.

In 1876 the federal government built a fully equipped life-saving station, manned primarily by Northwestern students. Their finest hour came in November 1889, when the steamer *Calumet* ran aground off Highland Park during "one of the fiercest blizzards known in that region in years," according to the station chief's log.

The Northwestern crew quickly towed one lifeboat north and arrived as the vessel was ready to break up. Lifelines fired by cannons fell short, so the crew had no choice but to brave the crashing surf. In three trips some 200 yards out, the Northwestern crew saved the entire *Calumet* crew of 18. Seven members of the Northwestern station were awarded the Gold Medal for gallantry, the highest honor of the United States Life-Saving Service. The Northwestern Life-Saving Station continued in service until 1931.

In the 1870s the federal government equipped the Northwestern Life-Saving Crew with a station, surf boats, and modern life-preserving apparatus.

Willard left Northwestern in 1874. Yet her impact on Evanston and on the nation grew as she went on to the presidency of the Women's Christian Temperance Union. By 1876 Fowler had left Northwestern as well to become the editor of the *New York Christian Advocate*, the most influential journal in American Methodism.

The tax question

The Fowler-Willard episode was but an early skirmish in the social life of a town where mores were rapidly changing. Another serious and longer-lasting controversy arose in 1874 when the interests of the growing town, and "gown," (still, as ever, in financial straits) collided directly over the issue of the University's tax exemption, as described in the 1855 amendment to Northwestern's legislative charter. The opening salvo was from the Evanston town council: a tax bill to the University for more than $10,000 in property taxes for 1873.

The tax question had been discussed and negotiated politely for several years – an aging Grant Goodrich himself had taken time to outline benefits that Evanston gained because of Northwestern. But the arguments moved neither side. Given the stakes, both devoted heavy resources to the case, with legal appeals and reversals continuing for several years. In 1878, *University v. People* reached the U.S. Supreme Court, which ruled in support of the University's exemption.

Even then, the issue refused to go away, and perhaps it was aggravated by Northwestern's response to its legal triumph. When word came of the high court's decision, Professor Oliver Marcy, acting president of the University, was naturally eager to share the good news, and he stopped his carriage to tell a group of students. Though mild-mannered in the extreme, Marcy embellished his announcement:

"You may build bonfires," he said, which the students did enthusiastically – perhaps too enthusiastically. The fires rose in "a blaze of glory," as a student recalled, and did nothing to salve the town's wounds.

Despite the bonfires, Marcy's term at the helm had a stabilizing influence on a university with a history of too many presidents with too-short tenures. Fifty-six years of age and white-haired when he was made acting president, Marcy had a gentle, conservative streak but a blunt manner. Shortly after assuming the position, he told the trustees that they were on a short road to failure. "Character is the growth of years," Marcy said. "As long as the occupant of the presidential chair is changed each three years, the institution must lack character."

Professor Oliver Marcy (1820–99) served as acting president from 1876 to 1881, though he disliked his administrative role. He was a scientist at heart, a devoted curator of the University Museum, and a thoughtful writer of essays insisting that the theory of evolution was truly harmonious with the word of God.

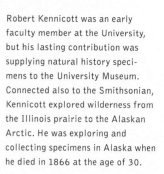

Robert Kennicott was an early faculty member at the University, but his lasting contribution was supplying natural history specimens to the University Museum. Connected also to the Smithsonian, Kennicott explored wilderness from the Illinois prairie to the Alaskan Arctic. He was exploring and collecting specimens in Alaska when he died in 1866 at the age of 30.

The University Museum began as a "cabinet of curiosities." But with Oliver Marcy as its curator, it grew into a substantial natural history collection with undeniable bits of adventure woven in.

Henry M. Bannister's spyglass was probably with him when he accompanied Robert Kennicott on a Western Union Telegraph expedition to Alaska in 1865–66, which took Kennicott's life. Bannister, class of 1863, reported on the scientific observations made there, which helped persuade the United States to purchase Alaska from Russia. Bannister later became a physician and published widely on mental illness and nervous disorders. He died in 1920.

Tug-of-war became a varsity sport in 1887. Northwestern won a major competition in Chicago in 1889, eliciting high praise from the school paper. "Our Tug-of-War team is the only athletic element we have that does credit to the institution," the *Northwestern* observed. The Purple claimed the title of champion again in 1890 and 1891, after which interest in the sport slackened.

Northwestern's 1888 five-man tug-of-war team won a tournament hosted by the Union Athletic Club (UAC) at the Casino Club in Chicago.

While University athletics existed mainly in the male realm, female students at the Woman's College engaged in gymnastics and other modes of physical activity, although their athletic endeavors, unlike those of the men, were not open to spectators.

INTERCOLLEGIATE ATHLETICS

Athletics at Northwestern generated passions, ire, organizational frustrations, and every so often, a modicum of fame for the University.

Baseball was the first intercollegiate sport on campus, and the Northwestern nine's first game was played in 1871 against a nearby team called the Prairies. The Northwesterners prevailed 24–13. A week later they met again, Northwestern winning 43–18. This was an era of indifferent pitching and gloveless fielders, and scores were consequently high.

A league called the College Baseball Association of the Northwest took form around 1871 when the Silver Ball trophy was donated by the Women's Educational Association. Northwestern, Racine College, and the University of Chicago competed for the championship. Racine most often came out on top and Chicago at the bottom, though Northwestern was champion in 1875.

The Western College Baseball Association was organized in 1881 with Racine, Wisconsin, Michigan, and Northwestern. A high point of Northwestern sports in that time was a playoff in Milwaukee between Wisconsin and Northwestern for the 1889 championship. Northwestern was down by four runs in the bottom of the ninth inning and came back to win 12–11, and the streets of Milwaukee were alive with purple banners.

While other sports had their practitioners – track and tug-of-war attracted the purest of athletes – football gained a foothold at Northwestern in the early 1880s. The first intercollegiate game was against Lake Forest University in 1882. But some deplored football and discouraged its growth. An article in the *Northwestern* about a game played out East noted that "blood flowed as freely as at a prize ring entertainment."

But emotions ran in football's favor, and for several years the Purple, as Northwestern's team was called, played in not just one league but two. Success was spotty until 1896, the first formal year of the new Western Conference and the greatest year for Northwestern's dazzling halfback Jesse Van Doozer. That year represented another turning point, as the conference (eventually the Big Ten) led its members to establish faculty athletic committees, enforce eligibility rules, and bring money from university treasuries for athletic purposes. At Northwestern this meant new bleachers (at Sheppard Field in 1891), tennis courts (in 1895), and other improvements in an athletic program that was now a full-fledged part of the University.

In 1875 the University diamond was etched out in the rough near what is now Deering Meadow. By 1888 the team picture showed that even if the Northwestern nine was outplayed on occasion, they were rarely outdressed.

Marcy's scientific approach

Marcy's passion was for science and teaching. A New Englander by birth and a former teacher at Wilbraham Academy in Massachusetts, he arrived in Evanston in 1862 and quickly undertook active fieldwork in natural history. He coauthored a monograph, *Enumeration of Fossils Collected in the Chicago Limestone*, in 1865. He later made geological studies for the U.S. government in the wilderness of Montana and Idaho.

Marcy believed devoutly in the importance of firsthand observation, and thus he became the central figure in the creation of the University Museum. This museum, initially an old-fashioned "cabinet of curiosities," had been begun by Robert Kennicott, a part-time member of the faculty in the 1850s and one of the nation's leading naturalists at that time. (He died exploring Alaska in 1866.) Kennicott's passion was collecting and preparing botanical and zoological specimens; before he died he left a large selection of birds, reptiles, fish, insects, crustaceans, and other specimens in a small room in the University Building, which only a few dignified with the term "museum."

Members of the class of 1875, including three women, pictured on the steps of University Hall.

In 1870 Marcy made certain that a room in the new University Hall was allocated to the purpose of a true museum and that a taxidermist was hired to help collect new specimens and mount them. Indeed, the professor's museum work was hardly trivial. Darwin's *Origin of Species* had been published and was throwing scholars into urgent discussion. Marcy's writing on the subject cited evidence that evolution was scientific fact but also guided by higher authority. "It is no part of our purpose, here, to discuss the question, 'How God brings new forms into being,' but to show that there is a God in nature, or something besides matter in motion," Marcy wrote in the *Northwestern Christian Advocate*. For proof he turned directly to the fossil record. Citing the development of fish, for example, he showed how evolution was no step-by-step process. Great leaps ahead were unexplained except as the work of God.

Marcy's museum ignited at least one incident of interclass rivalry. In 1876, the story goes, an Eastern professor was in Chicago with an exhibit of natural history specimens, one of which was the best whale skeleton then known. Because the bones of this marine mammal were for sale, Northwestern's class of 1877 resolved to make the specimen a gift to the University Museum. But so did the class of 1878, whose members got the jump when they found the skeleton's owner in a Chicago barbershop and negotiated the $700 price as he was being shaved.

For the class of '78, the tale of the whale represented a triumph over upperclassmen, and the younger students could not stop boasting. The whale was soon mounted in the University Museum, along with the bones of a Himalayan elephant and an Irish elk. Then, quite unexpectedly, something new was placed within the ribs of the whale. It was a human skeleton, which carried the label: "Gift of '77."

Marcy was amused, perhaps, but on the whole he found it hard to be mirthful. He was still acting president of an institution whose mortgage payments were draining the treasury, and the only budget reduction possible was in faculty salaries. By 1880 Marcy had had it; he wrote trustee Orrington Lunt a letter that sounded like a resignation: "The question now arises, will I insist on my petition for a change in the presidency. I have thought the matter over and concluded that it is right and just that I should still insist upon it." The board ignored him.

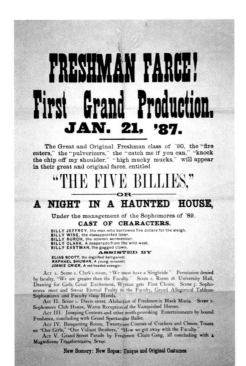

Whoever decreed that freshmen should be seen and not heard had not made himself clear at Northwestern when the Freshman Farce was produced in 1887. In this case, first-year students seemed intent on making their presence known by whatever means possible. Members of the community who dared attend *The Five Billies* were not disappointed. "It is just literally convulsing the people," reported the *Northwestern*.

In 1874 the Osson Literary Society was formed for women, resegregating this extracurricular activity. Those students who voiced an opinion considered the move a step backward, but the administration made the concession to the forces of conservatism at the Woman's College. The battle to cloister the coeds, however, was a losing one.

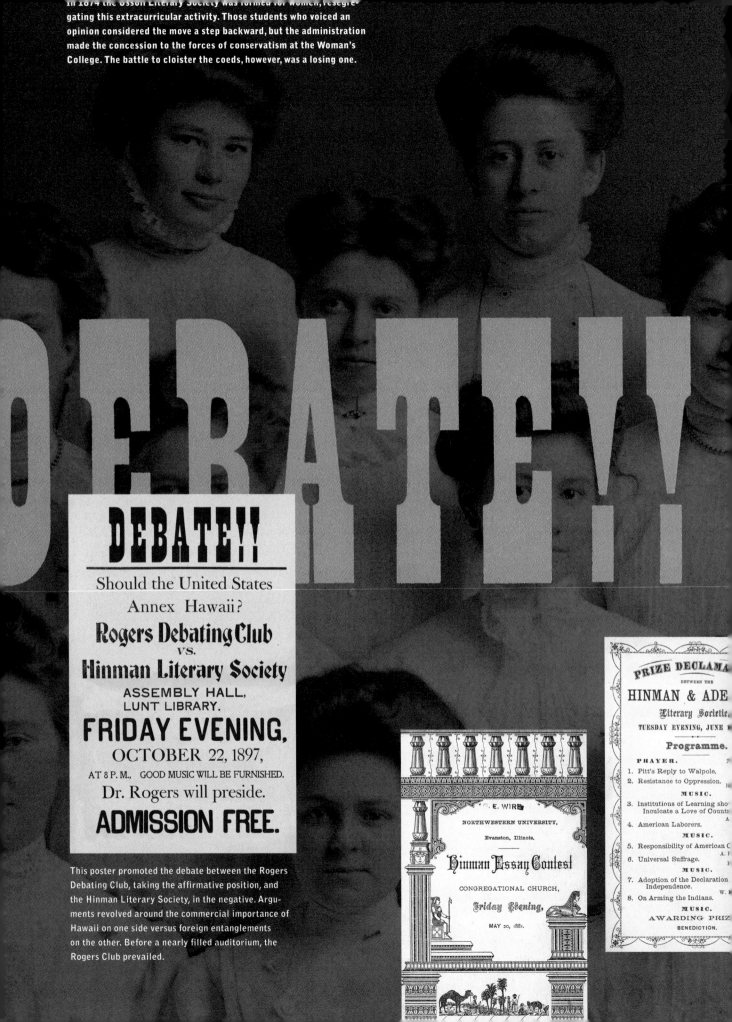

DEBATE!!

Should the United States
Annex Hawaii?

Rogers Debating Club
vs.
Hinman Literary Society

ASSEMBLY HALL,
LUNT LIBRARY.

FRIDAY EVENING,
OCTOBER 22, 1897,
AT 8 P. M., GOOD MUSIC WILL BE FURNISHED.

Dr. Rogers will preside.

ADMISSION FREE.

This poster promoted the debate between the Rogers Debating Club, taking the affirmative position, and the Hinman Literary Society, in the negative. Arguments revolved around the commercial importance of Hawaii on one side versus foreign entanglements on the other. Before a nearly filled auditorium, the Rogers Club prevailed.

E. WIRE

NORTHWESTERN UNIVERSITY,
Evanston, Illinois.

Hinman Essay Contest

CONGREGATIONAL CHURCH,
Friday Evening,
MAY 20, 1881.

PRIZE DECLAMA
BETWEEN THE
HINMAN & ADE
Literary Societie
TUESDAY EVENING, JUNE

Programme.

PRAYER.
1. Pitt's Reply to Walpole.
2. Resistance to Oppression.
   MUSIC.
3. Institutions of Learning sho
   Inculcate a Love of Count
4. American Laborers.
   MUSIC.
5. Responsibility of American C
6. Universal Suffrage.
   MUSIC.
7. Adoption of the Declaration
   Independence.
8. On Arming the Indians.
   MUSIC.
AWARDING PRIZ
BENEDICTION.

LITERARY SOCIETIES

It "distinguished itself for the elasticity of its constitution," wrote an early chronicler of the Hinman Society, Northwestern's first literary society and the first extracurricular activity at the University. Oration, debate, and scholarly discourse constituted the formal purpose of the Hinman and a succession of other literary societies in the 19th century. But in the youthful spirit of democracy, votes were often taken to suspend rules, admit women to their meeting rooms, elect President Lincoln an honorary member, assess dues, waive dues, or levy a fine (in one case) of half a bushel of peanuts for a trumped-up and presumably hilarious charge.

Yet early Northwestern students took their debates seriously — sometimes on issues as far-flung as the political situation in Utah, other times on those closer to home, such as the place of science in Northwestern's curriculum.

In 1860 the Adelphic Society was created as a counterpart to the Hinman, and in the spirit of brotherhood, the two sometimes held joint meetings and debates. Openness of spirit was usually the rule. This was demonstrated again in 1872 after Northwestern became coeducational and the first woman destined to graduate, Sarah Rebecca Roland, became an Adelphic member.

The seriousness of the literary societies waned little by little, and a meeting with a scheduled oration or debate might be quickly transformed into a social mixer or dance, for which reason the resegregation of the sexes was regarded by the women's dean as expedient. The Ossoli Literary Society (named for the feminist and transcendentalist Margaret Fuller Ossoli) was created for Northwestern women in 1874. Ossoli meetings were evidently solemn, so much so that it was hard to get men to attend as guests.

Ultimately the Hinman, Adelphic, and other literary societies were the victims of changing times. In a letter to the editor of the *Northwestern* in 1889, an undergraduate lamented the loss of "higher attainment in our literary societies." Why? "I refer to the fraternity system which is considered by many the arch-foe of the literary society." Literature did not die, but by the early 20th century, literary societies were a relic of a more formal past.

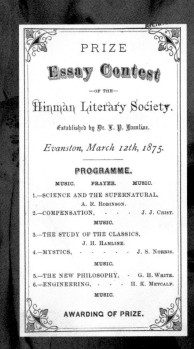

PRIZE
Essay Contest
—OF THE—
Hinman Literary Society.

Established by Dr. L. P. Hamline.

Evanston, March 12th, 1875.

PROGRAMME.
MUSIC. PRAYER. MUSIC.
1.—SCIENCE AND THE SUPERNATURAL,
A. R. ROBINSON.
2.—COMPENSATION,   -   -   J. J. CRIST.
MUSIC.
3.—THE STUDY OF THE CLASSICS,
J. H. HAMLINE.
4.—MYSTICS,   -   -   -   J. S. NORRIS.
MUSIC.
5.—THE NEW PHILOSOPHY,   - G. H. WHITE.
6.—ENGINEERING,   -   -   H. K. METCALF.
MUSIC.

AWARDING OF PRIZE.

Northwestern's earliest social events revolved around literary societies, which featured prayer and music as well as declamations that reflected campus interests. Classics, science, and the supernatural were all regarded as appropriate subjects to discuss at these formal occasions.

Another Marcy letter provides further insight into his administrative travail. "I think I have received nothing on my salary for this year," he wrote the University treasurer at the end of 1880. "My bank account is balanced on the wrong side.... An order for $100 would serve me till Jan. 1st."

A review of the baseball situation

After the Civil War, baseball became the national pastime, and it was quickly adopted by Northwestern, whose first team was organized by 1869. The team was called the Purissimas because of the pure skill they exhibited on the diamond. They played all comers initially and did well enough, though their 1874 game against the professional Chicago White Stockings (today's Cubs), champions of what would become the National League, resulted in a 34-2 defeat. Ultimately, Northwestern found that a collegiate league was most satisfying, as rivalries could develop, the campus could get involved, and inevitable procedural arguments could be worked out in an established forum.

By 1871 the College Baseball Association of the Northwest was established, and a Silver Ball trophy was donated by the Women's Educational Association, which may have provided spectators at the games as well. Competition for the Silver Ball was intense; when Northwestern won it in 1875, some coaxing was required before the old University of Chicago, the previous champion, would give it up. Chicago was protesting that Northwestern's catcher did not attend class and might not have been enrolled at all. But Chicago was "soon convinced that their suspicions were groundless, and now the Silver Ball lies in the University book store, where it can be seen at all hours of the day," wrote the first campus newspaper, the *Tripod,* with justifiable pride.

Joseph Cummings (1817–90) was the last of Northwestern's unbroken line of pastor-presidents – he was a former president of Wesleyan – and probably the most effective. Realizing that private contributions were key to a healthy institution, Cummings engaged a fundraising director, and Northwestern quickly found money for a new science building and other projects.

In 1876 the University was still land-poor, and trustees were often in dispute over how much of its endowment property should be sold. Conservatism prevailed, and as land values increased in Evanston, the balance sheet of the University improved. This meant above all that the faculty was paid on time, an irregular occurrence in the early history of Northwestern.

This early baseball league appears to have been too small to survive. Limited to colleges on the same rail line – Chicago, Northwestern, and Racine College – rivalries intensified and in 1880 turned bitter when Northwestern and Racine finished the regular season in a tie for the championship. A playoff was called for, but bickering quickly clouded plans for the game.

Racine claimed that Northwestern was carrying ineligible players. Northwestern countered that Racine's legal position must have been devised by "the most expert expounder of the Mohammedan Koran," in an article entitled "A Review of the Baseball Situation" in the *Vidette,* another campus newspaper. The article further accused Racine of dodging Northwestern, which had beaten them badly in the final game of the regular season. Racine would not play and would not relinquish the Silver Ball. Northwestern told Racine to keep it and dropped out of the league.

The *Northwestern* concluded, "We congratulate [the team] that she has withdrawn from a league in which the regulations of the constitutions are apparently of so little weight in deciding a dispute."

The next year a new league, the Western College Baseball Association, was organized, and its games were well reported by the campus press. It was unexplained why the new league, with Northwestern, Michigan, and Wisconsin, also included the craven Racine College. Old rivals apparently were hard to shed.

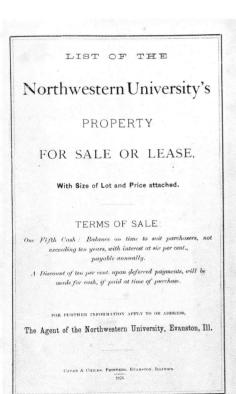

When New York industrialist Daniel Fayerweather funded Northwestern's new Hall of Science, dedicated in 1887 on a site just west of today's Fisk Hall, he remained an anonymous donor. Designed in the Romanesque style by Holabird and Roche, the building is thought to be the first in the Chicago area erected specifically for instruction in science. Fayerweather kept the extent of his fortune from the leather trade a secret until he died in 1890. In his will he left an additional bequest to Northwestern, which fought off a legal challenge from his family. Fayerweather Hall, as it became known, was torn down in 1953.

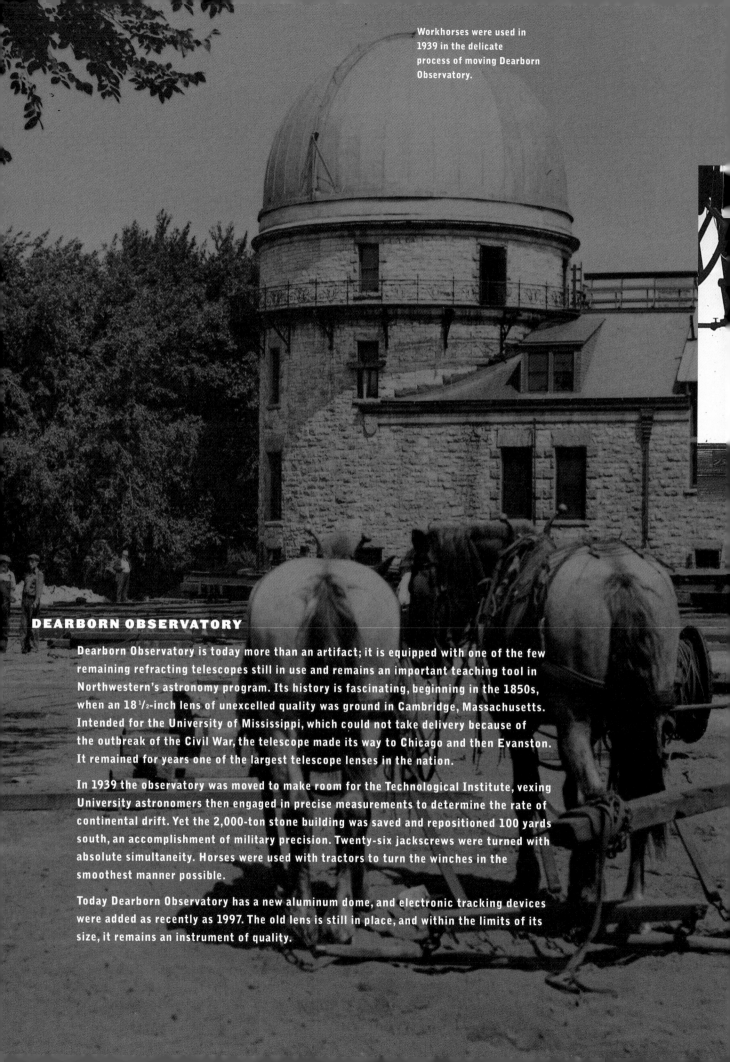

Workhorses were used in 1939 in the delicate process of moving Dearborn Observatory.

DEARBORN OBSERVATORY

Dearborn Observatory is today more than an artifact; it is equipped with one of the few remaining refracting telescopes still in use and remains an important teaching tool in Northwestern's astronomy program. Its history is fascinating, beginning in the 1850s, when an 18 1/2-inch lens of unexcelled quality was ground in Cambridge, Massachusetts. Intended for the University of Mississippi, which could not take delivery because of the outbreak of the Civil War, the telescope made its way to Chicago and then Evanston. It remained for years one of the largest telescope lenses in the nation.

In 1939 the observatory was moved to make room for the Technological Institute, vexing University astronomers then engaged in precise measurements to determine the rate of continental drift. Yet the 2,000-ton stone building was saved and repositioned 100 yards south, an accomplishment of military precision. Twenty-six jackscrews were turned with absolute simultaneity. Horses were used with tractors to turn the winches in the smoothest manner possible.

Today Dearborn Observatory has a new aluminum dome, and electronic tracking devices were added as recently as 1997. The old lens is still in place, and within the limits of its size, it remains an instrument of quality.

President Cummings takes the helm

In 1881, John Evans, still president of the Board of Trustees (despite having left in 1862 to become governor of Colorado Territory), donated $50,000 to Northwestern on the condition that the University match it with $150,000 in outside contributions. These were found "under the blessing of Providence," as the trustees reported when the money was raised. This paid the University's accumulated debt of $200,000 and for the first time in years put finances on a stable footing.

In 1881 a new president, Joseph Cummings, arrived. Cummings, a true patriarch of Methodism, had been president of Wesleyan University for 17 years, and now at 75 years of age was well past the point when most men retired. But he remained a figure of force and power, and it was said that beyond his abilities as an administrator he also loved the classroom and continued to teach. Such versatility was appreciated by the trustees, who supported him, and the students, who respected him deeply. Yet there was another constituency whose esteem for the new president was particularly important: rich benefactors, whose purse strings Cummings was skilled at loosening.

Frequently and with increasing emphasis, Cummings warned the board that new sources of revenue were essential. "The necessity for this change is becoming urgent and the peril of losing influence great," he wrote in his report to the trustees in 1884. On a personal note, he said that he had been "greatly embarrassed by the limited available funds of the university," made worse by the trustees' irritating unwillingness to incur new debt.

Cummings took the bold move of hiring a special agent to solicit funds and not wait for the "spontaneous gifts of the church," Northwestern's usual manner of raising money. Hired to perform this important task was the Reverend Robert Hatfield, a Methodist elder who would receive a commission of 10 percent on all funds secured through his efforts. Hatfield got right to work, mailing letters and a University prospectus to rich Methodists wherever they might be. Most of these communiqués naturally fell on blind eyes.

One blessed missive, however, was passed from its recipient to an elderly acquaintance in New York City. And Providence was kind. The New Yorker, Daniel B. Fayerweather, said that he had never heard of Northwestern University but was impressed as he read about its plans for the future. In this case, Hatfield was requesting funds for a science building, a crying need at this time, because physics was taught in two small recitation rooms in University Hall, and the chemistry lab was crowded into the basement. After appropriate follow up by Hatfield, Fayerweather made a contribution of $45,000.

Initially, Fayerweather declined to be identified as the donor of Science Hall, as it was called, and his name remained a secret until his death in 1890, when his will allocated an additional $100,000 for Northwestern and when the apparent reason for Fayerweather's reticence was revealed. The *Northwestern* explained:

George Washington (Jupiter) Hough sitting at the Dearborn Observatory eyepiece a few years before his death in 1909.

CAMPUS JOURNALISM

Campus journalism had taken many forms and many voices since it began with the first issue of a monthly called the *Tripod* in January 1871. News was not the *Tripod*'s specialty, rather it was more of a forum for students and professors to write at length on academic subjects such as local geology and moralistic topics such as "The Pleasures of Hard Work." Reporting consisted of coverage of campus activities, such as the doings of the Good Manners Club. Out of character was an 1872 article – perhaps a kind of hallucination – called "A Hasheesh [*sic*] Dream."

In 1878 the independent *Vidette* was launched. It was published twice monthly, and the next year the *Tripod* was twice monthly as well, issued on alternate weeks with the *Vidette*. The *Vidette* was newsier and had a humorous side, editorializing about campus affairs – against hazing, for instance – and printing profiles of the baseball team. " 'Greased Lightning' is the cognomen of the pitcher Hall," it reported in the spring of 1878. "He is very fleshy ... and takes prayers in the university."

The *Tripod* and *Vidette* merged in 1881 to form the *Northwestern*, a journalistic enterprise that changed to once-a-week publication in 1888 and thrice-weekly in 1903, when it was rechristened the *Daily Northwestern*. Throughout this period the newspaper excelled in covering milestones such as the death and funeral of President Cummings in 1890. It covered sports in detail. It revealed less than complete commitment to press freedom, however, objecting with fury to a negative article in the *Chicago Tribune* about life in the Woman's College. "There ought to be a statute," the *Northwestern* opined, "which would regulate the lawless careering of these journalistic pirates.... "

Campus journalists had business acumen. They could and sometimes did beg or borrow the use of presses in Evanston and Chicago. Local merchants, meanwhile, eagerly paid for advertising. In 1887 editors created the for-profit Northwestern University Press Company to publish the *Northwestern*. This group went on to found the *Evanston Press*, and at least one of the group, Edwin Llewellyn Shuman, class of 1887, went on to journalistic distinction as literary editor of the *Chicago Record Herald*.

The *Northwestern* saw some competition when the short-lived *Northwestern World* was launched by antifraternity men in 1890. This paper outperformed the *Northwestern* when a local dry goods dealer advertised in both to determine which would draw more buyers. But like many a good protest, the *World* died; the *Northwestern* was returned to dominance, where it would remain throughout the 20th century.

The *Northwestern* was born January 28, 1881. Student run, it came out initially every two weeks and enjoyed its status as an official University publication. This special issue of the newspaper was sent far and wide as a promotional flyer for the University.

The *Vidette* began publication in January 1878, making Northwestern a two-newspaper campus for a few years.

When the literary societies launched the *Tripod* in January 1871, the editors explained that the name represented "a tolerably good synonym for these words: Oracle, Offering, Examiner." A fourth pillar would have been advertising, which enabled Evanston's only newspaper at the time to prosper rapidly.

Northwestern's first woman gradu-
ate, Sarah Rebecca Roland, was
the lone female to receive a degree
in 1874. Roland was from Freeport,
Illinois, and later married John A.
Childs, owner of the *Evanston Index*.
She died in 1937 in Pasadena,
California.

The old oak was depicted on the class
of 1885's commencement invitation.

For more than a half-century, the
old oak stood as the "the emblem
of the University," as Frances
Willard called it, "sending its roots
deep into the soil and spreading
them out far and wide." Located
southwest of University Hall, it was
said to mark an old Indian trail
with its great armlike branch pointing south and east. Class photos,
such as this one of the class of 1880,
taken around the old oak became
a tradition. When the tree died in
1905, a portion of the trunk
remained for several years covered
with a blanket of ivy.

Hatfield became a master of fundraising, so good that the trustees found it best to change his commission arrangement to a $2,500 annual salary. By 1889 the University had a new men's dormitory. It also had built Dearborn Observatory that year, a fine structure at the end of Noyes Street designed by Henry Ives Cobb (who also designed the Newberry Library in Chicago). This served as further evidence that science education, despite evolutionary debates in certain religious circles, was on a firm foundation at Northwestern.

Indeed, the observatory had a curious history, dating back to 1863, when the telescope, with an 18½-inch lens, was the largest in the world. Made in Cambridge, Massachusetts, initially for the University of Mississippi, it never made it to that destination because of the Civil War. This enabled the old University of Chicago to acquire it and Chicago lawyer J. Y. Scammon to provide money for a suitable tower and dome to mount it. This facility, on Chicago's South Side, was named Dearborn after the maiden name of Scammon's late wife, a descendant of a Revolutionary War general for whom Fort Dearborn was named.

When the University of Chicago became defunct in 1887, Northwestern received the telescope, which was already world famous and would become more so. While being tested in Cambridge, for example, it was involved in the discovery of a companion star to Sirius, the brightest star in the heavens. At Northwestern, where sandy soil kept vibration to an astronomically happy minimum, Professor George Washington Hough embarked on a wide range of investigations, among them those of the planet Jupiter, for which the professor became known as "Jupiter" Hough.

Cummings ushered in these and many other positive developments at Northwestern. His death from heart failure in May 1890 brought on a moment of heartfelt mourning at Northwestern and throughout Evanston. As the *Northwestern* reported, "Immediately upon receipt of the sad intelligence by professors, classes were dismissed. At noon the faculty and students convened in the college chapel." Much of University Hall, including Cummings's office, was draped in black. Two days later the late president, dressed in academic robes, lay in state. "As the silent procession filed slowly by, students and friends paused for a moment to gaze for the last time upon the noble countenance so typical of Christian strength and beauty."

At his funeral in the First Methodist Church, Cummings was eulogized for his "wonderful simplicity, his tenderness and sweetness of disposition as a pastor, his energy and capability as an executive and financial manager," the *Northwestern* reported. Such a blend of qualities was deeply valued at Northwestern, although the importance of fiscal awareness would very shortly overshadow the luxury of pastoral virtue in the interests of a larger and more powerful University.

a   *Orrington Lunt*
    Library (1894)
    Now Lunt Hall.

b   *Annie May Swift Hall*
    (1895) Pictured.

c   *Music Hall* (1897)
    Now Human Resources.

d   *Fisk Hall* (1899)

Lincoln

Orrington

Sheridan

Noyes

Foster

Emerson

Sherman

University

Chicago

Hinman

Clark

**NORTHWESTERN'S
EVANSTON CAMPUS
1890–1900**

*BUILT DURING
THIS PERIOD*

BUILT PREVIOUSLY

RAZED

TOWARD A MODERN UNIVERSITY

As the century drew to a close, the dreams and schemes of the University's founders were being realized. In the final decade of the 1800s, Northwestern, with 2,700 students, became the country's third-largest university, after Harvard and the University of Michigan. Its academic departments were evolving, with emerging disciplines such as economics and political science added to the curriculum in the College of Liberal Arts and five professional schools established in Chicago.

Northwestern had become a true university—an institution of many dimensions. As the trustees searched for Joseph Cummings's successor, they understood that they no longer needed a traditional pastor-president but rather a skilled administrator with one foot in the modern world. Cummings himself had insisted on as much before his death. His successor, he wrote, must be "first of all a man of good executive abilities…he must be a man in whose judgment businessmen will have confidence."

The 1890s also represented a turning point in American society. It was a period of progressive ideas and modern organizations as well as the "quest for goodness in bigness," as Northwestern historian Robert Wiebe described it in his 1967 book *The Search for Order.* At the University, the impulse to expand the institution was inspired by this prevailing philosophy, and the trustees' impatience was increased by news that oil magnate John D. Rockefeller was launching the new University of Chicago with seemingly unlimited infusions of cash.

In 1890 a committee of trustees, headed by William Deering of the Deering Farm Implement Company, embarked on a search for a president to guide Northwestern into the new century. They soon found a person "eminently qualified," Deering said, to head a large organization. The man was Henry Wade Rogers, dean of the University of Michigan Law School, which had grown during his tenure to become the largest law school in the nation. Rogers, although 37 years old, represented worldly perspectives; he was also the son-in-law of an eminent Methodist minister from New York, which clearly swayed the trustees in Rogers's favor as well.

The trustees knew that Rogers was a progressive. What they should have predicted were inevitable clashes between their brilliant new president and the old guard of the University. Initially these clashes were mild. For instance, at Rogers's inauguration that fall, Orrington Lunt, now a venerated elder, opened the ceremonies with a message of caution. "The seats of learning ought to be as essentially conservative as they ought to be slow to run risks or enter on dangerous experiments," he said. Rogers later rose to deliver his inaugural address, and although he spoke in a spirit of conciliation, he took what appeared to be the opposite view. "We must not hesitate to make changes in the established order of things," the younger man said.

William Deering (1826–1906) made his fortune as the founder of the Deering Farm Implement Company, which later merged with the McCormick Harvesting Machine Company to form International Harvester Company (now Navistar). President of the University's Board of Trustees from 1897 until 1906, Deering gave more than $1.2 million to Northwestern in his lifetime. Fisk Hall was one of his major contributions. He also headed the committee that hired Henry Wade Rogers as president in 1890.

Henry Wade Rogers (1853–1926), the first Northwestern president without a divinity degree, represented the progressive spirit of his time when he consolidated and modernized the University's many components. After leaving Northwestern in 1900, he became law dean at Yale, and later he was a U.S. Appellate Court judge.

While acknowledging "the principle that Christianity is true, that it is the basis for our civilization, and the beginning of wisdom," Rogers asserted that the work of Northwestern was not "narrowly sectarian." The University must embrace "every description of knowledge that, rising above mere handicraft, could contribute to train the mind and faculties of man," he said.

Rogers makes a move

In fact, Northwestern had been moving in a worldly direction all along. Largeness of purpose, for example, had motivated the University's affiliation with its professional schools: the Chicago Medical College (1870), Union College of Law (1873), the Illinois College of Pharmacy (1886), and the University College of Dental and Oral Surgery (1886). But the schools operated autonomously and with little direction from the administration in Evanston.

"While this relationship persists," Rogers said, "the University can hardly be considered a university except in name."

Rogers's solution was bold: the new president quickly took the step of moving his office to the Chicago building that was home to the law school. Rogers's objective was to take a greater role in directing the professional schools and to maintain more contact with captains of industry. While Evanstonians raised their eyebrows when Rogers, who lived at 1819 Sheridan Road in Evanston, boarded the commuter train like an ordinary businessman, those at the Chicago-based schools, significantly, did not object. The professions were not then in uniformly high repute, and the schools seemed eager to strengthen their ties with Northwestern.

Under President Rogers (front row, black mustache) the College of Liberal Arts faculty had one foot in the Old World, with scholars such as Robert Baird, professor of Greek (top row, second from right), and another in the new, with John Henry Gray, professor of political and social science (right side, holding cane). Dean of women and professor of French Emily Wheeler was the lone female on the faculty in this period.

"The so-called professions meant little as long as anyone with a bag of pills and a bottle of syrup could pass for a doctor," wrote historian Wiebe "[or] a few books and a corrupt judge made a man a lawyer."

Union College of Law

Rogers set up a system of deanships where each dean reported to the president. He appointed himself dean of the law school, an attractive post since this school had a distinguished past but also had much room for improvement. The history of Northwestern University School of Law dated back to 1859, when it was established as the law department of the old University of Chicago. Its faculty included some of the city's eminent attorneys, such as Northwestern founder Grant Goodrich and Evanstonian Harvey B. Hurd. Yet the school was nomadic in its early years, moving in and out of rented space in commercial buildings.

Early law students learned partly by lecture but primarily by witnessing skillful lawyers in court. During 1859, the school's first year, classes were suspended for at least a week when one of the state's best litigators was in Chicago to argue a case in appellate court. The lawyer was Abraham Lincoln, former congressman and at the time counsel to the Illinois Central Railroad. He left memorable impressions, partly as a cheerful man, "though I thought a great deal of it was forced," remembered one student. Another student was struck by Lincoln's constant repetition of legal points in arguing before the jury, which ruled in his favor.

In 1873 Northwestern agreed to assume joint control of this law school, which was renamed the Union College of Law. The agreement provided that the University of Chicago, which was foundering financially, and Northwestern would both contribute $2,000 yearly toward the subsidy of the school, and that either university could acquire full control if and when the other failed to meet this obligation. This occurred in 1886, when the old University of Chicago was on the verge of bankruptcy and extinction.

Then as now, law school training was rigorous, though not without light moments.

One Northwestern alumnus remembered his education with the adage that the law was "a jealous mistress, begrudging every moment not spent in her adoration or service."

Another recalled the story of an ill-prepared fellow student accepting quiet coaching from classmates as the professor, a Socratic pedagogue, drilled him without mercy. The interrogation was proceeding relatively well under the circumstances until two classmates offered opposing answers to the same question. When the professor demanded a response, the young man hardly missed a beat. "The authorities are divided on that point, sir," he said, and a good portion of the class erupted in laughter.

Among the professional schools in Northwestern's early years, the Union College of Law was arguably the most rigorous. Students were consumed with the peculiar logic of evidence, contracts, and pleadings, and many went on to become politicians of note. Here the class of 1877 poses, properly attired, with the faculty.

By 1888, the requirements for a law degree were already increasing, and, a few years later, Northwestern University School of Law would expand to a three-year course. Gone but not forgotten were the days when the best way to train a lawyer was "to set him down in a law office and let him grow," as a graduate reminisced.

Vol. 8. No. 23.   Midsummer Number.   July, 18 1888.

NORTHWESTERN.

Union College of Law.

The Fall Term begins Sept. 19th.

A full course of instruction in the science and practice of Law is offered, requiring two collegiate years of 36 weeks for its completion. The diploma, with the degree of LL. B. conferred after such a course, is accepted by the Supreme court as satisfactory evidence of qualifications for admission to the Bar.   For circulars address

HENRY BOOTH, Chicago, Ill.

CHICAGO MEDICAL COLLEGE,

The Medical Department of Northwestern University.

SESSION 1888-9.

N. S. DAVIS, M. D., LL. D., Dean.

The Collegiate year begins on September 25th, 1888, and continues six months.
The course of instruction is graded, students being divided into first, second and third year classes.
Qualifications for admission are either a degree of A. B., a certificate of a reputable academy, a teacher's certificate or a preliminary examination.
The method of instruction is conspicuously practical, and is applied in the wards of Mercy and of St. Luke's Hospitals daily at the bedside of the sick, and in the amphitheatres.
FEES IN ADVANCE: Matriculation, $5.00; Lectures, $75.00; Demonstrator, including Material, $10.00. Hospitals: Mercy, $6.00; St. Luke's, $5.00. Laboratory, $5. No extra fees for private classes or Microscopical Laboratory. Breakage (returnable), $5.00. Final examination, $30.00, February 1.

COR. PRAIRIE AVE. AND TWENTY-SIXTH ST., CHICAGO.

FACULTY.

H. A. Johnson, M. D., LL. D., Emeritus.
H. O. P. Roler, A. M., M. D., Emeritus.

N. S. Davis, M. D., LL.D., Dean.
Edmund Andrews, M. D., LL. D., Treas.
Ralph N. Isham, A. M., M. D.
John H. Hollister, A. M., M. D.
S. J. Jones, M. D., LL. D.
For further information or announcements, address,

M. P. Hatfield, A. M., M. D.
John H. Long, Sc. D.
E. C. Dudley, A. B. M. D.
John B. Owens, M. D.
O. C. DeWolf, A. M., M. D.
Walter Hay, M. D., LL. D.
F. C. Schaefer, A. M., M. D.
I. N. Danforth, M. D.

W. E. Casselberry, M. D.
W. W. Jaggard, A. M., M. D.
N. S. Davis, Jr., A. M., M. D.
F. S. Johnson, A. M., M. D.
Frank Billings, M. D.
E. Wyllys Andrews, A. M., M. D.
Frank T Andrews, A. M., M. D.
G. W. Webster, M. D.

FRANK BILLINGS, M. D., SECRETARY,
735 State St., Chicago, Ill.

UNIVERSITY PRESS CO. PRINT.

The Medical School built a surgical amphitheater for 500 spectators in its affiliated Mercy Hospital in 1902. Students and visitors from all over the world were drawn to the surgical clinics of Dr. John Murphy, whose breakthroughs in the treatment of appendicitis and intestinal disorders were demonstrated in performances like this one.

This photo of a physiology laboratory in 1900 shows a relatively new way to teach, employing modern instruments and improved laboratory techniques in the study and practice of medicine.

Although students were still admitted to the pharmaceutical schools to prepare for drugstore jobs, Northwestern's School of Pharmacy placed the education of pharmacists on a more professional footing with its course leading to a degree as a pharmaceutical chemist. In the 1890s this was an advanced and necessary profession. While the work that druggists once performed was being done by manufacturers, pharmaceutical chemists were being called on to perform the laboratory work now important to the practice of medicine and public health.

ILLINOIS COLLEGE OF PHARMACY, CHICAGO.
Time Card for the Winter Term, 1889--90.

SENIOR CLASS.		JUNIOR CLASS, DIVISION A.		JUNIOR CLASS, DIVISION B.	
Section 1.	Section 2.	Section 3.	Section 4.	Section 5.	Section 6.

N. B.—The classes are divided into sections for convenience, only; Senior students partially employed in drugstores are assigned in Section 1, and the Juniors so employed in Sections 3 and 5. The required work occupies at least three and a half days each week. Each member of the Senior Class receives 32 hours instruction weekly; each Junior student, 31 hours weekly. Besides the required work (that specified in this Time Card), there will be special lectures at 8 o'clock P. M. on Thursdays, which are very instructive and interesting, and all students—both Seniors and Juniors—are expected to attend these special lectures, if possible, those employed in drugstores being excused if necessary.

Students are requested to preserve this Time Card for reference.

In 1896, when Northwestern increased the law degree requirements from two years to three, enrollment took an unwelcome dip, but it recovered completely a year later. Under Henry Wade Rogers and his increasingly serious curriculum, the law school joined the ranks of the elite law schools of the nation. The quality of instruction was soon matched by the qualifications of the students, and in 1900 the school boasted an entering class of 10 students with undergraduate degrees from Harvard, Yale, or Northwestern and 15 students from the University of Chicago.

Northwestern University Medical School

Like the law school, the Northwestern University Medical School grew from modest origins. Founded in 1859 as Chicago Medical College, it was the creation of Dr. Nathan S. Davis, a clinical physician with strong ideas about the rigors of medical education. Davis, previously a professor at Rush Medical College, had been at odds with the Rush administration over a variety of issues. One was the length of the course, which Davis insisted should be increased from Rush's current requirement of 16 weeks a year for two years.

Rush refused to act on this issue, and so Davis was eager to move on. His opportunity came in 1859, when he affiliated with a new institution, Lind University, and started a medical department, attracting other dissidents from Rush. This move ignited a rivalry with their former school. When Davis usurped Rush's affiliation with Chicago's Mercy Hospital, for example, Rush retaliated, writing that the Lind doctors were "phantoms in black, traitors and charlatans."

Lind was soon bankrupt, but Davis was tenacious; under him the school survived as Chicago Medical College. Davis was also an innovator. Early on, he developed what became known as the "graded curriculum," the teaching of medical courses in step-by-step succession. Traditionally, medical lectures were delivered with little regard to prerequisites. Davis was recognized as the first medical educator to insist that "the mastery of one [course] made the mastery of the next easier," he said, "and the accomplishment of the whole more comprehensive and complete."

The Illinois College of Pharmacy, founded in 1886, became the School of Pharmacy of Northwestern University in 1891 and was located in the laboratories of the Medical School. It was recognized as one of the leading schools in its field, employing modern laboratory techniques developed through advancements in medical research.

EARLY GRADUATES IN THE PROFESSIONS

Northwestern's professional schools were new in the late 1800s, but their futures were foreshadowed by the distinguished graduates they turned out in the early years.

The Chicago Medical College also turned out eminent practitioners who broke new ground. Daniel Hale Williams, class of 1883, went against the odds, becoming one of the first African American graduates and a founder of Provident Hospital, which served the city's black community. Williams was also the first African American appointed to the Illinois State Board of Health, and he was surgeon in chief of the Freedman's Hospital in Washington, D. C.

Kenesaw Mountain Landis moved to Chicago from Indiana to enter the law school class of 1891. After graduating, Landis was quickly recognized as a lawyer of intelligence and character. Among his achievements, he became a federal judge and passed down the ground-breaking antitrust judgment against Standard Oil in 1905. In 1920 he became the first commissioner of baseball in the wake of the Chicago Black Sox scandal, when the national pastime needed a virtual dictator.

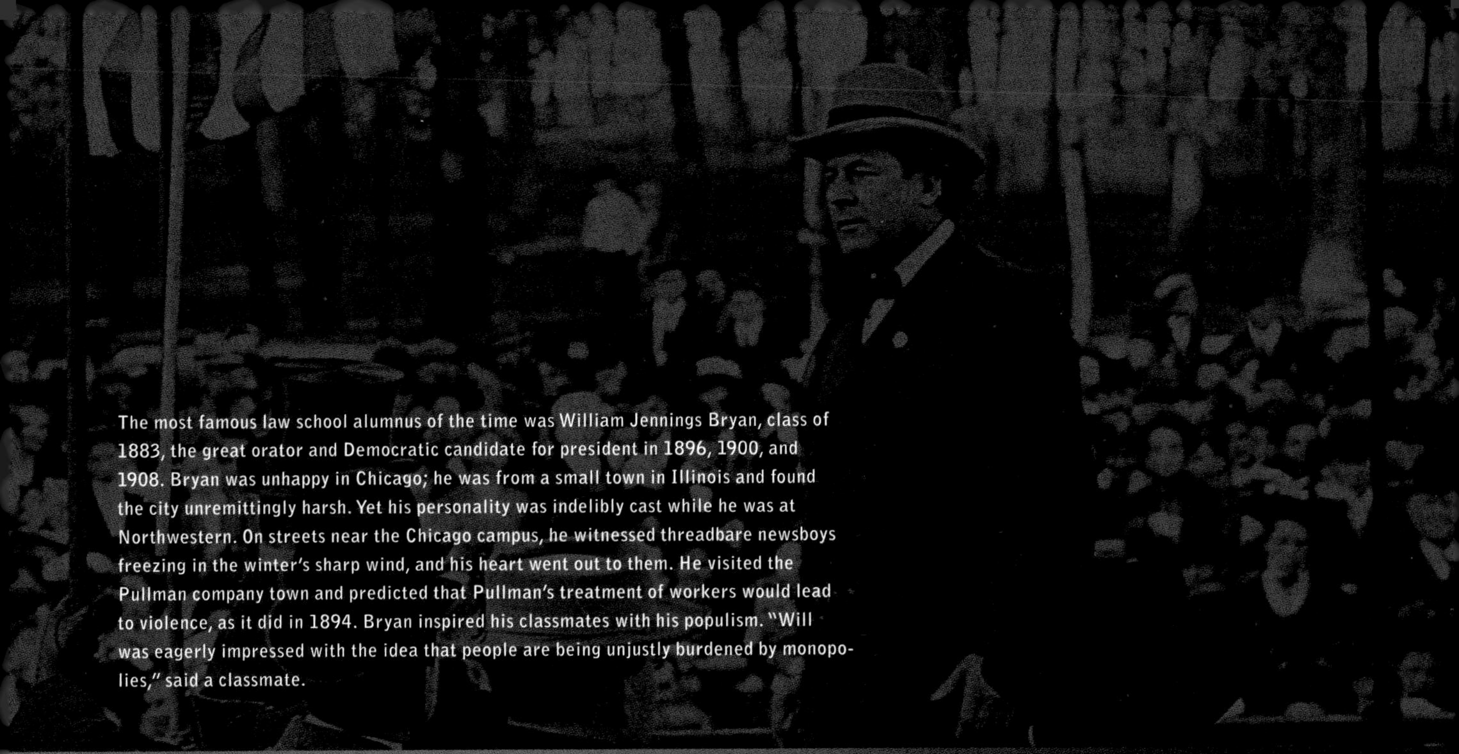

The most famous law school alumnus of the time was William Jennings Bryan, class of 1883, the great orator and Democratic candidate for president in 1896, 1900, and 1908. Bryan was unhappy in Chicago; he was from a small town in Illinois and found the city unremittingly harsh. Yet his personality was indelibly cast while he was at Northwestern. On streets near the Chicago campus, he witnessed threadbare newsboys freezing in the winter's sharp wind, and his heart went out to them. He visited the Pullman company town and predicted that Pullman's treatment of workers would lead to violence, as it did in 1894. Bryan inspired his classmates with his populism. "Will was eagerly impressed with the idea that people are being unjustly burdened by monopolies," said a classmate.

There are few names in American medicine that are better known than Mayo, though that was hardly the case when Charles H. Mayo graduated from Chicago Medical College in 1888. Fresh out of school, Mayo joined his brother William in a surgical practice in Rochester, Minnesota. Energetic and innovative, they established what became one of the most famous medical institutions in the world, the Mayo Clinic.

In a speech at the cornerstone ceremony for Northwestern's new Chicago campus in 1926, Mayo remembered his professors. "With a few accurate instruments, and without methods of precision, they had to wrest the secrets of disease from grudging nature," he said. "Medicine is both an art and a science, and both make appeal to the true physician."

In 1870 Northwestern sought and arranged an affiliation with Chicago Medical College. This relationship provided Davis with a small subsidy, shared faculty, and little more; but he maintained complete administrative autonomy. Nevertheless, the relationship seemed to have considerable symbolic meaning for the University.

When President Haven conferred Northwestern diplomas on medical graduates that spring, he expressed conspicuous pride. "Your profession is as old as the clergy," he said. "Doctors are the great prosecutors of science and free thought."

Despite ambitious goals, the Medical School's facilities were primitive and remained cramped even after its move to a new building at 26th Street and Prairie Avenue in 1870. Particularly notorious were the dissecting rooms (used only when cold weather permitted), where medical students earned a well-deserved reputation for rough manners.

"Many a properly raised young man blew his first tobacco smoke across the dissecting table," wrote an early graduate. "Tradition had established that it was impossible to endure the odors of the dissecting room unless one smoked...."

As late as the 1890s, medical students were regarded as the University's rowdiest bunch, largely because of dissecting room antics. Visitors to gross anatomy class were often greeted with unprovoked verbal abuse. Most memorable was a delegation from Garrett Biblical Institute, who found itself at the receiving end of a barrage of spare body parts.

The Woman's Medical School

Frank discussion of anatomy seemed inappropriate in mixed company at the time; hence medical education at Northwestern remained decades behind the rest of the University with respect to coeducation. In 1869 the Chicago Medical College enrolled three women, though that experiment came under attack when male students petitioned against the policy. Within a year the administration concluded that "certain clinical material was not as ready in coming forward... in the presence of a mixed class," and enrollment of women was abandoned.

The experiment in coeducation had a lasting impact, fortunately, because one of the women enrolled that year was Mary H. Thompson, a graduate of New England Female Medical College. The first female surgeon in the United States, Dr. Thompson came to Chicago in 1862. She helped establish the Chicago Hospital for Women and Children in 1865. After a year at Chicago Medical College, which she attended to receive additional training, she joined one of her professors, gynecologist William H. Byford, to establish a teaching faculty at the women's hospital.

At Northwestern Medical School a hard line remained against enrolling women. Dean Davis, for instance, insisted that medicine was a male domain, except

Northwestern University

Woman's Medical School

CHICAGO.

~

1896-97.

The annual announcement is an authorative statement of rules, conditions and fees for the current year only, extending from July 1st of the year it is published to July 1st of the following year. All questions regarding conditions for entering the college, course of study and graduation, are referred to the *Secretary*. All questions regarding fees or other financial matters are referred for decision to the *Treasurer*. All questions concerning scholarships and all conditions to missionary students, are referred to the *Dean*. The college will in no way be responsible for statements made by other members of the faculty or other persons which do not correspond literally with the published rules.

Northwestern University was among many schools that recognized the need for female physicians but found the presence of women in medical classes inconvenient. The solution was affiliation in 1892 with the Woman's Medical School, many of whose graduates distinguished themselves in missionary and charity work. The Woman's Medical School was discontinued by the University in 1902.

The Woman's Medical School was founded in 1870 on Chicago's near West Side in a hospital for women and children that was later named for one of its founders, Dr. Mary Thompson. Thompson was credited as the first female surgeon in the country when she attended Chicago Medical College (later Northwestern University Medical School) in 1869. After organizing the Woman's Medical School (which eventually affiliated with the University), she helped guide female physicians into careers.

for "a few singularly constituted women." Nevertheless, the Woman's Medical School, which burned to the ground in 1871 in the Chicago Fire, recovered and grew as an independent entity at Paulina and Adams Streets. By 1879 seniors at the college competed with men for internships in hospitals around the city, though to little avail at first. The women performed poorly in surgery exams, largely because opportunities for training in that area were limited. Also that year, several qualified women graduates were denied positions at the city insane asylum on the grounds that females ought not be exposed to such a place.

Attitudes changed as women physicians grew more determined. Dr. Mary Bates, class of 1881, became the first woman to complete a successful internship at Cook County Hospital. Another important step forward came in 1892 when the woman's college became affiliated with Northwestern University, which purchased its property, then a converted mansion located not far from County Hospital, with $35,000 raised in bonds.

The Woman's Medical School of Northwestern University flourished for several years, its enrollment peaking at 137 in 1893. Enrollment trailed off in the next few years, though its doctors continued to bring distinction to the school and the University. Graduates made notable contributions in missionary work, especially in Asia, where ingrained customs sometimes presented medical problems unknown in America. In China, Lucy Gaynor, class of 1891, wrote home describing deformities caused when the feet of young girls were bound tightly. Progress was made, Dr. Gaynor wrote, only after the mission school closed its doors to girls unless their feet were unbound.

Women students in the School of Speech assembled on the steps of Annie May Swift Hall in the 1890s.

Annie May Swift Hall, dedicated in 1895, commemorated meat packer Gustavus F. Swift's daughter, an elocution student of Robert Cumnock before her premature death. The $12,000 that Swift provided to build the Venetian-style building near University Hall superseded Dean Cumnock's wish to have the building named, as had been planned, after himself.

Despite the importance of the Woman's Medical School, enrollment continued to decline. Coeducational medical schools were now common and were seen as a more advanced setting for women students.

Thus, in 1902 Northwestern disbanded the school. Although this was an unavoidable economic decision, things were made worse by a trustee who said, "It is impossible to make a doctor out of a woman." At Northwestern, the prejudice continued, and women remained barred from enrolling in its medical school until 1926.

A school for speakers

Although Northwestern was modernizing, one of the University's fastest growing disciplines in this period was also one of the most traditional – oratory. This was due largely to the powers of Robert McLean Cumnock, founder of Northwestern's School of Oratory, who was as much an entrepreneur as a scholar. While oratory was an old-fashioned discipline, and, some said, an anachronistic one, Cumnock transformed the field into something dynamic and established the foundation for what later became the School of Speech.

Cumnock was a humble-born Scot who moved with his parents to the mill town of Lowell, Massachusetts. He worked his way into the Methodist prep school Wilbraham Academy in Massachusetts and then attended Wesleyan University, where his gifts in elocution were refined. After graduation in 1868, Cumnock was hired by Garrett Biblical Institute, where he trained future ministers to deliver sermons with drama and fire.

In Evanston, Cumnock found other ways to use his skills. He took a part-time faculty position at Northwestern, where his classes were instantly popular. He also went on the Chautauqua circuit. Chautauqua talks were big events in those days, featuring talented and often stirring speakers on subjects that were frequently religious and always culturally inclined. Chautauqua was a kind of intellectual's vaudeville, and soon Cumnock became a star. Fame brought more students to Cumnock's classes, and in 1878 Northwestern created a two-year program leading to a certificate in oratory, useful for "teachers of elocution and public readers."

Robert McLean Cumnock began as a Northwestern teacher of elocution courses that attracted primarily divinity students and women. The popularity of his classes and the expansiveness of his personality motivated the University to incorporate Cumnock's courses into a full-fledged course of study, and the School of Oratory became a recognized, degree-granting component of the University in 1894. Cumnock's school expanded its appeal by training preachers, actors, and platform speakers in an age of religious revival and grandiose political rhetoric.

The University exercised little control over Cumnock, whose compensation came from tuition paid by his students. This arrangement caused no discernible jealousy among other faculty members, but Cumnock's stature baffled many of them. Elocution was then in low repute, due partly to the attempt of "modern" orators to devise a science of ditones, tritones, and pectoral and nasal projections. But Cumnock had no patience for such transparent pseudoscience. He regarded oratory as an art, and he practiced it with obvious skill.

Cumnock's courses grew in popularity, and in 1892 the trustees rewarded their rising enrollment by establishing a full-fledged, degree-granting program, the School of Oratory. The professor continued to govern his curriculum autocratically, however, and when students once petitioned him to add extemporaneous speaking and debate to the course list, Cumnock refused. Oratory was heroic, he believed, not topical. To prove his point, he would devote an entire class period to a Robert Burns monologue, which he performed with an elaborate Scottish burr.

In 1893 the trustees accepted a plan Cumnock presented to build a new building, provided Cumnock found the donors, which he did when he secured a bequest from meat packer Gustavus F. Swift. The building, completed in 1895, was named after Swift's daughter, Annie May, who had become ill and had died several years previously as a Northwestern undergraduate. Because of its "Venetian" style it drew praise as the most elegant building yet on the Northwestern campus. It was also highly suitable to its purpose, as evidenced by the fact that it has continued to house the same school, later renamed the School of Speech, for more than a century.

Music at the University

The 1890s were a turning point for another school that might have been marginal except for the personal vision of one individual. Northwestern's Conservatory of Music, founded by Oren E. Locke as a part of the Woman's College, hit a low point in 1891. With only 40 students enrolled and a talented faculty wholly dependent upon revenues from tuition, music's future at Northwestern was in doubt. But then Peter Christian Lutkin, a renowned church organist, was made director.

Lutkin expanded the curriculum broadly in his first year, despite the lack of students. The problem, he believed, had been that the conservatory was limited to instruction in piano and voice, with some organ and violin training mixed in. Lutkin quickly organized new courses in both theory and practice and fashioned a curriculum not just for professional musicians but for schoolteachers and musical amateurs as well.

Peter C. Lutkin served as dean of the School of Music at Northwestern from 1883 to 1931. He came to national prominence as an educator by building one of the nation's first music schools situated within a degree-granting university.

The School of Music presented frequent recitals on campus and at nearby churches. One of the University's earliest chapel choirs is pictured here in 1898 on the steps of Lunt Library.

Music's popularity at the University in the 1890s encouraged a variety of musical styles and organizations, such as the Mandolin Club, shown here in 1893.

When Music Hall was opened in 1897, it was small, but it enabled the School of Music to move its rehearsal rooms from the Woman's College (now the Music Administration Building), where the din of music education was distracting to residents.

His ideas were promising, but revenues continued to fall short of expenses. Lutkin soon found these financial troubles too distasteful and prepared to return to the private music school he operated at his home on Indiana Avenue in Chicago. As a last-ditch effort, however, he made several recommendations – primarily that the conservatory be brought into the College of Liberal Arts and its director made a professor.

These changes seemed doubtful, especially when President Rogers wrote, "I do not believe that the interests of the college will be materially affected should the conservatory be discontinued."

But then, to the surprise of just about everyone, a groundswell of support on the board, led by trustee James H. Raymond, resulted in the acceptance of Lutkin's proposal. He was made a professor and chair of the music department.

Lutkin quickly broadened the music department's offerings, and enrollment increased. Courses were taught in music history, covering the evolution from oratorio to opera to classical and modern composers. The curriculum also trained students in harmony and counterpoint and became as intensive at Northwestern as it was in major conservatories.

Dean Lutkin himself was happiest when he was teaching church music. Organists should be "the best trained of all musicians," he said. He even encouraged his students to study theology to better understand religious music. With these developments under way, and with enrollment swelling to 200, the music department was elevated to new status as the School of Music in 1895.

The Orrington Lunt Library was built in the classical style in 1894. With gas *and* electric illumination and a capacity for 90,000 volumes, it was intended to be a library for the ages, though it was replaced in 1933 by Deering Library. Lunt then became the administration building, which it remained until 1942. After wartime service housing the Naval Radio School, it was turned over to the mathematics department in 1945.

Lunt Library was thoroughly modern for its time. A reading room was flooded with natural light. A card catalog, book lift, and speaking tubes made this building an efficient venue for learning.

Greeks and barbarians

In the 1890s discussion of the role of fraternities ran hot in the student press as well as in faculty circles. Greek-letter organizations had been on campus for years, and while they aroused suspicion in some places, Northwestern raised no objection when two such "secret societies" were created in the early 1860s. They disbanded during the Civil War, but the fraternity movement was revived at Northwestern when Sigma Chi formed a local chapter in 1869; by the turn of the century, eight fraternities and eight sororities had been established.

Sigma Chi's founding at Northwestern was marked by slightly cryptic circumstances. The story was that its initiation was conducted in the basement of the Baptist Church in Evanston, and for whatever reason, it was done without the permission of the church. While evil repercussions did not ensue from this furtive genesis, the event only reinforced the covert reputation of the fraternal concept.

Early members of Sigma Chi included George Lunt, class of 1872, son of Northwestern founder Orrington Lunt, and Lorin C. Collins, class of 1872, future speaker of the Illinois House of Representatives.

Members were respectable men, but as a group they maintained strange rituals, such as chanting in vacant houses and holding woodland retreats. Outsiders did not know quite what to make of it, but rumor was that the brothers also kidnapped goats, a practice that figured into the rituals of Sigma Chi and other fraternities.

Shortly after Sigma Chi came Phi Kappa Sigma, whose founders included undergraduate John M. Dandy, class of 1873, later editor and publisher of the *Chicago Saturday Evening Herald*, a newspaper of literature, drama, music, and "all matters pertaining to polite society." Despite the wholesomeness of Phi Kappa Sigma and Sigma Chi, an unseemly controversy tainted the entire fraternity movement in 1875. It unfolded when professors Cumnock and Henry S. Carhart lured members of these two fraternities into a proposed local chapter of Psi Upsilon, the professors' fraternity.

Psi Upsilon was regarded as a prestigious Eastern fraternity, and even University dignitaries were present to welcome members of the national organization at an elaborate dinner given for the delegation. Toasts were offered and plans were made for installation ceremonies. But then the unthinkable happened. Northwestern was blackballed by one anonymous chapter among the 15 then in existence. "Not the least crestfallen of those concerned were the Northwestern faculty men who were forced to suffer this final slip twixt cup and lip," a historian of Sigma Chi put it a few years later.

Lodilla Ambrose, class of 1887, was made assistant librarian of the University and de facto head of the library in 1888. Ambrose shepherded the growth of the library from a single room in University Hall to the Orrington Lunt Library in 1894 and remained a leader in modern library management. As she fought for resources for the library, she antagonized important University administrators, which may have led to her dismissal in 1908.

Even as fraternities grew, the progressive spirit of the times cast suspicion on all institutions that were not purely democratic. Northwestern's Greeks — secret, exclusive, and often luxuriously settled in off-campus houses — were hardly democratic. Thus, a backlash grew when a group of antifraternity men, so-called "barbarians," formed a society of their own, the Massasoits. Self-professed iconoclasts, they extracted a pledge from each member never to join a fraternity. They also launched a new campus weekly, the *Northwestern World*, in 1890.

The *World* published for only two years, but never was so much dust kicked up in campus journalism. From the outset the editors went after the *Northwestern*, the official campus newspaper, run by fraternity men. The *World* tweaked them ceaselessly for elitism and wrongheadedness, and the backbiting reached a crescendo when the *World* accused a *Northwestern* editor of getting his grade in elocution revised upward to qualify for an oratorical competition.

For students in the 1890s, pennants and other collegiate memorabilia were meaningful decoration in their rooms.

Nothing positive came of the dispute, though the Massasoits must have felt they were on the rise in the fall of 1891 when they engineered the election of L. H. Knox, class of 1892, a barbarian through and through, as senior class president. Knox's election suggested that fraternities were in decline, but that wasn't true. Within a year or so, the most irascible Massasoits graduated and left campus. The younger ones ended up joining new fraternities that were looking for members. The *World* ceased publication in 1892, and the Massasoits became extinct shortly thereafter.

The University administration watched these events without comment, though it was on record against another perhaps related aspect of college life: hazing and gratuitous violence on campus, which Rogers (perhaps erroneously) claimed was lessened during his tenure.

Dunking underclassmen in the lake may have been old-fashioned by this time, but the "cane rush," a mid-autumn brawl between freshmen and sophomores, was in full flower and was regarded by some outsiders, such as Chicago reporters in search of stories, as a charming bit of brutality.

The cane rush was scripted around the affectation of canes or walking sticks, used mostly to make menacing gestures at members of the rival class. Weeks of this behavior climaxed in a street fight, sometimes scheduled and sometimes not, with members of the winning class continuing to carry their canes for the remainder of the term.

A particularly vicious cane rush occurred one morning in 1891, when freshmen marched to chapel en masse, making a spectacle of themselves and their canes. This evidently antagonized the sophomores beyond restraint, and as the freshmen later marched down Chicago Avenue, they were ambushed by sophomores at Clark Street. Broken sticks and ripped coats were the result, and the sophomores prevailed. "Every cane that could be broken came to grief, and now those hundred canes furnish room ornaments for the sophomore girls," wrote the *Northwestern*.

Gamma Phi Beta was the largest sorority at Northwestern in 1896 and was noted for its literary accomplishments and scholarship. Most likely because of its stature, members were permitted to move to rented quarters in a duplex at 1918 Sheridan Road, the other half of which was the residence of President Rogers.

In the early 1890s, sororities were less free than fraternities to organize social events and to move into off-campus houses. Yet groups such as Omega Upsilon were promoters of something that everyone regarded as vital to the life of a university — school spirit.

Members of Phi Kappa Psi in 1898 were hardly warriors in the service of secret societies. The antifraternity movement had dissolved by this time, and so tame were the Greeks that the University administration was negotiating to allow fraternity houses on campus, though this was still a decade away.

NORTHWESTERN UNIVERSITY SETTLEMENT

"While we are studying economic theory we study also the human beings whose
lives compose that theory. In pursuing the doctrine of rent we do not forget the
man who pays the rent." This was how William Hard, onetime head resident at
the Northwestern University Settlement on Chicago's Northwest Side, described
the settlement's mission at the onset of the progressive era.

The settlement was created in 1892 through the collaboration of Northwestern-
trained sociologist Charles Zeublin and Emma Winner Rogers, the dynamic wife of
Northwestern president Henry Wade Rogers.

Zeublin began this work – modeled after Toynbee Hall in England – in a six-room
flat above a feed store on Division Street in Chicago and later moved to Chicago
Avenue, a neighborhood of ethnic diversity and poverty. Classes taught girls to
cook, garden, and sew; boys learned law, etiquette, and athletics. Later there was a
free medical dispensary and a legal clinic to save the "poor and unlettered," as a
Chicago newspaper described them, from "the people of speckled reputations who
live by robbing their neighbors."

By 1907 Harriet Vittum had assumed the post of head resident and would remain in
that position for 40 years. During her tenure she improved prenatal care in the
community, established a music school, developed boys' and girls' camps, and intervened in domestic abuse cases.

In the most direct ways, the settlement reflected the ideals of Northwestern
University. It was viewed as "an avenue opened between the great world of labor
and the great world of accumulated knowledge," as Hard wrote.

Emma Winner Rogers, wife
of President Henry Wade
Rogers, was a central figure
in the opening of the
Northwestern University
Settlement in 1892.

The pleasures of purple

If anything could neutralize such shenanigans, Rogers believed, athletics could. "Students work off their excess of animal spirits on the athletic field and in the gymnasium," Rogers wrote in an article for a magazine. The president liked intramural sports best, and he particularly liked tennis, for which he had Northwestern's first courts built in 1895. He was less enthusiastic about the big-time sports, baseball and football, but he supported them, at least at first.

Intercollegiate football at Northwestern began November 11, 1882, when the Northwestern eleven traveled to Lake Forest University (later College), where they were shut out. In following years, fall afternoons often featured intrasquad scrimmages and occasional games against other schools. By 1889 football was sufficiently organized to host a team from Notre Dame in what is now Deering Meadow. The game generated high excitement, though the 200 spectators were inexperienced and rushed on to the field after nearly every play. Despite the fans and the score – Northwestern lost 9–0 – The *Northwestern* reported that it was "the best football contest yet played in Evanston."

By 1890 football was generating campuswide interest, and the Northwestern University Football Association began seeking subscriptions of 50 cents to help pay the team's expenses. The *Northwestern*, always a booster of "university spirit," beat the drums for football.

"The prestige attending a winning college team is so great and the benefit to the college represented so considerable, that any honorable means should be employed to place a good team in the field," the newspaper proclaimed.

Football was not universally admired, however, as Charles D. Wilson, class of 1893, knew too well. Wilson was Northwestern's lineman par excellence, the tallest man on the team and "built from the ground up," as a *Northwestern* sportswriter wrote in 1891. "He is a star player, and great things are expected of him this year."

The Class of 1896.

In 1896, Jesse Van Doozer and Albert Potter, both class of 1897, were running backs on a Northwestern team that came within an extra point of winning the first Western Conference title.

The 1896 football program pictured one of the better Northwestern teams in the early years of football at the University. It was the first year of the Western Conference, which became the Big Ten.

Tennis courts were built at Northwestern in 1895, and by the next year the women of the University organized the Entre Nous Tennis Club.

Wilson was well known for another reason. Already a Methodist minister when he enrolled at Northwestern, he was quickly tagged "the fighting parson" in the Chicago papers. And while the Methodist bishop tolerated the nickname for a year, it galled him considerably. What the bishop should have realized was that Wilson was one of the hardest-working men on campus — he not only carried the middle of the Northwestern line but also traveled nearly every weekend to preach at churches throughout northern Illinois. But it wasn't enough, and the bishop finally ordered the parson to quit the team, which he did in his senior year.

Football progressed despite setbacks. Sheppard Field, with a large grandstand, was opened in 1891. In 1896 the Western Conference was organized, with the universities of Minnesota, Wisconsin, Illinois, Purdue, Michigan, and Chicago joining Northwestern in what would become the Big Ten a few years later. The inaugural season was a good one for the Purple, as the Northwestern team was known. They were undefeated through most of the season and were poised to be champions of the West. All they needed was a win in the last game of the season against Wisconsin.

It shouldn't have been a problem. Northwestern was at home, and the team had Jesse Van Doozer, class of 1897, who was considered the best running back in the West. But rain had left the field a morass, and Van Doozer could manage just one touchdown, after which Northwestern missed the extra point. Wisconsin had problems of its own; its team was held scoreless for the first three quarters, and it was looking like the glory was Northwestern's. But then a snap to Northwestern's punter went awry. The ball went all the way to the end zone, where most of the 22 players on the field collapsed on one another in the general area of the ball. When the mud was cleared, the referee ruled that a Badger had recovered the ball. The kick after the touchdown was good, and Wisconsin marched home the champion in the first season of the embryonic Big Ten.

As football grew in popularity, President Rogers had second thoughts about it. He even wrote letters to other presidents about banning the sport in colleges because it was too rough and professional in its seriousness.

Rogers won little support for this view, though, and he let it pass. Another issue was claiming his attention, and it was one that put extreme pressure on him personally.

Sheppard Field grandstand, just north of the site of the present-day Technological Institute, was completed in 1891. It continued as the University's athletic grounds until 1905, when Northwestern Field was opened on Central Street, where Dyche Stadium (now Ryan Field) was constructed in 1926.

EARLY WOMEN OF NORTHWESTERN

The women of Northwestern assumed a prominent role in campus life from the moment they were first admitted. Coeducation was established at the University in 1869, and Northwestern women quickly made a mark on the University and on the world beyond.

The third dean of women, Rena Michaels Atchison, had a long career of achievements. As an undergraduate at Syracuse University, she was a founder of Alpha Phi, one of the first Greek sororities in the country. At Northwestern from 1885 to 1891, she performed duties as house-mother to young women while breaking new ground in French literature. She was a Victor Hugo scholar of note, editing the French dramatist's work in an edition primarily for college teaching.

Progressive ideas provided important openings for women, especially in the law. Judge Mary M. Bartelme, an 1894 graduate of the law school, used raw courage in getting elected to a Chicago judgeship in 1923, but it was ceaseless compassion that raised her career to towering heights. On the bench, she specialized in the cases of troubled girls. Based on that experience, she opened her home to young women in need. This was the first of many "Mary Clubs," which became well-regarded as refuges for teenagers and as a major charity in Chicago society.

Nineteenth-century professional women faced many barriers, but those willing to persevere often found success. Northwestern's Catherine Waugh McCullough attended the Union College of Law when women were a novelty in the legal sphere. Graduating in 1886, she practiced law in Chicago and won such admiration that the male voters of Evanston elected her the first female justice of the peace anywhere in the nation. Serving in a succession of judicial posts in the years that followed, she pressed the cause of women's suffrage by word and example. And as the cause advanced, she accorded ample credit to the influence of coeducation in universities where "professors see not idealized women, but real women."

From the beginning the position of dean of women was filled by women who were pursuing useful and distinguished careers. Jane Bancroft Robinson assumed the post in 1877 (following Frances Willard) and remained until 1885, during which time she earned a PhD in French. In a time when doctorates for women were not common, Bancroft went on to study in Zurich and Paris and returned to the United States to take charge of the Women's Home Missionary Society of the Methodist Episcopal Church. Women, she believed, had a special role in mending the social fabric; this belief also inspired her to found the American Association of University Women.

Rogers under pressure

In 1898 the United States declared war on Spain, and most Northwestern students and faculty were quick to demonstrate their support of the war when they attended a mass meeting in Lunt Library. The meeting was to encourage students to enlist, which few did, but patriotic fervor was definitely in the air. Rogers spoke at this meeting as well, though his words were cautious. War was serious business, he said, and students ought to think twice before rushing to fight on foreign soil.

While the Spanish-American War was in progress, Rogers at first did not oppose it vocally, but when the conflict continued the following year, and American troops occupied the Philippines, Rogers held back no longer. His views on the subject were strong and already known among his friends, so when a large anti-imperialist meeting was organized in Chicago, Rogers agreed to be the featured speaker. Rogers's view was that the war was fought "to give liberty to the people of Cuba. The people of the Philippines have the same right to be free and independent."

Rogers instantly felt the wrath of Evanston. The local paper, the *Evanston Index*, charged that the president "should have been more circumspect than to take part in a meeting of such a character." Within a few days, a countermeeting was called in Evanston with the purpose, wrote the *Index*, of showing that

"the majority of prominent citizens of the city are loyal to the administration and have no sympathy with the views of the president of the University."

Rogers lasted as president for another year, but he was under constant pressure. In June 1900 he resigned with a letter that stated, "All that I had hoped to accomplish has not been attained, but I have the satisfaction of knowing that the University is in excellent condition." The resignation made headlines in Chicago, but it was never clear just what did Rogers in. The *Daily News* suggested that he was not a money hustler as compared to William Rainey Harper at the University of Chicago. Perhaps more on target was the *Index*, which stated, "A large majority of those who are most influential at Northwestern would prefer at the head a man who is a staunch Republican."

More sinister was a possibility published in a letter to the editor of the *Chicago Evening Post*. It came from an anonymous member of the Board of Trustees, who

The roots of the band program can be traced back to informal groups organized to play at football games. By 1903, the band received the sponsorship of the School of Music, marched in parades, and was under the directorship of the appropriately named Professor Charles S. Horn.

said that Rogers's dismissal was the result of a "conspiracy" among members of the board's executive committee. Their objective, wrote the dissident, was elevating Robert D. Sheppard, business manager of the University, to the presidency.

Conspiracy or not, Sheppard was too close to the center of the controversy, and he was not offered the position he clearly wished to have. It was just as well. Sheppard would soon cause considerable embarrassment to the University, and the embarrassment would have been far worse had he been president. For some years, it was revealed, Sheppard had been soliciting loans in the name of the University and of Garrett Biblical Institute, which he also represented, and putting the proceeds into real estate ventures of his own. While lenders believed they were secured by the full faith and credit of Northwestern or Garrett, some of Sheppard's investments went sour. A considerable scandal ensued, which resulted in Sheppard's resignation and his departure from Evanston in disgrace in 1909.

Rogers, meanwhile, went to Yale, where he joined the law faculty and was eventually made dean of the law school. In 1913 he was appointed by President Woodrow Wilson as judge of the United States Circuit Court of Appeals in New York City, a position he held until his death in 1926. Rogers was succeeded at Northwestern by able administrators who recognized that he had been a progressive and modern president who had ushered, or pushed, the University forthrightly into the 20th century.

Fisk Hall, designed by Daniel Burnham, was completed in 1899 and housed Northwestern's Preparatory Department, after whose principal, Herbert F. Fisk, the building was named. When the school, later called Evanston Academy, was disbanded in 1917, the building went on to house the departments of English, Romance languages, and botany (for which a greenhouse was attached to the front for several decades). In 1954 it became the home of the Medill School of Journalism.

a   **Chapin Hall** (1901)

b   **Swift Hall of Engineering** (1909)

c   **Patten Gymnasium (old)** (1909) Razed in 1940.

d   **Men's Housing Quadrangle** (1914) Original buildings; additions later.

e   **Harris Hall** (1915) Pictured.

f   **Music Practice Hall** (1915) Moved in 1925.

Lincoln

Orrington

Sheridan

Noyes

Foster

Emerson

Sherman

University

Chicago

Hinman

Clark

NORTHWESTERN'S EVANSTON CAMPUS 1900–1920

BUILT DURING THIS PERIOD

BUILT PREVIOUSLY

RAZED

THE UNIVERSITY
COMES OF AGE

Northwestern begat Evanston, but the two evolved separately, and they marched to different drummers. Evanston's reputation stressed harmony with the world and with God. "It is said that when a resident of Evanston dies," the *Chicago Herald* explained in 1890, "and his spirit knocks for admission at the pearly gates of Paradise he has but to utter the magic words 'From Evanston' and the good St. Peter admits the applicant without further question." The feeling locally was that "Evanston is a perfect Arcadia."

The University, on the other hand, was a place of modern ways and mild social anarchy. The occasional street brawl, an expression of class rivalry, was cause for concern. More persistent, perhaps, was the increasing number of students, unshaven and indifferently dressed, on streets otherwise noted for churches and a growing panorama of spacious Victorian homes.

Students were not barbarians, but to longtime Evanstonians they symbolized the encroaching world outside. Evanston was growing. It had a new streetcar line to Chicago that brought strangers to town in greater numbers than ever before.

Evanston's small-town atmosphere was further disrupted when South Evanston – more urban and hardly an Arcadia – was annexed in 1892. While growth was inevitable, Evanston's hostility toward change was easily transferred to the increasingly progressive milieu of the University. Consequently the dismissal of President Henry Wade Rogers represented a victory for the conservatives. Then in 1902 the old guard initiated something even more chilling: the "inquisition" of Professor Charles W. Pearson.

The Pearson inquisition

Charles Pearson was, by most accounts, a kind and wonderful man of wide-ranging intellect. Born in England in 1846, he sailed the world as a crewman on a merchant ship before settling down in Evanston and enrolling at Northwestern. After graduation he became a Methodist minister – following in his father's footsteps – and then returned in 1872 to teach at the University. By 1881 Pearson was a professor in the English department, a poet, and an author of essays on theological topics. It was this latter activity that led to his fateful collision with the town.

In January 1902 Pearson published an article in both the *Evanston Index* and the *Evanston Press*. Entitled "Open Inspiration vs. Closed Canon and Infallible Bible," it expressed ideas that the professor had discussed freely with colleagues in the past – that the Bible was in some respects fictitious.

"Modern preaching lacks truth and power because so many churches cling to an utterly untenable tradition that the Bible is an infallible book," he wrote. The Bible, in short, was based partly on myth.

Although Pearson was known as a religious man, his published views elicited a harsh reaction locally. The Sunday following the publication of the article, the Reverend J. J. Parkhurst, pastor of the First Methodist Church (and also a Northwestern trustee), preached emphatically against the article and asked all who believed in the Bible's unerring truth to stand. The entire congregation rose except for Professor Pearson. As adverse publicity heated up, and as the president of Garrett Biblical Institute decried Pearson's views and demanded his resignation, the trustees formed a committee to investigate what the Chicago papers termed a "scandal."

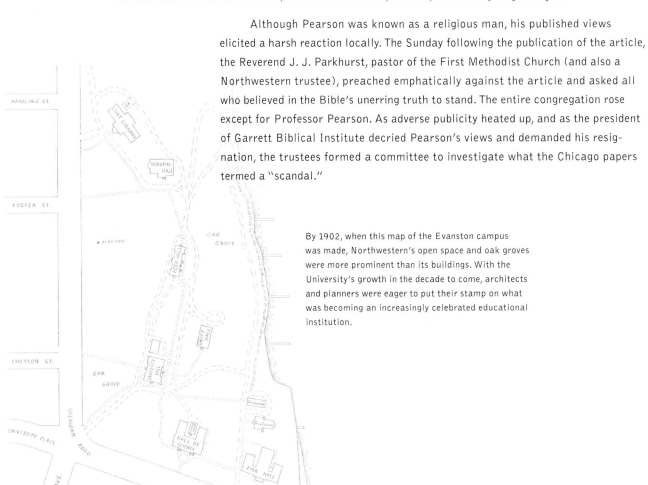

By 1902, when this map of the Evanston campus was made, Northwestern's open space and oak groves were more prominent than its buildings. With the University's growth in the decade to come, architects and planners were eager to put their stamp on what was becoming an increasingly celebrated educational institution.

Volume

Students in front of Old College in 1890.

EVANSTON ACADEMY

Northwestern established its Preparatory Department in 1859 as a way of preparing students for college. In the early years of the University, this need was so great that faculty and trustees sometimes worried that "Prep" would overshadow the rest of the University.

Enrollment outpaced that of the University for years, peaking at 701 in 1892. Fisk Hall, named for Herbert Fisk, who served as principal from 1873 to 1904, was built in 1899 to accommodate the prep school, renamed Evanston Academy in 1905. But enrollment was declining, largely because of the growth of public high schools in Illinois. In 1917, the University's board determined that the old school had served its purpose, and it was closed at the end of the school year. Fisk was converted to other uses, and a chapter from Northwestern's pioneer days was brought to a close.

Evanston Academy grew more independent as its enrollment increased, even publishing its own newspaper – the *Academian* – as early as 1896.

The Academian

EVANSTON ACADEMY

No. VII.   JANUARY 14, 1909   ice Ten Cents

Campus oratory competitions were nearly as popular as sports. In 1908, Evanston Academy had three students entered among some 40 high school students from five states competing for medals in the annual Interscholastic Declamation Contest. The Academy's Myron Kafer was a finalist and took home this medal and watch fob.

There was nothing unusual about rivalry between the classes in the 1903–04 school year. The students who produced these inflammatory pamphlets were perhaps more literate than usual, but this era's classes were rarely shy about brandishing broomsticks and canes, standard weapons in the class wars of the period.

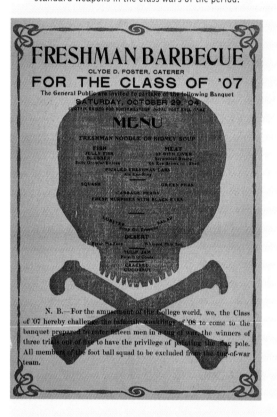

Proclamation

When in the Course of College Events

it became necessary for the class of '06 to sever their connection with the laws of good sense and common decency, a certain respect for the opinion of the Disciplinary Committee demands that we declare the causes that thus impelled THEM to the separation:

We Hold these Truths to be Self-Evident:

That all Sophomores are created brainless, that they are endowed by their creator with certain depraved hallucinations, that among these hallucinations are the following: That they own the earth by right of discovery; that their brain-sick babble can intimidate their natural superiors, the Freshmen; and that their cheap, long-delayed, crack-brained procs are a real terror to the world.

NOW WHEREAS these aforesaid irresponsible, brain-ruptured double flunkers of '06, in order to notify the world that such a contemptible organization still presumed to exist; and to provide some avenue of escape for the surplus bile engendered by their sleepless nights and continued defeats, have in their idiotic twaddle cast aspersions upon the mighty prowess of the glorious class of 1907; AND WHEREAS these same before-mentioned idiotic weaklings attempted weeks after the conflict to recoup their defeat at the flagpole by daubing the pole with COWARD'S WHITE (their true emblem), be it known to all that we accept their slobbering challenge unconditionally.

The gauge is down.
We will give no quarter.

We will choose our own headgear, be the volcanic emissions of torrid atmosphere from "Easy" Mark and his gang to the contrary notwithstanding. We will drag them to battle by the hair of their hollow hatracks and thrash their quivering forms into dog meat. We will pound their pudding pates into the subsoil so deep that the coroner will have to draw them out with an onion poultice and a scrubbing brush.

We Have
Spoken

Northwestern was led into the 20th century by an interim president firmly entrenched in the 19th. Daniel Bonbright was one of the grand old men of the faculty, having arrived as a classics professor in 1858.

As the trustees were widely regarded as conservative oligarchs, the tide against Pearson was rising. The committee initially included Professor Daniel Bonbright, acting president of the University after Rogers's departure. But seeing the tide turning inexorably against Pearson, Bonbright excused himself from rendering judgment in the matter, citing his personal friendship with the accused. This quickly sealed Pearson's fate. He resigned from Northwestern, left the Methodist Church, and became pastor of the Unitarian Church in Quincy, Illinois, where he died in 1905.

Mild anarchy and student life

While the University had lost its innocence, it remained a youthful and thriving place – not always harmonious but often remembered as colorful and charming.

Northwestern had rich students and poor ones, and many of the poor ones learned the art of economic survival early on. Joseph Dutton '01 captured this struggle in a chapter of the 1905 University history entitled "Working My Way Through." Initially, Dutton had stoked fires, sifted ashes, and shoveled snow in exchange for a room in one of the big Queen Anne houses near campus. He later moved up to the position of steward in a local boardinghouse, making $300 or $400 a year over his own expenses by keeping fellow students in room and board. Dutton found the work agreeable, despite his indifferent aptitude for the kitchen and an especially odoriferous incident with boiled rhubarb left on the stove too long.

Also remembered from this period were the more trivial but vastly more entertaining dramas of restless youth. At a freshman dance one night in 1902, for example, the gas lights went out unexpectedly, and the party was plunged into darkness. As boys shouted in fright and women fainted, the scene was a "reign of terror," according to a Chicago newspaper with a taste for sensation. For many long minutes the party was paralyzed, until several freshmen finally made their way to the front door. There they were turned back by the hooligans who had shot off the lights, who were quickly recognized as Northwestern sophomores.

Although they had been humiliated in the presence of women, the freshmen quickly devised a plan to lower their class president out a window and locate the police. By the time this was accomplished, the sophomores had dispersed, and no arrests were made. But the freshmen marched home in high dudgeon and vowed ardently to get even. Fortunately, the school year ended before any real damage could be done.

There was always class rivalry. The following fall, for example, the same class of 1905, now sophomores, was the target of a freshman plot to kidnap couples on their way to a social affair. Plans were made to incarcerate the men and spirit the women to a freshman dance in Rogers Park. The plot was uncovered because of loose-lipped freshmen, but that only ignited a series of threats and counterthreats. Any freshman seen near the sophomore dance would have a ducking in frigid Lake Michigan, sophomores warned. Freshmen countered with a promise that the kidnappings would be carried out.

Clubs and other societies in this period were inspired by many ideas, some strange. Very little is known about this photograph from the University Archives. One assumes that the precise pretext for the meeting was lost in the time between the call to order and the last drop of whatever beverage filled the large glass magnum in the front row.

"Trouble between the classes is brewing," reported the Chicago *Inter-Ocean*, "and the juniors have offered their support to the freshmen in the event of any class war." Serious violence did not materialize, however, and the newspaper dropped the story.

Women engaged in the restless spirit of college life, too, though more gently. In the eternal battle between the sexes, one victim was a less than fortunate undergrad named Charles Dickens '03. Dickens was "one of the ablest literary men in the student body," as the *Index* described him in its report of the events that ensued, but he was also a touch gullible. And he had the misfortune on the evening in question of returning his escort, Grace Mercer '04, to her residence far too late for easy excuses. Although Mercer appeared to sneak in undetected, the following day brought to the young man an entirely unwanted message. Mrs. Sergeant, the faculty resident, sought an interview with him, the *Index* said. Sincere apologies were in order.

Obediently, Dickens arrived at Woman's College at the appointed time, endured a scorching rebuke from Mrs. Sergeant, and was left chastised. Only later did Dickens learn the humiliating truth — that the scolder was an impostor, an undergraduate with a talent for the stage, and nearly a dozen young women were in the next room, listening and stuffing handkerchiefs in their mouths to keep from laughing out loud.

The beginning of the new century brought a period of loosened mores. Dating was common, and some Northwestern women became expert at scaling the walls of Willard Hall (as Woman's College was then called) to avoid the consequences of violating curfew. Many people took a laissez-faire attitude to such goings and comings, but there was also resistance to the onset of the budding romances at Northwestern. One anonymous professor, for instance, offered his sarcastic opinion of snuggling or spooning in public in the 1902 *Syllabus*: "When you have completed your daily pairing off and when you sit in loving contiguity on the several stair landings of the university buildings 'studying together,' holding each other's hands, or casting languishing glances, don't mind the disapproving glances of any professor. He's simply jealous — that's all."

"While royal purple and old gold are beautiful colors and produce a pleasing effect when combined, it would be much better, it is thought, to have a single color represent the university," stated an article in the *Northwestern* in 1892, when purple was officially adopted. This was the second change in school colors, the first coming in 1879 when purple and gold replaced black and gold in the University's athletic regalia. By the 1890s, a single color was regarded as more dignified and was also standard at Eastern colleges. "Northwestern should not be behind her eastern sisters," the newspaper noted.

The 1912 football team could muster only a record of 2-3-1.
Then as now, alumni were important to the University,
and football was important to the alumni. Homecoming that
year was played at Northwestern Field, site of the school
gridiron (now Ryan Field), since the athletic program had
outgrown old Sheppard Field on Sheridan Road.

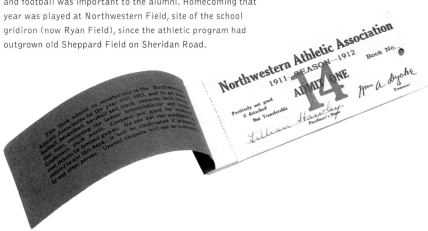

The 1901 football team.

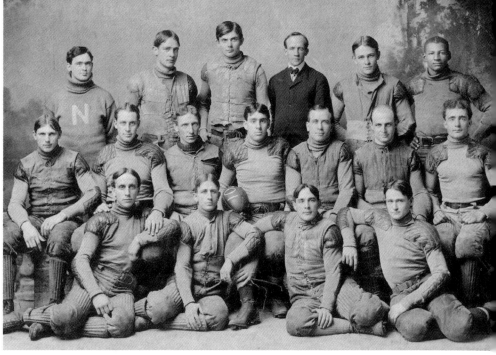

To later fans, the early Northwestern football
uniform (worn by team captain Charlie Ward '03,
later longtime secretary of the alumni association) resembled something more gladiatorial
than athletic — not too far from the views held
by the administration, which discontinued
varsity football in 1906 and 1907 because of
its violent nature.

1885

1943

1929

1932

THE SYLLABUS

The first yearbook issued from the fertile imaginations of Northwestern undergraduates was called *Pandora* after the source of all chaos, which this annual for the school year 1883–84 was not. It was a tame student publication that listed faculty, classes, officers, and organizations in a dutiful way.

The following year, *Pandora* was replaced by the *Syllabus*, a name whose explanation was not recorded, though the first *Syllabus* in 1885, like those of most succeeding issues, exhibited a structure as rigid as the outline of any first-year Latin course. Literary flair crept in, of course, with reflective prose about college life. In 1886, for example, an essay signed by the perhaps weary seniors observed that their greeting to old Northwestern four long years before had been "but the prelude to a farewell." They claimed to be "worthy models for succeeding classes." Actually, it did not appear that the freshmen were paying that much attention to their elders. Their class essay that year recounted with pride the exploits of "one heroic freshman" who sneaked into the cloakroom at a sophomore supper and threw every overcoat and wrap out the window.

The *Syllabus* always has been a handsome publication. For its first nine years it was published by the fraternities. (Thus, its pages devoted to Greek-letter social organizations were designed with the flourish of royal proclamations.) In 1894 the yearbook was taken over by the junior class, a custom that continued until 1946. Yearbooks in this period were identified by the juniors' graduating class year, so the 1920 *Syllabus*, for example, actually chronicles the 1918–19 school year.

Almost from the beginning, the *Syllabus* advanced the cause of the semiserious. In 1929 the caption for a photo of a railroad tank car marked with the letters of Delta Tau Delta suggested that the car carried a shipment of hooch from Ontario. In another caption, a line of baby carriages was identified as a traffic jam at the School of Music.

More straightforward on this subject was Professor Alja R. Crook. Crook was a confirmed bachelor with a Van Dyke beard and the aloof air of a scientist. But there was one thing that jolted him, and that was the spectacle, or even the thought, of students kissing. When a reporter from Chicago discovered Crook's views on the subject, his opinions quickly became a matter of public record. Then began a kind of crusade, albeit a short-lived one, when a group of male and female undergraduates formed the Northwestern University Anti-Kissing Society. Promising to follow Professor Crook's teaching, they dedicated themselves to the proposition that kissing was disgusting and demoralizing and "entirely unnecessary in respectable courtships."

Quite naturally, the effectiveness of the Anti-Kissing Society, not to mention its sincerity, was suspect. And not many months after it was created, the society was delivered a death blow when two leading antiosculators, John W. McClinton '03 and Frances C. Lemery, briefly enrolled in the School of Music, were engaged to be married. "The society is at once disbanded and it is rumored that several other important announcements may be expected in the few days remaining in the college year," according to a Chicago newspaper.

Northwestern University in Chicago

Northwestern remained focused on the idea of becoming a larger and more consolidated university, and in 1902 the institution took a step forward by purchasing Chicago's Tremont House hotel on the southeast corner of Lake and Dearborn Streets. The site of the Tremont and its name were fabled in Chicago lore; the Tremont was best known as the headquarters of Lincoln's inner circle that engineered the Republican nomination in 1860. That hotel burned in 1871, but it was rebuilt and two decades later purchased by Northwestern. It was a stately edifice in the French Second Empire style. The purchase and renovation revealed the trustees' taste for Loop real estate (the LaSalle and Jackson property was still paying handsome dividends). But the University's main objective was to house the professional schools, though the Medical School would remain physically separate, close to its teaching hospitals, and largely independent.

The impact of the new Northwestern University Building, as it was called, was underlined by plans for President Theodore Roosevelt to participate in a ceremony to dedicate the law school's new quarters. Unfortunately, Roosevelt fell ill and canceled, sending his most recent nominee to the U.S. Supreme Court, Oliver Wendell Holmes, in his place. Pageantry for the occasion was as impressive as anything ever conducted by the University – it took place over the three-day inaugural of the University's new president, Edmund Janes James, in October 1902. Processions of alumni and faculty passed through rows of students in caps and gowns. Holmes used a diamond point to scratch his name and the date into a glass panel on the wall and then gave a memorable address, reflecting in part on the humble origins of this school and the stately new quarters now before him.

"It has been affirmed that the law was and ought to be commonplace," Holmes declared. "I almost fear that the intellectual ferment of the better schools may be too potent an attraction to young men, and seduce into the profession many who would be better elsewhere." But Holmes went on to express approval for Northwestern and especially for his friend Dean John Henry Wigmore.

"I feel quite sure, from his printed work, that his teaching will satisfy the two-fold desire of men; that it will send them forth with a pennon as well as with a sword, to keep before their eyes in the long battle the little flutter that means ideals, honor, and yes, even romance, in all the dull details."

Such praise from one of the most eminent legal minds of the age certainly must have set Wigmore's heart aflutter. It also affirmed the decision he made to accept the Northwestern deanship the year before; the offer had come when he and a number of colleagues were offered positions in the new University of Chicago Law School. Julian Mack was the only faculty member to jump ship.

The Tremont Hotel, located at Dearborn and Lake Streets, became the Northwestern University Building in 1902. Thoroughly renovated for academic use, the building gave the University a downtown identity and consolidated three of its professional schools located in Chicago.

John Henry Wigmore joined the Northwestern University School of Law as a professor in 1893. He was dean from 1901 to 1929, during which time he increased the size of the school and its ambition to be "a Law School of the highest character." Wigmore also was a towering legal scholar, producing his *Treatise on Evidence* in 1904–05. Wigmore summarized his work by observing, "The general rules are based on shrewd experience in human nature."

NORTHWESTERN UNIVERSITY
Equal Suffrage League
WEDNESDAY EVENING, APRIL 6, 1910

Music Hall, Evanston

———PROGRAM———
Violin Solo . . . MISS WINIFRED GOODSMITH
Reading . . . . MISS PEARL OSBORNE
Vocal Solo—"The Cry of Rachel"—Salter
MISS EDITH COX

"How the Vote Was Won"
Cicely Hamilton and Christopher St. John
Produced for the first time at the Royalty Theatre, London,
April 13th, 1909

Staged under direction of MISS DOROTHY HORNING
Press Agent MISS JESSIE CAMPBELL
Business Manager MISS RUTH CARTER

CAST OF CARACTERS
Horace Cole (an Englishman) Mr. Eugene A. Luther
Ethel (his wife) . . . Miss Carol Albright
Winifred (Ethel's sister) . Miss Marguerite Raeder
Agatha Cole (Horace's sister) . Miss Elizabeth Fox
Molly (his niece) . . . . Miss Corinne Kahlo
Madame Christine (a distant relative)
Miss Pearl Winters
Maudie Spark (his cousin, a music-hall star)
Miss Lucile Morgan
Aunt Lizzie . . . . Miss Ruth Waring
Lily (his maid-of-all-work) . Miss Mildred Nevitt
Gerald Williams (his neighbor) . Mr. Ray F. Bruce
SCENE—Living-room in middle class English home.

PATRONESSESS
Mrs. J. Scott Clark   Mrs. Henry Crew   Mrs. U. S. Grant
Miss Eleanor Harris   Mrs. Thos. F. Holgate   Mrs. Wm. E. Hotchkiss
Mrs. Wm. A. Locy   Miss Mary Ross Potter   Miss E. I. Raitt
Mrs. Amos W. Patten   Mrs. Rob't R. Tatnall   Miss Minnie Terry
Mrs. A. H. Wilde

Northwestern and Evanston constituted a center of suffrage activity during the long fight for women's right to vote, which American women finally won in 1920. Feminist sentiments were definitely in the mainstream in 1910, at least locally. Patronesses of the program at left were the wives of many of Evanston's most powerful men.

Wigmore would continue as dean of the School of Law until 1929. In that time he demonstrated the notion that, although the law was designed for the common man, its great, inspired minds were indispensable. In cultivating potential donors, Wigmore revitalized the school's alumni association. Among the alumni was Elbert H. Gary, class of 1867, then president of U.S. Steel and namesake of Gary, Indiana; from him Wigmore obtained a series of contributions, initially for expensive and rare books on international law, making the school's library one of the most impressive in legal education.

State-of-the-art dental education

Another resident of the Northwestern University Building was the Dental School, which located its clinic on the top floor of the renovated hotel. Beneath a sky-light running the length of the building, the clinic featured 135 state-of-the-art dental chairs, each with an instrument table and fountain cuspidor. Lecture halls downstairs were suited for the steadily improving standard of dental education.

The Dental School took justifiable pride in its efforts to bring dentistry, until that time a brutal tooth-yanker's trade, into the realm of modern science.

"Dentistry is a calling which within the last few years began to pass from the stage of a mere mechanical calling into that of a learned profession," said University President Edmund James at the 1903 graduation of 175 students.

Professionalizing dentistry had taken time, however. Back in 1888 the University College of Dental and Oral Surgery, then loosely affiliated with Northwestern, attempted to increase its course of study from two years to three – the nation's first dental school to do so. Enrollment plummeted and the school came close to dissolution. Then in 1891, the college came under the full control of the University, which motivated Chicago's best dentists to join the school's faculty.

The Dental School clinic was located on the top floor of the Northwestern University Building. Students were responsible for recruiting their own patients, which not only provided subjects for their training but introduced a larger public to modern dentistry.

Dr. Greene Vardiman Black was a leader in bringing dentistry into the 20th century. Late in his career he undertook the deanship of the Dental School and raised its stature while elevating that of the profession at large.

Dance cards had dual utility. They maintained order at dances and provided colorful keepsakes. Their importance was manifest in their careful and sometimes elaborate designs.

Delta
Tau
Delta

CO-OPERATE!
Your dancing is objectionable.
If continued you will be asked
to leave the floor.

N
1912

CHI·OMEGA

The freshman class play at Ravinia Theater in May 1912 was about a Professor Trig who is beset by his suffragette wife – so much so that he promises his soul to the devil should he ever surrender to her feminine charms again. After three acts and numerous songs written by classmates, the denouement was sad for the professor, but the play gave the audience a good time. The score later went on sale at the college bookstore.

Fight songs were big at Northwestern in this period, as they were at campuses throughout the country. The "Military March" – this version was published in 1912 – did not rise to the level of a classic. "Go! Northwestern Go!" later became "Go! U Northwestern," the long-lived standard for the marching band, alums, and fans. Its composer, Theodore Van Etten '13, penned it while a senior in the School of Pharmacy, after an unexpected victory against Indiana prompted him to write the school's victory song. Years later, in 1940, Van Etten was made an honorary letterman and member of the N Men's Club.

Northwestern University Dental School quickly assumed professional leadership and enrollment grew.

Of critical service in these years was Dr. Greene Vardiman Black, who was a faculty member since 1883 and considered the father of modern dentistry because of the many technical developments attributed to him, such as the use of gold-foil fillings and the invention of the foot-powered drill. Since the Civil War, Black had used his training as an MD to bring true research methods to dental subjects. His papers, such as "The Formation of Poisons by Micro-organisms" and "Pathology of Dental Pulp," were many and widely read. Black became dean of the Dental School in 1897 and in 1900 was honored by being made president of the National Dental Association. By then he was a true elder but was still engaged in energetically defending his school and his profession from the showers of evil attention that sometimes rained on dentistry. In 1899, for example, Chicago was exposed as the center for "irregular" dental schools, otherwise known as diploma mills, and while Black and many of his colleagues were probably guilty of having ignored this problem in the past, he headed a governor's task force that helped eradicate such schools.

Ultimately the diploma-mill furor brought attention to the distinguished scientific work being done at Northwestern. Among important publications of the period, *Prosthetic Dentistry* was published by Northwestern professor Dr. James Harrison Prothero. His work constituted the best encyclopedia to date on restorative techniques, from inlay construction to dentures, and also on the bioscientific considerations necessary to make dental work an asset and not an infectious liability.

Black and Northwestern were on the battle lines of another conflict in 1904, when the Fourth Annual Dental Congress in St. Louis decided to exclude a distinguished Chicago dentist and former student of Black's, Charles E. Bentley, from the proceedings because he was an African American. European and Latin American dentists at the congress strongly supported Bentley. The Americans were less supportive, although Dean Black took a strong antiracist stand and did much to place the University on the right side of this persistent issue.

Throughout this early period of the Dental School, Greene Vardiman Black represented the good work done at Northwestern. Before he retired in 1915, he had taken dentistry out of the dark alleys and into the light of modern science. "He is also a musician, an artist, a linguist, a machinist, besides being a physician and surgeon as well as a dentist," wrote his successor as dean, Dr. Thomas Gilmer.

The James administration

The "University idea" had taken hold at Northwestern, and the institution was growing on many fronts. Still, the problem of sustained leadership beset the administration. Power remained with the Board of Trustees, which was a partial cause for the swift departure of Edmund James as president. James resigned in 1904 after only two years, saying that the trustees' ambitious plans for the University were impossible to fulfill when those same trustees prohibited his

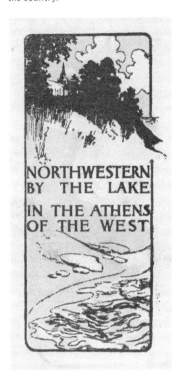

This 1901 brochure featured the buildings of the University in Evanston and Chicago. Its title reveals a confidence that came from growing maturity and distinction; Northwestern was at this time the third-largest university in the country.

NORTHWESTERN BY THE LAKE IN THE ATHENS OF THE WEST

"Sing a Song of College Days"

Looking from the North Window –
Music School – University Place – Willard Courts –

Alna
5/26/20

Tony's Passport Picture
Yokohama – August 1919.

"The Crow's Nest"
(Room 24 .Willard Hall)

Emmy in the "Patriarchal
Robe"
June 1919.

Mr. and Mrs. Edward Stone of Montreal, Canada, announce the engagement of their daughter Katharine Doris to Helmuth Christian Hay of 1134 Greenleaf avenue.
Tribune 5/9/20

Frexy Hough – 5/26/20
Syllabus Day

Trip to the Sag – Lemont, Ill. May 1, 1920.

Katherine Mason   The Crow   Myrtle Clancy.

Edith Sternfeld '21 availed herself of many social pleasures of college life. Scrapbooks like this one provide an intimate glimpse of the life of a student, an aspect of the University that is not easily seen in the official yearbooks and campus newspapers of the time.

INTIMATE VIEWS FROM AFAR

If students from one century could ever penetrate campus life in another, their time travel vehicles might be old college scrapbooks. Scrapbooks, lovingly kept by many students in that era, recorded memories and immortalized triumphs when Evanston was quiet and when the small events of college life were savored.

Among the many scrapbooks surviving in the University Archives is this exquisite example that belonged to Edith Sternfeld '21, an artist and later a professor of art at Grinnell College in Iowa. Much from Sternfeld's life at Northwestern is contained in this ledger-sized, purple-bound album, emblazoned with a large "N" on the cover. Sternfeld participated in most tag days, evidently. In her Friendship Party Book classmates and acquaintances at a YWCA affair wrote a few lines about their affection for her.

Scrapbooks were kept by men as well; they were often filled with news clippings about athletic contests and, often enough, about pranks and brawls of undergraduates. But the women applied real thoughtfulness and care in assembling their scrapbooks in a time when student publications, which also recorded moments from student life, were dominated by men.

administration from incurring debt. In truth, James was also an indifferent fund-raiser. At any rate, when he was offered the presidency of the tax-supported University of Illinois, he took it and left the problems of a private university behind.

While the James administration at Northwestern was otherwise uneventful, it represented, in retrospect, a turning point. "No more kite flyers," said William Deering, president of the Board of Trustees, after James resigned. He meant that Northwestern's president must be a realist, not a dreamer. From this time forward, Deering implied, the president should concern himself with the concrete needs of the University.

Seeking an architectural signature

Forging a single vision at the top was no trivial matter. The lack of one in this period led to, among other things, campus architecture that was anything but cohesive. Northwestern coveted architectural distinction: in 1905 it asked the Chicago architect Daniel Burnham to draw up a plan for the growing Evanston campus. Burnham, former architectural chief of the World's Columbian Exposition, was becoming one of the nation's leading architects and planners. His plan for Northwestern, however, led to nothing, though this was hardly due to lack of soundness or splendor. Rather, business manager William A. Dyche said it was "too radical and contemplates the destruction of all our present buildings," as he later wrote in a letter to a trustee.

In fact, Burnham never dreamed that Northwestern would raze the old campus to build a new one. Rather he was imagining a unified Evanston campus with a great quadrangle facing Lake Michigan and neoclassical-inspired buildings that could guide the designs of the future. Yet Dyche didn't even bother to show Burnham's plan to more than two or three trustees. Two years passed before he asked another well known architect, George Washington Maher, for another plan.

With offices in Chicago, Maher had earned distinction throughout the Midwest for his Prairie-style architecture, related in many ways to that of Frank Lloyd Wright, who was a few years younger. Presumably the architect was introduced to Northwestern by commodities broker James Patten, who was the Evanston mayor and future president of the Northwestern board. Maher had designed Patten's (now-demolished) home on Ridge Avenue, which was widely

Completed in 1910, the original Patten Gymnasium was a hallmark work of architect George W. Maher. It improved Northwestern's prospects in athletics and hosted the first NCAA national basketball championship in 1939, just months before it was razed.

extolled in the architectural journals of the day. Maher was a proponent of "organic architecture" and promoted a style that he insisted should be indigenously American. He rejected all European influence – no neoclassicism for him – which made nearly everything he did original. Sometimes it was marvelously unique, as in Patten's house built of massive limestone blocks.

As Maher developed a campus plan – not too different from Burnham's idea of quadrangles on the lake – he was also commissioned to design Patten Gymnasium and Swift Hall. Of the two, the gym could be called a masterpiece, a broad arch of a facade not only monumental but an echo of the great vaulted space inside. One can only imagine what Maher might have done had he designed an entire campus. Northwestern might have become an architectural wonder – the largest Prairie-style project of the period. But it was not to be.

Why did Maher lose the major part of the Northwestern job? It may have been because of Swift Hall, which was built to house the new school of engineering. Expertly proportioned, Swift may have dismayed some people, because it is a stark building, almost devoid of ornamentation, even though American tastes had not yet moved to such a modern look. Maher's disappointment at Northwestern may also have been caused by something else: his bewildering prose. As a wildly idealistic architect, Maher wrote essays about new "democratic" architecture that were frequently impenetrable.

"It may be the awakening of a loyalty toward the developing of our college architecture along the ideals expressive of Americanism," he wrote in an essay about his Northwestern plan. "It will see and comprehend possibilities in landscape and building that breathe of a democracy, here at hand."

Heck Hall, which housed mostly students from Garrett Biblical Institute, was gutted by fire in the winter of 1914. Pictured are students retrieving their belongings from the ice-covered building in the wake of the fire. The building, which was located in the center of campus where Deering Library was later built, was then razed.

Swift Hall, designed by architect George W. Maher and opened in 1909, housed the University's School of Engineering.

Shortly after Maher wrote these lines, the board decided to conduct a competition for its most pressing need at the moment: men's dormitories. Maher, who felt rebuked, entered the contest anyway, proposing a complex of horizontal buildings, "simple, dignified, and free from foolish conventionalities and thus contributing in no small measure to the educational features of the institution," as the architect described them. He didn't get the job. It went instead to Henry Hornbostel, a former colleague of Stanford White, the famous neoclassicist who designed New York's Grand Central Station. At Northwestern, Hornbostel produced brick dormitories in the neo-Gothic style, and they represented a handsome improvement to a campus that still lacked a coherent architectural stamp. But when the buildings of the so-called North Quads were finished, so was Hornbostel's work for Northwestern. Anything resembling a unified architectural vision for the University was another generation in coming.

Abram Winegardner Harris (1858–1935) was president from 1906 to 1916, which was among the most productive periods for the University up to that time.

The productive years of Abram W. Harris

The University progressed nicely during the next administration, that of President Abram W. Harris, who arrived in 1906. A Wesleyan graduate, Harris had held a number of positions before coming to Northwestern, including the presidency of Maine State College, which he transformed into a university. Harris was a builder at heart, and one task he undertook early in his tenure was establishing a new School of Commerce, an idea first advanced by President James.

Unfortunately James could not get his conservative trustees, commercial men for the most part, to embrace business training as a part of the Northwestern curriculum. James was less than diplomatic, certainly. "The average businessman," he said, "is ignorant and inefficient and cowardly. He is helpless in a crisis." His meaning was clear enough – that a broadly educated manager was more effective than a bullheaded one. But persuasive James was not, and it was left to his successor to win the battle by "the art of sweet reasonableness," as Abram Harris liked to describe his management style.

In a later article, "The College and Business Life," Harris wrote that the interests of colleges and businesses were beginning to come together.

"Business used to have a poor opinion of college men, and the achievement of college men in business gave some excuse for that view." He added, "The head of the most prominent banking corporation in the United States is a college graduate." This example served to elevate not banking but rather college education.

Bringing the business school idea to fruition took time. Harris and his colleagues wanted an elaborate curriculum of three years in a liberal arts–oriented program in Evanston, then a fourth year in Chicago with specialized business courses, taught by "men actively engaged in business." This was overly ambitious. Instead, Harris and Willard E. Hotchkiss, an economics professor, initiated the program in 1908 mostly with business courses offered at night.

The School of Commerce was a "commercial" success from the outset, with more than 250 students enrolling in courses in the first year. The catalogue included courses in accounting, commercial law, banking, finance, insurance, transportation, merchandising, and administration. Within two or three years, 500 students were enrolled (more than 200 of whom were women), but precious few were working toward a degree. Demand focused instead on the practical, a situation that forced Dean Hotchkiss to insist that the School of Commerce was not just a trade school and to repeat that the curriculum was "essentially an offshoot of [Northwestern's] economics work."

Still, the School of Commerce did teach the hard lessons of practical experience, and within a few years the school began to develop a teaching methodology that eventually became "the case method." This technique – not yet named – was initiated at Northwestern by Professor Arch Shaw, who had seen it used in legal education at Harvard Law School. Almost from its beginning, the School of Commerce brought business leaders to the lecture hall and classroom. The individuals described problems and options they faced, and students were asked to summarize possible outcomes of various decisions and strategies.

One real-world practitioner who lectured at the new School of Commerce was John Lee Mahin, a well-known Chicago advertising executive. In an evening lecture in 1911, when marketing was primitive and advertising often ineffective, Mahin explained how advertising dollars could be understood on a per capita basis. "Figures show," Mahin said, "the cost of newspaper and periodical advertising to be $1.75 per year." He compared that with $4 per capita for public education and $10 for "intoxicants." Mahin also asked the class to compare an advertising campaign with other promotional schemes, such as the distribution of free product samples, throughout Chicago. "The expense of distributing samples," he said, "at the rate of five cents per home reached would cover the cost of nearly 22 pages of advertising in every newspaper." The adman Mahin's analysis may now appear self-serving, but his point of view, along with those of many other lecturers actively engaged in business at the time, was an eye-opener.

The founding of the School of Commerce was a major milestone of the Harris administration. But it was also arduous. It was just one of many accomplishments

Some of Northwestern's most important figures achieved striking success outside the ivory-tower environment. Walter Dill Scott, future president of the University, was one. After training as a psychologist at Northwestern and the University of Leipzig, Germany (where he earned his PhD), he applied his experience to organizing the personnel administration of the U.S. Army in World War I. Scott's system eschewed the old-boy network in the military and devised quantitative techniques to evaluate soldiers for assignment.

NORTHWESTERN
UNIVERSITY
BULLETIN

Vol. XX, No. 22   Nov. 29, 1919

Published Weekly by Northwestern University
Northwestern University Building :: Chicago

Northwestern University
School of Commerce

Announces a Course in

PERSONNEL
ADMINISTRATION

Given by

PROFESSOR WALTER DILL SCOTT

Formerly, Chairman of the
Committee on Classification of Personnel,
United States Army

President, The Scott Company

Although Arthur Andersen did not receive a bachelor of business administration degree from Northwestern until 1917, he was a certified public accountant and part-time lecturer at the School of Commerce as early as 1910. Andersen later built Northwestern's accounting department to preeminence before leaving the faculty in 1922 to devote his full energies to his firm, Arthur Andersen & Company. He remained connected to the University as a member of the Board of Trustees and its president from 1930 to 1932.

Tuition, uniforms, and incidentals were provided free to each trainee of the Students' Army Training Corps. Each was ordered to prepare "in anticipation of his call to the colors, for active national service."

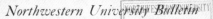

Northwestern University Bulletin

SEP 21 1918

LIBRARY

The
Northwestern University Unit
of the
Students' Army Training Corps
of the
United States Army

Company A of the Reserve Officers' Training Corps at the entrance to the Patten Gymnasium, which building contains a drill hall 215 by 120 feet in size and a gymnasium exercise room with 7200 square feet of floor space

Volume XIX, No. 16   November 9, 1918

Published Weekly by Northwestern University
Northwestern University Building
Chicago

[Entered as Second Class Matter Nov. 21, 1914, at the Post Office at Chicago, Illinois, under Act of Congress of Aug. 24, 1912. Accepted for mailing at special rate of postage provided for in Section 1103, Act of Oct. 3, 1917, authorized on June 14, 1918.]

In 1918 most men were not just students, they were also military trainees in the Students' Army Training Corps.

Women were essential to the war effort. Some Northwestern women left school to serve as nurses. Faculty wives, pictured here preparing medical kits for use on the front, were members of the local Red Cross chapter.

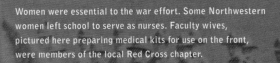

REPORTS FROM THE GREAT WAR

The Western Front was a world away when Northwestern students developed a romantic attraction to World War I. Among the first to succeed in getting to France were members of a local company of YMCA student relief workers. Among them was Jack Barker '17, who was assigned to visit English infantry camps, where he played ragtime on the piano and then asked his audience to sign pledge cards of "Christian allegiance."

Herbert Taylor '17 exhibited an entrepreneurial side as a YMCA worker, purchasing French bars frequented by Americans and turning them into alcohol-free hotels. Taylor's operations were funded in part by a scheme to exchange dollars for francs at an exorbitantly favorable rate. "So unusual has been Mr. Taylor's businesslike efficiency that many of his large staff of assistants outrank him in point of seniority," stated the *Chicago Daily News*, affirming the blend of capitalism and the Lord's work that infused, one hoped, many Northwestern students.

World War I forced members of the Northwestern community to turn their attention away from the ivory tower and toward the real world and its dangers. By 1918, the reality of the battlefront overcame romantic attitudes surrounding war, but it did not dampen students' willingness to serve. Another major contribution of Northwestern was to organize more than 200 doctors, nurses, and enlisted personnel from Chicago to operate a field hospital at Comiers, France, 15 miles from Boulogne.

Base Hospital #12, as this unit was known, received a heavy blow early, on May 19, 1917, just a day after leaving New York on the transport ship *Mongolia*. During target practice on the open sea, powder caps from a fired shell boomeranged and struck several nurses on a nearby deck, killing two. The nurses were from Chicago hospitals, not Northwestern, but their deaths were among the earliest American casualties of the war.

World War I sharpened the continuing discussion of the proper role of women in modern society. A case in point came with the story of Frances Poole of Evanston, who did not graduate with her Northwestern classmates in 1911 because she left school to become a welfare nurse. Later, when the first American men fell in Europe, she enlisted in the Red Cross and was assigned to a military hospital in upstate New York. She was still caring for bedridden veterans when the influenza epidemic hit the nation in 1918. She contracted the deadly flu herself but kept working until pneumonia set in, and five days later she died.

When Poole was brought home to be buried, she joined some 65 Northwestern men and women who lost their lives in service in World War I. "She had wanted to come home with colors flying," wrote the *Syllabus*, "and so she did."

This "service flag" from the Northwestern University School of Law commemorated those who fought. The flag exhibits 363 blue stars, each one representing a student or graduate in military service during the war. Yellow and white stars are thought to represent casualties; there were three when the flag was made toward the end of 1917.

of the president, who retired from the University in 1916 to take a less-demanding position with the Methodist Episcopal Church in New York.

The Great War

World War I interrupted the work of Northwestern, but it forced positive change in the life of the University. As the first truly national emergency since the Civil War, the Great War encouraged all of the University's schools to work toward a common objective. War has always galvanized universities, and this one drew the emphatic support of the students, faculty, and administration in Evanston and Chicago. Months before America entered the war, for example, Professor Thomas Holgate, who succeeded Harris as acting president, offered the services of Northwestern to the government for a department of military science. Such a department would include courses in "the art of war, the history of war, camp practice, sanitation, and the like," promised a University publication at the time.

Northwestern's eventual role during the war was less lofty. A formal department was not established, though courses in military technology were taught, and in 1918 the Evanston campus became a site for the Students' Army Training Corps, which enlisted most male undergraduates in the college as officer trainees. The SATC engaged less in the "art of war" and more in raw military discipline – with uniforms, marching, and students barking orders at other students.

It's no surprise that many aspects of military training were less than inspiring for many Northwestern scholars. When it was over, one student-trainee remembered that, among other lessons, it provided an early taste of military regulation, including a splendid bit of nonsense involving marching to class. This was to be done in units, though this cadet found himself marching alone as the sole member of his unit to a certain class. He was, moreover, often late for that class because as leader he was required to make a report of attendance of the unit at the class.

Beanies had been in evidence at Northwestern since the 1880s, when freshmen were compelled by domineering sophomores to wear them. Over the years, the wearing of beanies ebbed and flowed. The quaint custom reached a high pitch around the time that Mary Merle Piper '19 wore this one – any freshman caught bareheaded risked a good dunking in the lake. Beanies were worn into the 1950s, when freshmen could remove them and burn them in a bonfire if and when they defeated sophomores in a three-legged relay race.

Completion of Patten Gymnasium, dedicated in 1910, broadened athletic programs for women as well as men. The Woman's Athletic Association (WAA), which financed the bloomer uniforms for the basketball team, was founded in 1911 and raised money originally through sandwich days. A year later WAA raised funds with a minstrel show, which became annual and evolved into the present-day Waa-Mu Show.

The May Pageant represented traditional rites of spring on campus. This one in 1916 involved a performance that was described by the *Daily Northwestern* as an "airy fantasy," an idealized version of nature, performed in dance and music. Although May celebrations in ancient times were enmeshed in the symbolism of fertility, this one featured the dominant note of flag-waving patriotism and growing excitement over women's suffrage.

LOST NORTHWESTERN

In its early decades, Northwestern was building a university for the ages, at least when finances permitted. In styles that harked back to the old truths, Northwestern architecture turned mostly to Europe, to the Italianate (Old College), the French Second Empire (Heck Hall), and the Romanesque (Fayerweather Hall) styles. In one case (the original Patten Gym) it turned to an American architect, George W. Maher, who made forging an American style his lifelong mission. Many of these buildings were distinguished works of architecture, but they did not set a unifying tone for the growing campus, and when modern efficiency demanded, they were razed mostly without protest.

Of all of Northwestern's architecture, the original Patten Gym might be the most memorable and distinctive. The great arching structure, built in 1910, had few precedents on campus or anyplace else. The gym was razed in 1940 to make room for the new Technological Institute.

12004. Northwestern Gymnasium, Evanston, Ill.

View of campus circa 1914.

D GYMNASIUM & OLD COLLEGE, NORTHWESTERN, EVANSTON, ILL.

The first building of the University eventually became known as Old College. Originally on the northwest corner of Hinman Avenue and Davis Street, it was moved in 1871 to a site near present-day Fisk Hall, where it housed the prep school, and was moved again in 1898 to the north to make room for Fisk. When it was finally razed in 1973 shortly after a lightning strike that set off the building's sprinkler system, it had served for many years as the home of the School of Education.

Heck Hall, the first substantial masonry building on campus, was erected in 1867 as a dormitory for the Garrett Biblical Institute. It burned in 1914 — "mice and matches" was the ambiguous cause stated in the *Evanston Index*. Deering Library now stands on the site of Heck Hall.

116 B.

Heck Hall

Copyright 1907 By C R Childs, Chicago

Biblical Hall, Northwestern University, Evanston, Ill.—3

Memorial Hall was dedicated by Garrett Biblical Institute in 1887. It was the work of W. W. Boyington, who had designed Chicago's Water Tower two decades earlier. In 1923 Memorial Hall (fondly known as the Little Red School House) was turned over to Northwestern, and it housed the School of Commerce. It was razed in 1970 to make way for Leverone Hall, quarters for the burgeoning Graduate School of Management.

a **Business Office** (1923)

b **Garrett Evangelical Theological Seminary** (1924)

c **Dyche Stadium** (1926) Now Ryan Field.

d **Women's Housing Quadrangle** (1926) Original buildings; additions later.

e **Locy Laboratory** (1928)

f **Seabury-Western Theological Seminary** (1929)

g **Deering Library** (1933)

h **Willard Hall** (1938)

¾ mile west on Central

Lincoln

Orrington

Sheridan

Noyes

Foster

Emerson

Sherman

University

Chicago

Hinman

Clark

NORTHWESTERN'S EVANSTON CAMPUS 1920–1939

BUILT DURING THIS PERIOD

BUILT PREVIOUSLY

RAZED

CHAPTER 5

Levy Mayer Hall
(1926)

**Ward Memorial
Building** (1926)
Pictured.

Wieboldt Hall (1927)

Thorne Auditorium
(1932) Razed in 1982.

**NORTHWESTERN'S
CHICAGO CAMPUS
1920–1939**

i

j

k

l

Chicago

Superior

Huron

Fairbanks

McClurg

Lake Shore Drive

5

WALTER DILL SCOTT AND
A GREATER
NORTHWESTERN

**The University came to a crossroads in 1920 when the revolving
door of the president's office spun again. Lynn Harold Hough,
a minister and theologian, was appointed to the post in 1919
with high hopes that his eloquence and "sterling character" would
bring flocks of new supporters to Northwestern. Unfortunately,
Hough resigned after a year and two months in office – discouraged,
perhaps, by postwar inflation and the University's ominous financial deficit.**

**Frustrated but determined, the Board of Trustees embarked
on another presidential search. There was reason for optimism,
despite the Hough setback. Enrollment was up – from 4,100
students before the war to 6,800 in 1919 – and the board saw an era
of prosperity on the horizon. Northwestern was on the verge of
greatness, they believed, and the institution could attain it with
stable leadership and a large endowment.**

**If ever there were a university president for his time, it was
Walter Dill Scott, class of 1895, who was appointed to be the ninth**

president of Northwestern. Scott was an Illinois farm boy with an innovative spirit and Midwestern practicality who made it to college and graduate school and even achieved a successful career as an entrepreneur.

Scott's rural roots

It would be hard to imagine a success story more American than that of Scott, born in 1869 near Bloomington, Illinois. He was barely an adolescent when his father became disabled, forcing the youngster to work the family farm, sometimes single-handedly. At age 12, Scott was doing the spring plowing himself, but as he plowed he studied his lessons, reading grammar and history books while the horses rested between furrows. With the encouragement of his mother, a schoolteacher, and through sheer force of will, he kept the farm going and got through school, eventually winning a state-supported scholarship to college. He entered Northwestern, albeit late, at the age of 22.

Age didn't matter, evidently. Scott became a prominent member of the student body virtually from the time he arrived. He played on the football team, for example, though he was told it was ill-advised because he was slight and might easily be hurt. Scott persevered, however, spending the summer between his first and second years hiking and conditioning. He became a three-time letterman in the sport, even breaking a finger in a hard-fought contest against the University of Chicago.

Though Scott was stubborn, he was not rebellious. Nevertheless, he did play a leading role in the senior class burlesque before graduating in 1895. It was a mock chapel exercise; Scott portrayed then-president Henry Wade Rogers and affected the manners of an old-fashioned schoolmaster (which Rogers actually was not), looking stern as the students parodied religious customs and sang:

Fifty freshies grew up fast;/Seniors we became at last.../Soon we'll sit in other schools/Teaching many little fools.

Truth and psychology

Scott's college studies were not foolish at all but were serious work, primarily under philosophy professor George A. Coe. Fortunately for Scott, Coe was uncommonly open to new ideas. "It is of the utmost value to the whole cause of truth," Coe said, "that the mind, before attaining the relative fixity of maturity, should for a

Walter Dill Scott (1869–1955) was a psychologist, and for a short period, a consultant, before ascending to the presidency of Northwestern in 1920. He was the first alumnus of the University to hold the position.

By the 1920s the women's physical education program was growing, with as many as four instructors in the department. "In gymnastic classes," wrote the *Syllabus* some years earlier, "attention was paid to corrective and rhythmic exercises, which aimed to produce control through a responsive relationship between mind and body...."

Northwestern's Orchesis was an honorary member of the local chapter of a national dance organization. Started in 1924 as an offshoot of the women's physical education department, Orchesis engaged in interpretative dance, a predecessor to modern dance. In early performances, students choreographed and performed works with titles such as "Mood o' the Mist" and "Flames."

Sophomore Hop dance card.

time assume an utterly free and questioning attitude toward everything." This was hardly a conservative position, and it enabled Scott to work closely with his professor to study psychology, then considered a new branch of philosophy.

Scott embraced the theory of utilitarianism, highly popular with philosophers of the day, which judged human actions in terms of their effect on human happiness. Eventually, Scott chose psychology as his profession, though not by a direct route. His first ambition was to serve as a Christian missionary in China. Thus, after graduating from Northwestern, he attended a Presbyterian seminary to prepare. The call never came, however, so in a career move as radical as it was resolute, Scott moved with his new wife to Germany, where he studied with leading scholars of experimental psychology at the University of Leipzig. He completed his PhD dissertation entitled "The Psychology of Impulses Historically and Critically Considered," then returned with his new degree (after a short stint as an instructor at Cornell University), to Northwestern in 1900 to start a new department of psychology.

Scott was a soft-spoken man, but he did not avoid controversy even when it appeared dangerous to his career, and psychology was easily controversial. It led him, for instance, to hypnotism, which he sometimes practiced with students in his office in Old College.

Before long, hypnotism became something of a novelty among a group of undergraduates, and they began putting friends in trances. On at least one occasion, this led to an emergency call from a group of students who had put a subject in a trance and could not pull him out.

This might have become a scandal, except that Scott's brother John, then a professor of classics at Northwestern, found out about the episode and prevailed upon his brother to curtail recreational hypnotism immediately.

Scott challenged academic convention in other ways. He consulted with businessmen in Chicago and New York and wrote extensively on the psychology of advertising, placing articles in popular magazines such as *Harper's Weekly*, something that galled the traditionalists on the Northwestern faculty. Scott believed, for instance, that a printed ad should appeal directly to one or more of the physical senses. That his ideas made perfect sense, however, was initially less important to some colleagues than the fact that he was using scholarship for practical work, which was hardly encouraged and sometimes deplored in the ivory towers of the time.

Prejudice against practical work was still rife at Northwestern when Scott was made president, and many senior members of the faculty protested the appointment. At issue was the growth of modern social science; many professors believed it came at the expense of Greek and Latin, which was probably true. Perhaps worse, just before his appointment Scott had been head of his own consulting firm, which must have seemed like a total surrender to commerce. But the trustees held firm in their choice, and Scott soon demonstrated that he was a keen scholar as well as an effective leader. In less than a year, most of his detractors admitted that the "business psychologist," as Scott was sometimes described, understood with rare acuity the delicate ties that were necessary between the University and the real world.

Sybil Bauer '27 was a sophomore in the School of Speech when she was one of five Northwestern students to compete in the 1924 Paris Olympics. Bauer became the world's greatest backstroker in her day, taking the gold medal in the 100-meter event in Paris and later breaking the men's record in the 440-yard backstroke.

In 1924 the Northwestern swimming team won its eighth Western Conference (Big Ten) championship (its second in a row) when Richard Howell '26 (below right) and Ralph Breyer '25 (below left) dominated conference freestyle events. Both went to the 1924 Paris Olympics. Breyer participated in the gold-medal 800-meter relay team that also included Johnny Weissmuller (who later became Tarzan of the silver screen). When Howell and Breyer returned for the 1925 season, they helped Northwestern win its ninth conference championship.

William Droegemueller '28 was a standout on Northwestern teams in the mid-1920s, which was a golden age for Northwestern track and field. Droegemueller was a pole vaulter who broke the Olympic record when he cleared 4.1 meters in the 1928 games in Amsterdam. He only took the silver medal, however, Sabin Carr of Yale cleared 4.2 meters in the same event.

Elizabeth Robinson '34 (second from left) took gold in the 100-meter dash at the 1928 games at Amsterdam.

OLYMPIANS IN PURPLE

Before the Olympics were televised and its champions were full-blown media stars, athletes competed for the love of sport and rarely missed a class or lecture for a practice or photo shoot. Those were the days when Northwestern was among the nation's leading colleges turning out medal winners whose names never made the bright lights but whose moments of triumph were as sparkling as any multimillion-dollar endorsement contract.

Even in the 1920s, when Northwestern's success in team sports came hard, its track and swimming teams were strong because of top-flight coaches and the members' personal tenacity. Determination was certainly the case with Northwestern's first gold medal winner,

Sybil Bauer '27, who trained largely by herself at school and hotel swimming pools before she took the gold in the 100-meter backstroke at the Paris Games in 1924.

Bauer was not the only Northwestern athlete in Paris that year. So well represented was the Purple at the '24 Games that President Scott attended with his wife and claimed, with exaggerated pride, that he didn't see a single event in Paris that a Northwestern student didn't win. Northwestern brought home three gold medals that year.

Northwestern students won more medals in Olympiads to come, several in track and field and one in figure skating when law school graduate Ronald Joseph '54 took third in the pairs event at Innsbruck in 1964. But win or not, almost all Northwestern participants came back awestruck by the Olympics, not then a steppingstone but a genuine reward for years of training and hard work.

William Porter '48 was a hurdling legend in Wildcat track history. In 1948 he won the conference title in both the high and low hurdles; later that year his career climaxed with an Olympic gold medal in the 110-meter hurdles at London. His time was 13.9 seconds, then an Olympic record.

Annette Rogers '37 (center) took the gold medal in 1932 in the 400-meter relay and placed sixth in the high jump.

Jack Riley '32 helped the Wildcats win their first Big Ten wrestling crown in 1931. Riley won the conference and national championships in the heavyweight division. In the 1932 Los Angeles Olympics he took the silver medal.

Nancy Simonds '59, Northwestern's hope in the 1956 Melbourne Olympics, won a silver medal as a member of the 400-meter freestyle relay team.

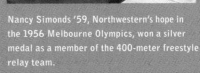

Dyche Stadium, dedicated in 1926, was designed by architect James Gamble Rogers. The stadium had the antique feel of a Roman aqueduct but at the same time used the advanced concept of curved grandstands, maximizing the number of spectators sitting close to the action. The west grandstand of Dyche Stadium held 25,000, an amazing number for college stadiums at the time, though plans were already being considered for three decks on either side and an eventual seating capacity of 80,000.

The team that christened Dyche Stadium in the 1926 season was worthy of a football stadium regarded as among the finest in the country. The '26 Wildcats went 5–0 in the conference and shared the Big Ten championship with Michigan. They were led by Captain Ralph "Moon" Baker '27, a "triple threat" because he could run, pass, and score field goals with his thrilling drop kick.

The 1924 football team was small and inexperienced and had just a 4–4 record, but it earned the name "Wildcats" after *Chicago Tribune* writer Wallace Abbey '23 was dazzled by its performance against Coach Amos Alonzo Stagg's University of Chicago powerhouse team. Many times that day the Monsters of the Midway were "stopped dead by a Purple wall of wildcats," wrote Abbey in his account of the game. The next week the erstwhile "Fighting Methodists," as the Northwestern team was sometimes known, came within a touchdown of beating Notre Dame, and the Wildcat name stuck forever.

A new urban campus

Practicality was a strong aspect of Scott's character, and it was no coincidence that his first major move as president involved an ambitious but eminently practical plan to consolidate Northwestern's professional schools on a new campus on Chicago's North Side. Such a concept had been discussed for several years. As early as 1908, the University's business manager, William A. Dyche, class of 1882, had advised selling the Northwestern University Building at Clark and Lake Streets (for a hefty price), and moving the professional schools outside the Loop. The building, a former hotel, was too noisy and a "fire trap," according to the *Evanston Daily News* (which had its own not-so-secret agenda to transfer all the schools to Evanston).

But for the most part the creation of a North Side campus was regarded as a step ahead, not just for Northwestern but for the city of Chicago as well. Trustees quickly set their sights on the Streeterville neighborhood — a rough back-street district at the time — and a chorus of civic voices gave ringing endorsement to Northwestern's making this move.

"Such a campus, ornamented by impressive buildings overlooking the blue waters of Lake Michigan, would make another beauty spot in the 'Chicago Plan' now gradually unfolding before us," wrote the *Chicago Evening Post.*

The *Post* referred to architect-planner Daniel Burnham's concept that public projects inspired private building, which led to a greater and more powerful city. With the Tribune Tower on one end of the new stretch of Michigan Avenue and Northwestern not far from the other, development of the Magnificent Mile, as it was soon to be called, was taking form.

A new Chicago campus, however, was bound to ruffle feathers in Evanston. The *Evanston Daily News* published many reasons why the professional schools ought to leave Chicago altogether. "Having the school in the heart of town is harmful, as a majority of the students are distracted from their studies by attending theaters, saloons, etc.," wrote Evanstonian C. J. Wendland in an opinion piece. "The standard of morality and soberness of downtown departments could be improved upon. This might be improved by moving the same to Evanston."

While the fear of student debauchery was probably overstated, there were trustees who agreed that Evanston was Northwestern's only real home. Among them was James Patten, a commodities broker, the former mayor of Evanston, and

A letter sweater once worn by Otto Siebenmann '27 is from a time when school spirit was elevated to unprecedented heights as Northwestern experienced a football renaissance in the 1920s. Pep rallies and other methods of pumping up fan interest were common occurrences.

president of the Board of Trustees, who favored locating the entire University in the suburb. Patten eventually resigned from the board over this question, also saying that the downtown campus plan was too ambitious financially.

Momentum was on the side of Streeterville. Early on, an imaginary rendering of the new campus appeared in *Chicago Commerce* magazine, accompanied by a quote from architect William Holabird.

Holabird said that the Chicago site possessed the potential for "nobility, a scope of beauty combined with educational and utilitarian possibilities equal to anything with which I have come in contact during my life as an architect."

This was typical hyperbole from an architect, but it was the kind of talk that helped loosen the purse strings of families who could make the plan for a new campus a reality.

Taking advantage of the momentum, the University embarked on a modern public relations program. The Campaign for a Greater Northwestern was inspired by Walter Dill Scott and his deft sense of advertising. But its success was assured by business manager Dyche. Dyche had held the position since 1903 and had vast contacts in Chicago that dated to before the Chicago Fire, when young William managed his father's pharmacy in the Loop and knew the likes of "Long John" Wentworth, Chicago's pioneer congressman.

The money came in. By June 1921, businessman Alexander McKinlock pledged $250,000 to purchase the Streeterville land in return for an agreement to name the new campus for his son, Alexander, an aviator killed in World War I. Due to business reversals, the McKinlock pledge was later revoked and the campus was renamed simply the "Chicago campus." But other large benefactors came forward, and the North Side plan became an exciting reality.

An architectural signature

Shortly after the Streeterville property was purchased, Scott declared that the new Chicago campus and its buildings should "make a positive contribution to the architecture of the city of Chicago." To accomplish this, the president and a committee of trustees quickly settled on a University architect. James Gamble Rogers was chosen with the expectation that he would establish a style not only for the Chicago campus but also for the considerable construction planned for Evanston in the next decade.

Rogers was up to the task; his most notable work at that time was the Harkness Quadrangle at Yale, and he would soon be completing the Presbyterian Medical Center at Columbia University. Clearly, Rogers's ability to handle large-scale commissions – and plenty of them – was key to his selection as Northwestern's master builder. Perhaps most important, however, was his mastery of historical styles. For other clients, Rogers had designed elaborate neo-Gothic and neo-Georgian buildings. Now, as Northwestern's official architect, he represented a signal that University leaders were looking not for modern or experimental buildings (Frank

Lloyd Wright and his followers were then in their prime) but for stately and familiar structures invoking the past.

By 1922 Rogers and his colleagues were put to work on the Chicago campus and almost simultaneously on the Women's Quadrangles in Evanston. Rogers was most interested in the larger buildings downtown; he had to be reminded by his employers to pay more attention to the dormitories. At any rate, his choice of collegiate Gothic for the Chicago buildings represented a logical, perhaps obvious, approach. Vertical and striking in profile, the Gothic style had become popular for tall urban buildings. At least one of the Northwestern buildings, Montgomery Ward Hall, would rise to the heights of a skyscraper.

Rogers's selection of the Gothic style for both the Chicago and Evanston campuses was regarded as appropriate also because of its endorsement by John Ruskin, the late English critic who wrote that the Middle Ages represented a high point in Western architecture. So pervasive was Ruskin's idea – he believed that Gothic form reflected honesty and moral uplift – that America's most famous colleges, including Yale and the University of Chicago, were making collegiate Gothic the overwhelming choice of higher education architectural styles in that period.

Collegiate Gothic also suited Rogers's ideas for the grand scheme that was developing for both campuses.

"When I think of the number of buildings that the Evanston campus will eventually hold," Rogers wrote, "I am quite sure that in spite of my first impressions, the Georgian will not be as capable of variety as the Gothic, which presents more freedom and picturesque composition and does not demand the symmetry that Georgian has to have."

Situated just north of Fisk Hall, Old College in the 1920s was a place where college fashions of the day were on display – raccoon coats, letter sweaters, and snap-brim fedoras.

THE CHICAGO CAMPUS

When a major new campus for Northwestern was proposed to be built on Chicago's North Side, it triggered a controversy almost as large as the plan itself. But with the power of the professional schools and key trustees behind the concept, the Chicago campus became a reality in 1921, when the University purchased nine acres of relatively undeveloped property in Streeterville, a rough neighborhood north of the Chicago River and on the shore of Lake Michigan. As the first major project of Walter Dill Scott's Northwestern presidency, the stately new campus was expected to cost $25 million.

Building something of this size had never been attempted at Northwestern, so the University launched the Campaign for a Greater Northwestern with elaborate brochures and other printed material, much of it guided by Scott's own expertise in modern advertising. To attract attention and wealthy patrons, Scott also commissioned a series of imaginary renderings for a stately campus to be included in a brochure stating that gifts would be "an investment for all time."

Gifts for individual buildings came quickly, most significantly from Elizabeth Ward, widow of mail-order magnate Montgomery Ward. Between 1924 and 1930, nearly $17 million was raised, primarily for buildings for the Medical and Dental Schools, the School of Law, and the School of Commerce. By 1927 Passavant Hospital also decided to locate on the campus, and plans for one of the most comprehensive medical centers in the nation began to take shape. In the 1940s Abbott Hall was constructed as a 20-story dormitory, and Wesley Memorial Hospital moved to the campus from the South Side, resolving the decades-long dispute over Wesley's obligations as a teaching hospital.

The principal donors were present at the Chicago campus groundbreaking on April 28, 1925. From left: Mrs. A. Montgomery Ward, Elbert H. Gary, Mrs. Walter Hirsch, President Walter Dill Scott, Mrs. Levy Mayer, William Wieboldt, Mrs. George A. McKinlock, and George A. McKinlock.

The A. Montgomery Ward Memorial Building, the largest University structure on the Chicago campus, was designed to house the Medical and Dental Schools. Its profile not only set the tone for the collegiate Gothic campus, but it blended with a Chicago skyline that was composed of an increasing number of modern skyscrapers.

The McKinlock Gate was created by the great wrought-iron artist Samuel Yellin to commemorate Alexander McKinlock, who had been killed in World War I. Although the Chicago campus originally was called the McKinlock campus, the Depression forced the family to revoke most of the $250,000 it had promised, and Northwestern's lakefront location was renamed the Chicago campus at the request of the family.

The architect James Gamble Rogers put a distinctive stamp on Northwestern, both on the Chicago campus and in Evanston.

George R. Thorne Hall was erected as a memorial to the partner and brother-in-law of mail-order merchant Montgomery Ward. Thorne Hall was Gothic on the exterior and modern in its interior (pictured in the background) and was described as a "demonstration of architectural acoustics." The auditorium was regarded as a place where discoveries in the professional schools would be presented in a public forum and would withstand the "criticism of the experts."

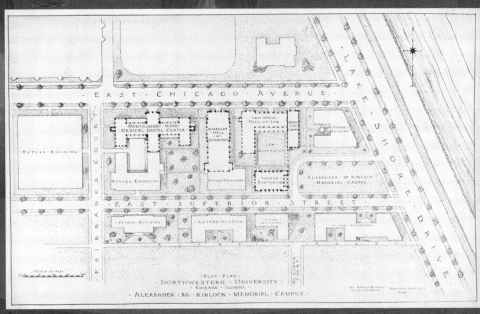

James Gamble Rogers produced this plan of the Chicago campus in 1925. It showed buildings that were underway and those that awaited funding before they could be added to the handsome lakeshore campus.

The Leighton Mount nightmare

Higher education remained a prime target for people who resented occasionally effete professors and sometimes-spoiled students. For the most part, President Scott, a poor-boy-made-good himself, could effectively deflect such faultfinding about Northwestern. Scott's public relations skills were tested, however, when a freshman named Leighton Mount '25 disappeared one night after the 1921 "class rush" – a brawl that was similar to the cane rush of previous decades.

The rush traditionally involved freshmen and sophomores, the latter asserting their authority and the former doing their best to overcome it. There was little doubt that Mount was involved in serious scrapping the evening of the class rush – some said he even ducked a sophomore in the lake. But he remained missing for a year and a half, until finally his decomposed remains were discovered under the Lake Street pier in Evanston. Police and a coroner's jury were determined to solve what looked like a vicious and senseless crime.

The situation had the makings of a media nightmare for Scott. For most of 1923, the papers speculated continually about the crime, and, not finding a ready suspect, they pointed accusingly at the University. Admittedly, Scott's explanations were tortured at first: He insisted that class rush was not hazing, which was coercive, but a voluntary tradition. Scott also intimated that Mount might have committed suicide, an unlikely suggestion that seemed to make the papers more aggressive and hostile toward the University.

The authorities never solved the crime, and the story ground slowly to a halt. But even when the case was officially closed, a perception remained that Scott's treatment of it was more concerned with its impact on University fundraising than with justice. Whether this was true or not, the University never broke ranks with Scott, particularly as reporters combed the campus for a suspect and made unlikely speculations. When Scott finally outlawed the tradition of the class rush, he did so with apologies about the loss of a long, if not particularly noble, school tradition. In the end, Scott reflected the prevailing view on campus that the University should not be embarrassed unfairly. Under harsh circumstances the president did not give in.

The Scrawl

Northwestern always had its dissenters; by the Roaring Twenties these dissidents had their own publication, a short-lived but sharp-edged literary magazine called the *Scrawl*. The *Scrawl* gazed into the looking glass darkly and often with a full dose of satire. In 1926, for example, the magazine took a less-than-respectful look at a semiofficial student council campaign to revive "college traditions." Who was behind all of this? wondered the *Scrawl*. Most likely it was women, "whose flagrant abandonment of Camel cigarettes for Chesterfields represented undoubtedly a severe wrench to the long-established Camel tradition of college women." The *Scrawl* writer noted with all due irony that Camels would be back at Northwestern as soon as the campus was reminded that Camels were stunningly popular everywhere else.

Volume V   Northwestern University, October, 1928   No. 1

The *Scrawl*, introduced in 1924, was the University's quarterly journal of literature and public affairs. It served as a mild scold, voice of satire, and chronicler of the vagaries of social life. As the University announced the Campaign for a Greater Northwestern, it fell to the *Scrawl* to warn that all this fundraising looked like a "boosters' Utopia," and, more critically, "a disease at Northwestern. Afflicted by it, the president, the deans, the professors and students are like so many puppets." The *Scrawl* was published until 1928.

The *Purple Parrot* was launched in 1921 as the campus's first humor magazine. In an early issue, an adventure entitled "So Help Me Register" ended when the writer "finally found where my adviser was hiding, under an assumed name, behind a barricade of broken barrels way up in the clock tower." In these two issues from 1923, the editors had their way with two sacred institutions on the Northwestern campus, equal rights for women and Homecoming.

The female members of the Class of 1926.

The *Scrawl* existed, evidently, to encourage rebellion. Thus, the magazine was quick to applaud a brave group of freshmen – the Class of 1929 – who took it upon themselves to defile the "senior log," a rustic bench near University Hall where seniors met and discussed the hot topics of the day. The freshmen regarded the senior log as a sign of undue privilege, or perhaps a symbol ready for bashing, and they painted it green.

Scrawl editors followed this story, eagerly quoting an upperclassman who said, "It seems that the yearlings do not realize the value and dignity of Northwestern traditions." The *Scrawl* had no patience for such haughty declarations and cited the upperclassman as just another of Northwestern's "self-constituted watchdogs." But in the end, the editors could only lament the incident's final outcome, which was an apology from the president of the freshman class, who promised "to prevent any reoccurrence of similar actions" and enforce conformity in the future.

Bernard DeVoto snipes

Northwestern's intellectual vitality was questioned in other ways. Bernard DeVoto, a young English professor, lambasted the University in a number of articles in popular magazines after he left the University in 1927. DeVoto, who would become one of the era's best-known and feistiest writers, penned a lengthy screed in 1928 entitled "Farewell to Pedagogy" for *Harper's Weekly*. In it he complained that scholarship was totally overshadowed in higher education by something much closer to job training, and the professors were going along with it.

"I am convinced that the greater part of the present plight of colleges is due to [a faculty of] uneducated fanatics," he wrote. "It is they who have debauched the curricula, violated the chastity of pedagogy, ravished the academic quiet of sane men, and created the noise and stink and smoke screen that envelop the profession."

Dean John Henry Wigmore of the School of Law had his troubles with the Board of Trustees; he believed they provided as few resources as possible for the law school. Wigmore was highly esteemed by his students, however, and in this picture from 1923 they presented him with a new suitcase before a trip to Europe.

DeVoto really felt that universities were bent on reducing every aspect of life to a "science" with "hideous jargon, chanting litanies whose terms are pseudo-scientific neologisms of no meaning whatever." DeVoto also took a jab at the typical university trustee, whom he called "a business man with a superstitious awe of education." In other articles along the same vituperative lines, DeVoto made one remarkable observation about women at Northwestern. "The men were Philistine, herd-minded, immature. The women," DeVoto wrote, "were liberal, individual, grown up."

Raising admissions standards

Whatever criticism came Northwestern's way, Scott was certain that the University could endure it if it maintained a high-quality product. One way to ensure this success was to start with the best raw material possible, and by the mid-1920s the University began to conduct entrance exams and raise overall standards of admission, which had been first come, first served at that point. The quality of the student body improved rapidly. By 1930 nine out of ten entering freshmen came from the top half of their high school classes, and six out of ten from the top quarter.

More experimental was Scott's well-publicized effort to enroll child prodigies as Northwestern freshmen. This program grew from his conviction that true genius was largely an acquired trait, and that a combination of high IQ (130 or higher) and a focused education could foster the spark necessary to develop rare intellectual gifts. "It may be his aim," wrote a newspaper about Scott's plan, "to see whether modern educational methods will fan [genius] into a flame or extinguish it like the snuffing of a candlestick."

In 1931 alumni who collected commemorative plates could choose among scenes of the Chicago or Evanston campuses. The plates were made in Staffordshire, England, by Spode-Copeland Sons.

A Glee Club jacket worn by Luther Noss '30.

THE N.U. CIRCUS

It's a wonder that the Northwestern Circus didn't last forever. In its time, it combined the University's well-known knack for theater with the highly developed sense of irony that any upper-level institution of higher education cultivates in its undergraduates. As an all-school activity, the circus involved hundreds and attracted thousands.

The N.U. Circus looked like just that, a circus, with a parade and even a midway with sideshows and booths. But during its prime in the 1920s and early 1930s, it was nothing like Barnum and Bailey. Among dozens of acts each year, "The Native Band of Hamberger Island" was an example of the originality of the circus; this band provided offbeat musical entertainment in a mock ethnographic vein. "A Life and Death Study in One Act" was a fair parody of the thespian histrionics sometimes performed on campus stages. Organized mostly by fraternities and sororities, the skits, stunts, and routines included contorted gymnastics, extravagant costumery, trapeze artists, and more than one elephant gracing the spotlights in the old Patten Gym "big top."

Having begun modestly in 1908 as a "county fair" outside old Willard Hall to raise money for the YMCA, the circus quickly grew into the biggest burlesque-cum-carnival-cum-fundraiser that anyone could imagine. When the circus ended after 1932—the biggest and best ever, it was said — it was not for of lack of interest but because it had grown so big. Planning took too much time away from the real purpose of the University.

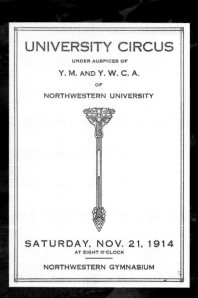

The "World's Greatest Collegiate Circus" was a three-ring affair and a "stupendous exhibition of youth, beauty, brawn, and mirth," as the program pointed out.

138

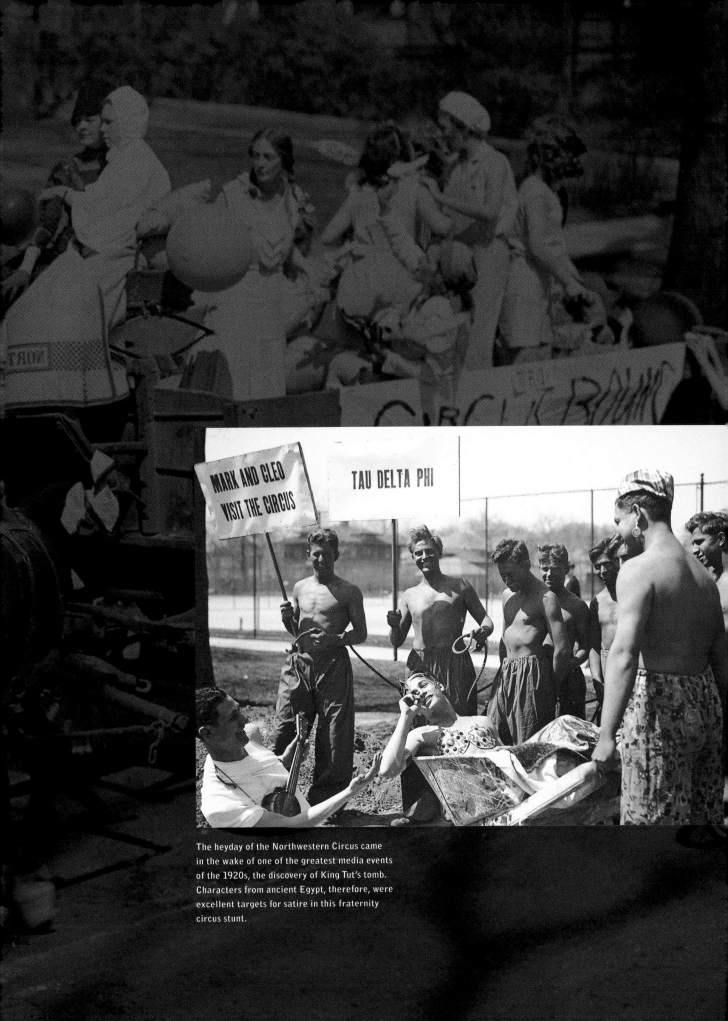

The heyday of the Northwestern Circus came in the wake of one of the greatest media events of the 1920s, the discovery of King Tut's tomb. Characters from ancient Egypt, therefore, were excellent targets for satire in this fraternity circus stunt.

MARK AND CLEO VISIT THE CIRCUS

TAU DELTA PHI

The success of Scott's child prodigy venture can be measured only anecdotally, but there was evidence that his effort may have been a success. One of Northwestern's first child prodigies, Harold Finley '33, entered the University at age 13, graduated cum laude four years later, and became successful in the investment business. He began his postcollege career at the Board of Trade and at age 19 received special permission to work on the floor of the New York Stock Exchange. While building his investment career, Northwestern's "dean of the prodigies," as Finley was called, also found the time and inclination to become an ordained minister.

A modern library

While the University kept one foot in the world of classical scholarship, it was modernizing in many ways. Among them was planning for a new library, overseen by librarian Theodore W. Koch. Koch arrived at Northwestern in 1919, replacing Walter Lichtenstein, a native German who had been dismissed the year before amid rumors that he was not entirely loyal to the nation at war. Whatever Lichtenstein's politics, he was a rare-book expert who may have been too "old school" for Northwestern. Although Koch was a passionate scholar of Dante and the Italian Renaissance, he was also eager to bring the University library into the 20th century.

Long past, Koch said, were the days when each course revolved around a single classic text. As more modern books became essential to coursework, Northwestern's library collection clearly lagged behind contemporary needs. The overcrowded Orrington Lunt Library lacked space, and ad hoc libraries were springing up elsewhere on campus — in the classics department, for example, and in the School of Commerce. The only solution — and Scott heartily agreed — was to replace the old Lunt Library with a larger building. This became possible when trustee Charles Deering gave $1 million for the purpose.

Koch had strong ideas on the design of a new library, and at least once he sent a handsome drawing by James Gamble Rogers back to the architect. The library, he insisted, should be designed "from within out."

In other words, its exterior architecture should serve the needs of the interior. Rogers's eventual design was successful, a massive Gothic structure loosely modeled after King's College Chapel at Cambridge University in England. Opened in 1933, it had a cathedral-like reading room, a large circulation desk, shelves for half a million volumes, and other features both utilitarian and "inspirational."

A School of Journalism

As Northwestern's curriculum modernized and grew, the University bridged the gulf between the ivory tower and the rest of the world as well as any institution in the nation. And it was happening in many disciplines. There were some areas, however, where the twain were not supposed to meet. Many people regarded journalism, for example, as beneath the dignity of serious academic inquiry.

Built during the Depression, Deering Library benefited from the availability of skilled labor. Masons constructed the building primarily of Lannon stone quarried in Wisconsin.

Deering Library opened in January 1933. It honors Charles Deering of Deering Harvester Company, who left $500,000 upon his death in 1927 for a new central library. Deering's heirs left most of the rest of the $1.25 million needed for this building, which had seating for 900 readers and shelving for 500,000 books.

The Deering Library circulation desk was substantial – noble on the outside and designed for efficiency from back to front.

A brochure for Medill stressed that this was a
true "journalism workshop" turning out men and
women ready for big-city newpaper work.

STUDENTS RECEIVE PERSONAL GUIDANCE IN WRITING NEWS FOR PUBLICATION

This corner of the city room in the Medill School of Journalism of Northwestern University shows the managing editor and his assistants busy at their work of criticising stories written by reporters in the course. At the left appears the bust of Joseph Medill, distinguished editor of the Chicago Tribune, for whom the school was named.

MEDILL SCHOOL OF JOURNALISM
IN PICTURES

THE TOWER
of the Chicago Tribune, one of the newspaper plants visited by students on their Field Trips.

H. F. HARRINGTON
Director of the Medill School of Journalism of Northwestern University, Evanston and Chicago.

WORKING TO MEET THE "DEADLINE"

Here you see advanced students writing copy and making-up the first page of the Daily Medillian, a mythical newspaper which goes to press once a week.

True enough, the reputation of newspapers, especially in Chicago, was marked by reporters with rumpled suits and hangovers. The image was not universal, of course – many papers had their resident intellectuals – though anything like a professional school education for the majority of those in the newsroom in any metropolitan daily seemed, well, a stretch of good sense.

That changed in 1920, when *Chicago Tribune* reporter Eddie Doherty decided that newspaper work could be formally taught, and that the *Tribune* itself might be willing to support the idea of a journalism school. Doherty was partly right. *Tribune* owner Joseph Patterson told Doherty that a school for reporters sounded like a fine idea, and if Doherty could find someone to run it, the paper might get involved. "We passed the buck and thought it would sink out of sight," remembered Patterson, who had just launched the *New York Daily News*, soon to become the nation's largest-circulation daily.

It did not sink, however. Doherty quickly got Ralph E. Heilman, dean of Northwestern's School of Commerce, intrigued and willing to develop the concept. Within a few weeks, President Scott was meeting with Heilman, Doherty, Patterson, and Patterson's cousin Robert R. McCormick, and they quickly came to terms: The *Tribune* would contribute $12,000 a year to a new school of journalism – named for Patterson's and McCormick's grandfather, Joseph M. Medill.

Everyone seemed agreed on the division of labor. "Dr. Scott said that he would take my money but not my advice," quipped Patterson at the school's dedication in 1921.

A liberal arts curriculum was naturally a strong element of journalism education at Northwestern. But everyone involved also agreed that the learn-by-doing approach was indispensable. Medill students were subjected to the gruff tutelage of John C. Carroll, a copyreader at the *Tribune*, who applied the pressure of real-world journalism in a class that used sophisticated reportorial simulations. With recordings as well as live actors performing roles in fictional news events, students witnessed stories as they unfolded, took notes, and wrote their stories on the spot. One such exercise was about a school fire, a disaster that killed 40 children. As the school principal, fire chief, and assorted others breathlessly described what happened, students turned out their stories under deadline pressure and Carroll's terse critiques.

On a different level, a Medill course entitled "Problems in Contemporary Thought," featuring speakers and debates on a variety of subjects, was developed as a course for journalism seniors. "Can Science Accept God?" for example, featured a dialogue between a seminary president and a philosophy professor. Clarence Darrow, Carl Sandburg, Jane Addams, and Bertrand Russell were among the speakers brought to campus not just for students, but in some cases, also for the public, which often turned out en masse.

THE NORTHWESTERN–UNIVERSITY OF CHICAGO
MERGER PLAN

It might have been the Universities of Chicago, or Chicago–Northwestern University. But
the proposed merger of Northwestern and the University of Chicago never got quite so
far as to settle on a name. Northwestern President Walter Dill Scott truly believed that
the merger could produce "one of the world's greatest centers of learning." But tradition and a few legal uncertainties stood in the way.

The merger concept was first raised in 1933 during the Depression, when enrollment at
Northwestern was down and faculty salaries had been reduced twice since the stock
market crash of '29. It represented something more than a financial strategy, however,
as both Scott and Robert Maynard Hutchins, president of the University of Chicago,
believed a union of the two schools would combine strengths of extraordinary complemen-
tarity. Northwestern excelled as an undergraduate university and in its professional
schools. Chicago was highly regarded particularly in graduate studies and research. A
merged university was viewed as a way of eliminating redundancies and promoting
above all "a community of scholars," as Hutchins described it.

The idea ran into instant trouble. There was doubt, for example, about Northwestern's
local tax-exempt status if the University were so radically altered. The press also
disliked much about the proposed merger. The *Chicago Tribune* printed negative commen-
taries, and the *Evanston Review* called it a "Rockefeller Plan to Wipe Out N.U." John D.
Rockefeller, the founding donor of the University of Chicago and creator of the former
Standard Oil monopoly, was suspected to be behind the merger idea (which he likely
was not).

Ultimately, Northwestern pulled out of the negotiations. A pivotal dissenter was
Northwestern University Medical School, whose faculty of mostly practicing physicians
wanted nothing to do with the University of Chicago and its emphasis on research.
Most of all, the merger plan ran afoul of the pride, nostalgia, and tradition that many
Northwestern people associated with their university. While merger proponents
framed themselves as idealists, merger opponents were no less ardent about preserving
two major institutions of higher education in the Chicago area.

The **Daily** *renaissance*

Medill quickly made its influence felt on Chicago journalism. "One-time prejudice against college students by city editors practically has disappeared," wrote a columnist in the *Tribune* in 1930. The journalism school also affected the quality of the *Daily Northwestern*, though not fast enough for everyone on campus, particularly journalism majors. "The *Daily* staff doesn't cover the campus, the campus covers the *Daily*," wrote one Medill student in 1936. She meant that too many stories were rewrites of press releases and were too often squeezed into print by editors who got free tickets to a dance or concert that was mentioned in the paper.

Efforts to improve the *Daily* hit a high point in the fall of 1936 when a pair of seniors, Falcon O. Baker '37 and Julian Behrstock '37, became editors. "The first requisite of a college newspaper is that it express the prevailing tone of the campus," they wrote in an editorial in their first issue.

That fall, for example, they took a survey on a subject close to the hearts of many students – the food served in Goodrich Commons. The paper reported that 130 of 140 undergraduates questioned believed that quality was below par – "too starchy" – along with other shortcomings. To its credit, the *Daily* also reported dissenting views. "I think this whole uproar about the food is a farce," said one student.

More serious was the *Daily's* coverage of racial discrimination, already an issue on campus, since it had been discussed in Student Union–sponsored forums. But these sessions usually featured local politicians and ministers who insisted that bias wasn't something that could happen at Northwestern. As the *Daily* followed up, African American students and townspeople said discrimination was only too real. The paper went on to editorialize that the subject deserved serious attention, which little by little it got.

Homecoming in 1932 involved a pep rally, a bonfire, the *Frolics of '32* revue, and a "Beaver Contest," in which the contestant with the most substantial beard would be shaved in public. Ohio State beat the Wildcats 20–6 on Saturday afternoon, after which the Homecoming Dance at Patten Gym featured Mush Ling and his North Shore Orchestra.

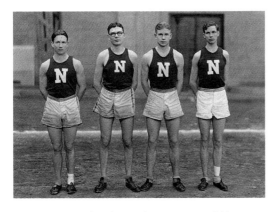

In the two-mile relay, the Northwestern team of Alvo Martin '26, H. Kastor Kahn '24, Don Calhoun '24, and Ralph Loveland '26 was Champion of the West in 1924, winning the Drake and Kansas Relays.

Champion Wildcats

In 1936 football was also destined to be news. Northwestern had a strong team with a chance to compete for the Big Ten championship. The excitement was tempered by a small flap that began with a story headlined "Wildcat Grid Team Called Professional," which concerned an article in *American Mercury* magazine contending that many leading colleges were running what amounted to professional football programs.

In articles that ran for several days in the *Daily*, a spokesman for the athletic department denied that its program was run for profit. But the whole controversy was soon overshadowed – the Wildcats were beating the tar out of the competition that fall, and the biggest headlines in the paper were crowing about the team's success. The *Daily* even came out with an extra edition after a game against Minnesota, which had a winning record of 21 straight games before coming to Evanston.

The Minnesota game was Homecoming at Northwestern, and despite a persistent rain, the crowd of 49,000 witnessed "one of the most spectacular punting duels" in Big Ten history.

The game remained a scoreless tie until the fourth quarter, when Bernard Jefferson '39, one of Northwestern's earliest African American stars, ran the ball to field goal range on the eight yard line, only to see the kick go wide.

Almost since the founding of the Western Conference, which became the Big Ten, Northwestern enjoyed underdog status. That made victories, such as those by the championship team of 1936, all the more sweet.

Bernie Jefferson had the balance and strength to be a top running back in any era.

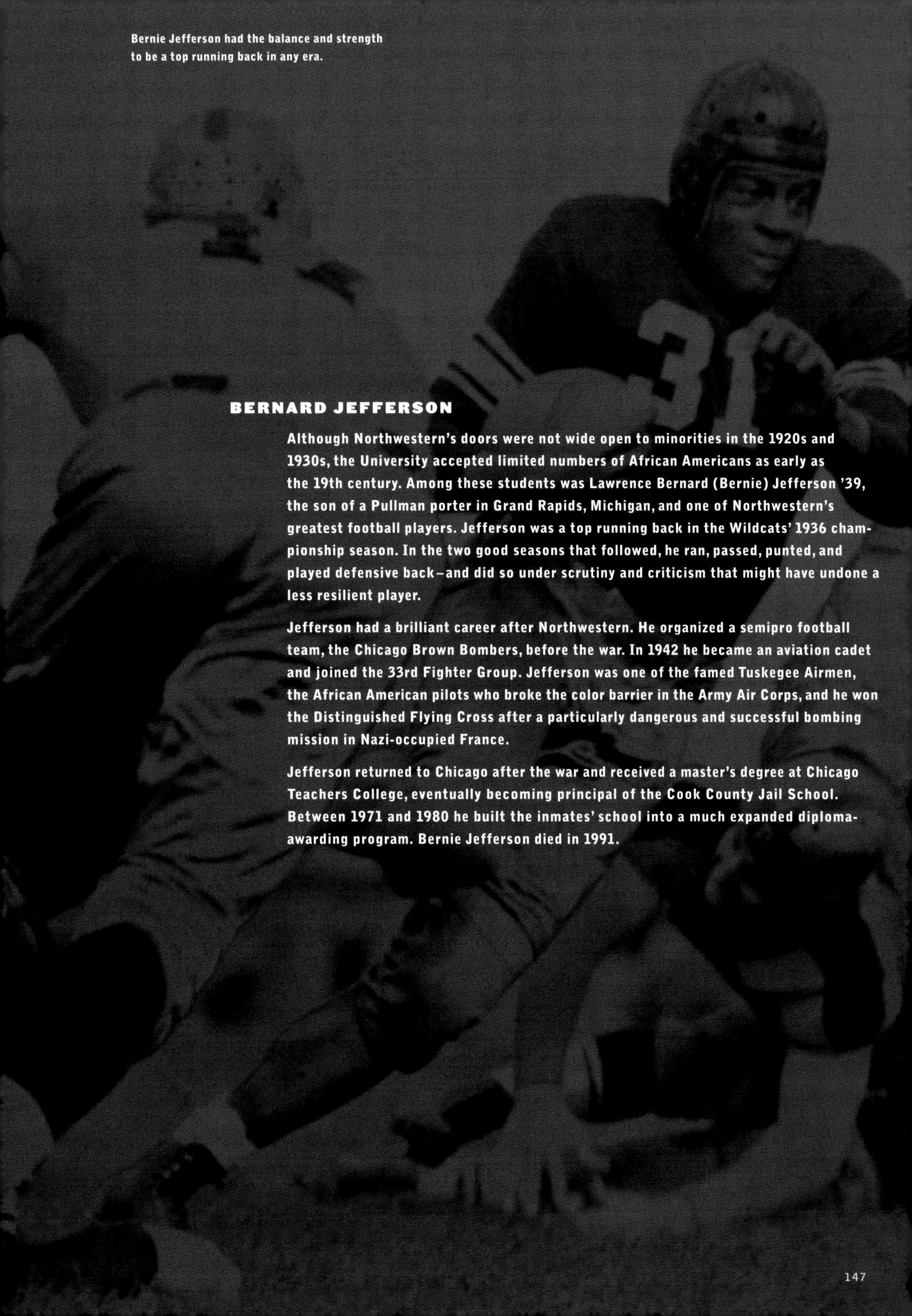

BERNARD JEFFERSON

Although Northwestern's doors were not wide open to minorities in the 1920s and 1930s, the University accepted limited numbers of African Americans as early as the 19th century. Among these students was Lawrence Bernard (Bernie) Jefferson '39, the son of a Pullman porter in Grand Rapids, Michigan, and one of Northwestern's greatest football players. Jefferson was a top running back in the Wildcats' 1936 championship season. In the two good seasons that followed, he ran, passed, punted, and played defensive back—and did so under scrutiny and criticism that might have undone a less resilient player.

Jefferson had a brilliant career after Northwestern. He organized a semipro football team, the Chicago Brown Bombers, before the war. In 1942 he became an aviation cadet and joined the 33rd Fighter Group. Jefferson was one of the famed Tuskegee Airmen, the African American pilots who broke the color barrier in the Army Air Corps, and he won the Distinguished Flying Cross after a particularly dangerous and successful bombing mission in Nazi-occupied France.

Jefferson returned to Chicago after the war and received a master's degree at Chicago Teachers College, eventually becoming principal of the Cook County Jail School. Between 1971 and 1980 he built the inmates' school into a much expanded diploma-awarding program. Bernie Jefferson died in 1991.

The 1939–40 handbook of the Women's Self-Government Association found that humor was one way of making the point that traditional family values were important to the decorum of student life at Northwestern.

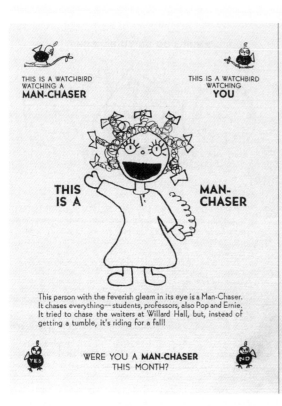

THIS IS A WATCHBIRD WATCHING A **MAN-CHASER**

THIS IS A WATCHBIRD WATCHING **YOU**

THIS IS A

MAN-CHASER

This person with the feverish gleam in its eye is a Man-Chaser. It chases everything—students, professors, also Pop and Ernie. It tried to chase the waiters at Willard Hall, but, instead of getting a tumble, it's riding for a fall!

YES NO

WERE YOU A **MAN-CHASER** THIS MONTH?

FRESHMAN DO'S AND DONT'S OR ELSE:

Hours:

| Every week night | Fridays and Saturdays | Sunday |

Exception:

Freshman women may have two ten o'clock permissions a week (which might profitably be spent at the Library).

Lateness:

A record shall be kept of the late minutes. Minutes are to be cumulative, beginning on the hour. If 15 late minutes are accumulated in 30 days, a girl must forfeit one 2 o'clock permission within two weeks.

Men's calling hours:

Week days	4 to 7:15 P.M.
Fridays	3 to Midnight
Saturdays	12 Noon to Midnight
Sundays	Noon to 8:30 P.M.

Mock political conventions at Northwestern began in 1908, when delegates made Robert LaFollette, the Progressive candidate from Wisconsin, the campus choice for president. In 1928, when this photo was taken, support was divided among Herbert Hoover, who eventually was nominated by the Republicans and won the election, and Northwestern law school alumnus Frank Lowden, class of 1887, who had come very close to winning the Republican nomination in 1920. But the students' choice in 1928 was Evanstonian Charles G. Dawes, who was then finishing his term as vice president under Calvin Coolidge. Dawes's political star did not rise, despite the endorsement from Northwestern students.

But the Wildcats kept the pressure on. When Minnesota fumbled, Northwestern scored. The Wildcat kicker missed the extra point, which made the rest of the game that much more exciting. Northwestern held on for a 6–0 win, and there was joy in Evanston. But the joy only lasted until Northwestern's game against Notre Dame, with the two undefeated teams vying for the national championship. It turned out that Northwestern's football fortunes could only go so far, and the Irish beat the Wildcats 26–6.

Campus politics

In the next few years the *Daily* matured considerably, largely because of events off campus. By 1939 turmoil in Europe was in full flame, and the editors of the *Daily* were not shy about covering global events and taking a stand. As was common at many large universities, the paper leaned mildly left. When Marxist economist Harold Laski was to speak on campus, the *Daily* editorialized:

"It seems incredible that Harold Laski is to speak in Evanston…. Evanston is dedicated to the philosophy of reaction; its populace forms the nucleus of the North Shore arch conservatives."

The *Daily* took the isolationist position against intervention in the European war. Columnist Stanley Frankel '40 led the charge, watching world affairs with one eye and the mood of the campus with the other. "I am one of those deluded individuals," Frankel wrote, "who is more interested in the artificial and abstract events in Chicago and Germany than in the concrete, real, here-now world of fruit lemonades and dream girls." In a 1937 column, trying to get his readers' attention, he chose his "All-International" gridiron eleven, with "Frank" Roosevelt at quarterback and Joe Stalin at right tackle. Stalin was "a veritable killer…hasn't shown much on offense but defensive work is unbeatable."

Frankel's view on the impending World War was that "America must stay out of this mess. Our ancestors came to this country to get away from the endless wars and battles and hates of the other hemisphere." But when the war came, the *Daily* joined other once-isolationist newspapers in supporting the military. Shortly thereafter, Frankel himself went into the Army and served with distinction in the South Pacific. His distaste toward war only increased, but in later articles and then a book on his combat experience, he tempered his former pacifism considerably. The heat of battle taught him that "once you're in a war the end justifies the means."

WAA-MU

Until 1929 Northwestern's talent on the stage was well known but had not yet become an institution. In that year a pair of seniors in Phi Delta Theta wrote and staged a first-class musical, which they called Waa-Mu, and one of the biggest names in college-produced musicals was born.

Although Joe Miller '29 and Darrell Ware '29 had every intention of producing a hit, the name Waa-Mu entered the Northwestern lexicon more or less by accident. The "Waa" stood for Woman's Athletic Association, which had been staging minstrel shows and musical revues since 1912. The "Mu" stood for Men's Union, which had put on comic operas for nearly as long. The two seniors reckoned that mixing the sexes on stage was desirable, though the WAA committee, which had a loyal following for its annual show, wasn't so sure it needed to share the spotlight with the men.

Miller and Ware got started by creating a topflight script. They also raised $1,200, borrowing $5 at a time from interested students. With little more than hard work, they produced and directed *Good Morning Glory*, and it was a hit even before the first curtain rose. "Campus interest is the highest yet for any single dramatic activity in University history," wrote the *Daily*. No one was disappointed, and the producers began working on the next year's show almost immediately.

Waa-Mu became an annual event, and it wasn't long before the biggest talents on campus were getting involved. In 1936 Walter Kerr '37 (later an eminent theater critic for the *New York Times*) was the principal writer for a musical revue entitled *It Goes to Show*, with a special barb for Eleanor Roosevelt:

Aside from all the worries of this New Deal that we've dealt,
It's work enough for anyone
Just to be a Roosevelt.

Waa-Mu's producers were demanding but flexible. In 1938 the board felt it didn't have a good enough script, so it staged George Gershwin's *Of Thee I Sing*, about a presidential candidate promising to bring more love to the White House. Leonard Rosenberg '41 (later Tony Randall) played an obstreperous Texas congressman in the play. Darrell Ware was soon off to Hollywood to write screenplays. Joe Miller remained at Northwestern, directing the show until 1975 and bringing Waa-Mu to legendary status. Several times the show traveled to Chicago after its Evanston run. In 1951, famed orchestra leader Fred Waring played original Waa-Mu songs on the radio. Waa-Mu did not actually inspire the construction of Scott Hall, completed in 1940, but it certainly helped make Cahn Auditorium, which was attached to the student center, one of the best-equipped theaters in the Chicago area.

As Waa-Mu evolved, politics became the show's perennial (though not exclusive) stock-in-trade. In 1941, writers included a skit with the German ambassador visiting the White House and drawing swastikas in the washroom. Waa-Mu went on hiatus during the war but returned in 1946 with one of the great comedy tandems in Northwestern stage history, Paul Lynde '48 and Charlotte Rae Lubotsky '48, later known on television as Charlotte Rae.

Through much of this period, Northwestern trained a constant stream of Broadway and Hollywood talent. Joe Miller, who became director of student affairs, deserves much of the credit. For nearly 50 years he infused Waa-Mu with the flash and polish that made a professional actor of many a hoofer on the Cahn Auditorium stage.

Waa-Mu 1981, the 50th anniversary show, gently spoofed Northwestern's history and reprised numbers from Waa-Mu's past.

In the early 1920s the Woman's Athletic Association had a successful run with musical comedies such as this one; by 1929 the musical had merged with the somewhat less successful comic opera produced annually by the Men's Union. Thus was spawned Waa-Mu, Northwestern's famed annual musical revue.

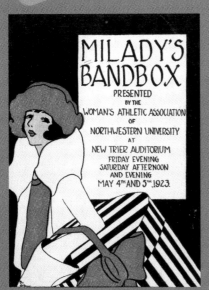

The Waa-Mu Show of 1952 depicted life in the big city — with street urchins, beautiful women, nosy reporters, and scam artists galore.

151

Wait a Minute, staged in 1941 with Louise Yates '43 and Robert Stone '41, harked back to days that were simpler, more carefree, and deserving of gentle satire insofar as haberdashery was concerned.

Joe Miller '29 (right), one of two originators of the Waa-Mu Show, made it a musical comedy (later a musical revue) of professional quality from its first production in 1929.

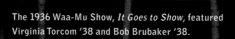

The 1936 Waa-Mu Show, *It Goes to Show*, featured Virginia Torcom '38 and Bob Brubaker '38.

In the Silver Jubilee of Waa-Mu in 1956, Warren Beatty '59 (right) showed a hint of the star quality that would propel his career as a leading man in the movies.

Present Tense, the 1969 Waa-Mu revue, touched on contemporary themes such as assassination, birth control, Biafra, and *Rosemary's Baby*. The show struck a more traditional note with a number entitled "Operatic Static." Future television and film star Shelley Long '71 (seated left) was a member of the cast.

Among Friends, 1960, featured Ann-Margret Olson '63 (far right), later the movies' Ann-Margret, in several skits that dealt in Waa-Mu's round-about way with romance and warnings about the undergraduate's next step, marriage and family life.

a **Patten Gymnasium (new)** (1940)

b *Scott Hall/Cahn Auditorium* (1940)
Pictured.

c **Technological Institute** (1942)
Original building; additions later.

d **Lutkin Memorial Hall** (1941)

³/₄ mile west on Central

Lincoln

Orrington

Sheridan

Noyes

Foster

Emerson

Sherman

University

Chicago

Hinman

Clark

NORTHWESTERN'S EVANSTON CAMPUS 1939–1949

BUILT DURING THIS PERIOD

BUILT PREVIOUSLY

RAZED

CHAPTER

e   ***Abbott Hall*** (1940)

**NORTHWESTERN'S
CHICAGO CAMPUS
1939–1949**

Chicago

Superior

Huron

e

Fairbanks

McClurg

Lake Shore Drive

6

NORTHWESTERN IN WAR AND PEACE

By nature, Northwestern's next president, Franklyn Bliss Snyder, was polite but direct. "I should like to see the next few years," he wrote, "chiefly concerned with bringing all our Schools up to the level which the best have already attained."

A member of the English faculty since 1909, Snyder had long lamented the relatively low salaries in the College of Liberal Arts, especially compared to those in the Medical School and School of Law. What he did not say – and didn't have to – was that low salaries were responsible for the mediocre quality of the faculty in some departments. Succeeding Walter Dill Scott as president in 1939, Snyder was now in the position to do something about it. Early in his tenure, he increased top salaries in the college to $9,000, and he never let go of the purse strings, reviewing each faculty salary himself and approving every raise.

Snyder operated with an iron hand, which meant that the president's distinct personal viewpoints often guided University policy. At least once he violated his own salary cap to hire an economist he could woo in no other way. He denied other faculty members raises when he was displeased, as in the case of philosophy professor Paul Schilpp, an ardent pacifist whose politics went against the grain and whose salary stayed the same between 1940 and 1948.

A strong conservative

Memories of Snyder are deeply etched. He was an ambitious English scholar and an opinionated conservative who did not mind clashing with more liberal members of his faculty. In his 10 years as president of the University, he succeeded in his primary objective, which was to raise the quality of academics at Northwestern, primarily in the liberal arts, to a level where it might compete with older and more prestigious institutions.

The son of a Congregational minister from Connecticut, Snyder had moved with his family to Rockford, Illinois, and attended nearby Beloit College in Wisconsin, graduating and showing enough promise in the humanities to make scholarship his life's work. He attended Harvard for graduate studies and received his PhD in English in 1909.

The 1939 inauguration of a medallioned Franklyn Bliss Snyder (1884–1958) as president of the University marked the beginning of a period of growth in the academic departments and enhanced prestige for the University.

In 1940 Northwestern's football victory over Notre Dame was cause for a campus celebration so intense that classes were dismissed "to give Northwestern students the entire day to relieve the emotional strain," according to one newspaper.

Over a period of several decades, students raised funds for building a much-needed student center, and in 1939 they had the added incentive of honoring the retiring president, Walter Dill Scott. The result was Scott Hall, with lounges, student activity offices, Cahn Auditorium, and, most important, the Scott Grill, which became the bustling social center of campus from the moment it was opened. At the 1940 dedication of the building, ex-President Scott said that the building would fulfill one of the highest ideals of modern education, "a socially adjusted personality."

Snyder's field was Scottish literature, and his dissertation was on the poet Robert Burns, a subject he continued to research until his *Life of Robert Burns* was published in 1922. The book was reviewed by the *New York Times* as a groundbreaking work:

"So careful at every point, so thoroughly documented is this work, that it might be regarded as an attempt at a corrected biography of the poet rather than as merely another 'Life' of Burns."

Specifically, Snyder clarified the record of the poet's alleged drunkenness — Burns was not a hopeless sot as previously thought. He also researched the writer's relationships of the heart and discovered that Mary Campbell, the subject of Burns's most fervent love poetry, may not have been the truest love of his life.

At Northwestern, Snyder's stature as an academic garnered him his first administrative post, as dean of the Graduate School in 1934. He easily took to administration and later rose to the position of vice president and dean of faculties. When Scott decided to retire several years later, Snyder was not the obvious choice to be successor; the Board of Trustees conducted a two-year search. But Snyder was finally elected unanimously with a signal that his administration would transform the University and particularly the College of Liberal Arts with a "quality of distinction," the term Snyder used as he struggled to place Northwestern among the nation's elite universities.

The Murphy bequest

While Northwestern's growth over the years had depended on decades of hard work and vision, some of the institution's most important steps forward could never have been predicted. One such step began in 1936 when President Scott received a letter from a man in Richmond, Virginia. R. E. Cabell professed to represent a client who was preparing to make a major gift to an American university "toward establishing or endowing a school of engineering." He said his client was considering Northwestern.

This news was welcome, if baffling, since the University had a weak engineering department at the time. But it had much improved its fundraising capabilities, and when the possibility of the large bequest was presented, Scott and his chief fundraiser, Thomas Gonser '24, sprang into action. They quickly identified the mystery donor, who turned out to be Walter P. Murphy, an inventor of railroad equipment with scores of patents to his name, ranging from better coupling equipment to improved refrigeration units for box cars. Further research revealed that Murphy had amassed a great fortune. However, he was exceedingly shy and enigmatic. Thus, Northwestern dealt very carefully with the opportunity and went to great lengths to make the benefactor comfortable with the University.

In drafting a prospectus for a new school of engineering, Gonser consulted two luminaries in the engineering profession: Charles Kettering, chief engineer of General Motors, and Herman Schneider, dean of the school of engineering at the University of Cincinnati. Gonser had perceived that Murphy was a practical man with little patience for abstract thinking; Kettering in particular was known for taking ideas and getting them into production. Schneider was a hands-on engineer as well as the architect of the well-established work-study plan at Cincinnati.

Murphy responded favorably. While other schools were being considered for the bequest, Murphy favored a university in or near Chicago, evidently because it was America's great railroad center but still did not have a major school of engineering. Murphy's attorney also had discussed the bequest with the University of Chicago, but that school proved to be too theoretical, and its president, Robert Hutchins, was evidently too aloof.

Murphy's concern all along was for "better trained and better prepared graduates in technical and engineering lines," as Walter Dill Scott later wrote in his short biography of Murphy.

While negotiations were in progress, Murphy remained mysterious. Toward the end of 1936, for example, he suspended talks because of his obsession with the presidential election that year. Then, small misunderstandings cropped up about what the new school should cost. Time passed, and the administration endured moments when the money seemed entirely lost. But finally in 1938 Murphy was convinced that Northwestern was a university after his own heart. He gave $6.7 million for scholarships, endowment, equipment, and a building that would be completed in 1942 and named the Technological Institute.

When Abbott Hall on the Chicago campus was completed in 1940, it was immediately taken over by the Navy for its V-7 midshipmen. By the end of the war, it began to serve the original purpose as a dormitory that would foster a collegiate atmosphere for students in the professional schools.

Annapolis of the Midwest

World War II delayed President Snyder's ambitions to build Northwestern's overall academic strengths. But he flourished as the University's wartime president nonetheless. While colleges all over America were deeply involved in the war effort, few were as active militarily as Northwestern. This was largely attributable to Snyder, called "the Admiral" behind his back because of his enthusiasm for military undertakings.

Naval training became the main activity on both campuses for the duration of the war. So expansive were U.S. Navy programs during the Snyder administration that Northwestern was nicknamed the "Annapolis of the Midwest."

Northwestern's relationship with the Navy grew out of its naval ROTC unit, one of six such University programs established in 1926. NROTC soon developed a small but strong curriculum on the Evanston campus, with courses such as celestial navigation, taught by astronomy professor Phillip Fox. Acquiring sea legs was another matter, of course. When a pair of 30-foot whaling boats arrived on campus in the 1920s, courtesy of the Navy, the NROTC unit was initially at a loss about how to use them. With help from the lifesaving station, a winch was rigged to move the heavy rowboats in and out of the water, and simple maneuvers were conducted on Lake Michigan. Eventually, saltwater cruises were de rigueur for midshipmen, and the NROTC unit grew in numbers and status.

With World War II brewing, a more extensive commitment to military readiness was called for, and Snyder appointed six students and six faculty members to a Committee on Student Morale. Pearl Harbor was nearly a year away when the committee was created, and its purpose was initially unclear. The *Daily* somewhat sardonically explained that it was to address "Northwestern children and our naughty habits, cribbing, cutting classes, leaving school" and other sins of commission.

ENGINEERING AND "TECH"

The architects of "Tech," Holabird & Root, used modern features of the day — large windows and artistic reliefs by artist Edgar Miller — for the graceful Lannon-stone building that has remained functional for 60 years.

In the 1920s, President Walter Dill Scott was well aware of the shortcomings of Northwestern's engineering curriculum. The program was largely theoretical, and most students graduated well versed in the physical sciences but weak in technical skills after just a few courses in civil and mechanical engineering. To build a stronger school of engineering, Scott gave serious consideration to a proposal to merge with Armour Institute, the Chicago technical college later renamed Illinois Institute of Technology.

The Northwestern-Armour merger looked like a sure thing in 1926, but it lost steam shortly thereafter, particularly when the Armour family informed Northwestern that it would donate little of the $10 million needed to make the merger worthwhile for the University. The merger also failed because Northwestern's faculty wanted to build a stronger engineering school themselves. However, it was not until 1939 that the $6.7 million bequest of Walter P. Murphy provided the means to build the Technological Institute, which was dedicated in 1942.

The school distinguished itself from the outset with an extensive cooperative education plan. In fact, Murphy's founding gift was contingent on the co-op program — a five-year system with 7 quarters of work and 11 quarters of study was adopted as the foundation of the new school.

Ovid Eschbach, who was formerly involved in recruitment of engineers for AT&T, was hired as the first dean, and the school's relations with industry flourished. Students worked at companies such as Bell Telephone and Allis-Chalmers for co-op credit; faculty members came from companies such as B. F. Goodrich and Corn Products. Walter Murphy evidently approved of the direction of these programs, for when he died in 1942, he willed an additional $28 million to the cause.

E-199—New Technological Institute, Northwestern University, Evanston, Ill.

The Technological Institute opened in 1942, incorporating the physical sciences and engineering disciplines in one facility. The objective was to turn out "better trained and better prepared graduates in technical and engineering lines," according to Walter Dill Scott's short biography of the building's donor, Walter P. Murphy.

Walter P. Murphy, a railroad-supply tycoon, gave $6.7 million in 1939 to create the Technological Institute. He willed the University another $28 million.

V-12 – the Naval Reserve Officers Training Program – was established on many campuses throughout the nation. Marching students became a common sight in Evanston after July 1943, when the first 1,000 candidates arrived to study and train in preparation for wartime service.

THE WARTIME CAMPUS

The fall of France to the Nazis in June 1940 began a period of intense wartime preparation for government, industry, and education throughout the United States.

Like most universities, Northwestern was eager to make its contribution, and within a few months students, faculty, and administration had begun a program of all-out readiness. Even before the United States entered the war, Dean of Faculties Frederick D. Fagg assumed the role of campus coordinator for the federal Office of National Defense Activities. He increased the size of the NROTC program, facilitated a number of defense-related technical research projects, and oversaw military-related academic work, such as efforts in the psychology department to improve Army personnel selection. (This echoed a ground-breaking Army personnel system devised by psychologist Walter Dill for the government in World War I.)

Northwestern also volunteered its facilities and was chosen as a site for a Naval Reserve Midshipmen's School, the V-7 program, which filled Abbott Hall, the newly completed dormitory on the Chicago campus. Between 1941 and 1945 V-7 turned out more than 24,000 ensigns. They were called "90-day wonders," and one of them was the eventual skipper of PT-109, John F. Kennedy.

A major Navy program on the Evanston campus was V-12, the Navy College Training Program, which placed uniformed trainees in class for a year and a half of continuous study, after which came active duty and officer's training. Many returned to Northwestern to finish their degrees after the war.

The Navy Radio School was yet another major training program, bringing apprentice seamen to the Evanston campus for 16 weeks of class at the Technological Institute. After classes in theory, code, and radio operations, some 6,000 graduates of this school came out with the rank of seaman radioman or radioman third class.

In all, Northwestern was responsible for 11 separate military programs for the duration of the war, including a Navy Flight School, an Army Signal Corps program, and the revival of Base Hospital #12, the Northwestern field hospital unit that had served in France in World War I, which established itself in North Africa and Italy during World War II.

peaks to nation tomorrow

eady!'--Pres. Snyder

AR SPECIAL

Ill., Monday, Dec. 8, Vol. 62, No. 45

western

Inland Press Association · International News Service

nyder pledges Northwestern d in telegram to Roosevelt

sident Franklyn B. Snyder morning sent the following an to President Roosevelt: orthwestern university is to renew its pledge that the resources of the university vailable to you for so long u may need them."

statement is in keeping the cooperation of the uni- ty during the past two years with the activities on the cam- turing the last war.

day more than 850 men are g an intensive course in the Navy's Midshipmen's Train- chool at Abbott hall on the ago campus. The first groups, rising a total of 2,493 grad- are now commissioned as ns in the Naval Reserve and on active duty.

the Evanston campus, the al R.O.T.C. has the largest bership in its 16 year history, men. With the largest Civil nautical authority class in area and the third largest in nation. Northwestern has ed out 315 licensed pilots dur- he past two years and is now ing 50 men.

its new Technological insti- the university is giving 15 ses on defense industry to than 600 men as part of the rnment-sponsored program to

University head gives message to men, women

"To the men and women of North- western:

"Every member of this univer- sity will do all in his power to help the national government win the war which Japan has forced upon us. The moment the first bomb fell on Honolulu this became our paramount duty — our greatest privilege. Till this job is done, nothing else really matters.

"Most of us are civilians. In war the first duty of the civilian is to keep calm, carry on his normal ac- tivities, and hold himself ready for what his government may ask of him. Nothing of value can be ac- complished by civilians in a state of hysteria.

"So—hold steady! I have asked the Student Governing board, the General Faculty committee, and the deans of all the schools, to meet today to formulate plans. Soon hereafter we shall hold a convoca- tion at which these plans will be presented to the student body.

"Meantime—I say it again— hold steady! The government will let you know when you are needed in the army or navy. Till you are called, the greatest service you can render yourselves and the nation is to continue your education for the years of peace that we are sure will return.

Franklyn D. Snyder."

N.U. faculty meets at 4:30 p.m. tomorrow in Lutkin hall

Deans of the university schools, meeting with President Franklyn B. Snyder and Fred Dow Fagg, dean of the faculties, late this afternoon, discussed methods whereby the university and its students may aid the government in the war against Japan, but em- phasized at the same time the students should pursue a normal life and continue their studies un- til their services are required by the government.

At the same time President Snyder called a second meeting of the General Faculty committee to be held at 4 tomorrow in Lutkin hall. Alpheus Smith, professor of English and chairman of the com- mittee, will preside. The first meeting of the committee will be held jointly with the Student Gov- erning board, the Student Defense commission tonight.

All-university convocation Wednesday

A joint committee of the Stu- dent Governing board, the Student Defense commission, and the Gen- eral Faculty committee met to- night to arrange final details and plan the program for Wednesday's All-University Defense convoca- tion. Time and Place will be an- nounced in tomorrow's DAILY NORTHWESTERN.

Present plans call for state- ments from President Franklyn B. Snyder, President-emeritus Walter Dill Scott, and chairman of the Board of Trustees, Kenneth Bur- gess; a statement from the SGB chairman, Julius Pewowar, on the responsibilities of students in the present crisis; and the presenta- tion of the Student Defense com- missions' program by chairman, Joe Lery.

Letters were sent out early this evening by the SGB and the de- fense commission asking for sug- gestions from students on new courses that the university might sponsor to aid students in assist- ing the national war effort.

House presidents should submit these suggestions by 1:30 p.m. to- morrow (Tuesday) in Dean Fagg's office, second floor, Lunt.

At the same time all men's house presidents were asked to fill out a questionnaires regarding the men from their organization now in the armed services. These should be returned immediately.

President Roosevelt

President Roosevelt will ad- dress the nation over the radio at 9 p.m. tomorrow night, it was announced early this eve- ning.

His address will be carried over all the major networks. It is presumed that he will describe the course of the war against the Japanese empire, and tell what counter-meas- ures have been taken by the United States armed forces.

WAR BULLETINS

The Lend-lease program will continue in full operation, Presi- dent Roosevelt announced today.

Japs bomb Manila

Manila (Mutual Broadcasting system)—The first bombs fell on the city of Manila itself from 3:30 to 7:35 a.m. this morning but the Japanese planes were driven out to sea by American navy planes with at least one Japanese plane shot down. No civilian casualties were reported.

West coast on full wartime basis

From the tip of Alaska to San Diego, the entire West coast is on a full wartime basis.

The possibility of air raids was admitted when all schools in the vicinity of the forts guarding the mouth of the Columbia river were closed and a complete blackout was put into force.

LaGuardia, Mrs. F.D.R. to fly to Los Angeles

Mayor Fiorello LaGuardia, di- rector of civilian defense, and Mrs. Roosevelt will fly to Los Angles tomorrow to survey that city's im- mediate defense needs, it was an- nounced tonight.

Dominican Republic wars on Japan

The Dominican Republic declared war on Japan today and the Cham- ber of Deputies unanimously past a "Solidarity with the United States" program.

Students tell of confidence in U.S. policy

With the nation plunged into a state of war with Japan yesterday, campus leaders last night express- ed faith and confidence in our na- tion's policy.

Julius Pewowar, president of the Student Governing board, made the following statement:

"With the United States now ac- tively engaged in war, the time for partisanship is at an end. To all of us who believe staunchly and firmly in freedom and democracy, national unity of spirit and of ac- tion is essential.

"I feel confident that the students of Northwestern and of universities and colleges throughout the land will stand solidly and irrevocably behind the efforts of our nation."

Coordinating all national defense efforts on the campus is the De- fense council. Said Joe Lery, chairman:

"We face a situation today which the Defense commission, in its six months of planning, had anticipa- ted. We feel that we shall be ca- pable of handling our part."

Said Connie Booth, head of the Women's Self-Governing associa- tion:

"I have felt for a long time that this campus has been thoroughly lacking in defense consciousness. I hope that the present situation will unify the students as it has the nation."

Dick Brahm, chairman of the See 'Student', page 2

tudents must conquer n educational dilemma

The months of tension, marked by an ever-mounting is in a war-torn world, suddenly culminated last night in Japanese declaration of war on the United States. The n for the future became clear and the people of our country d united in a determination to defend our way of life.

Yet, on university campuses, youth who stood ready to t were met with a dilemma. They were united in a will- ness to aid our country in whatever way possible, but that y willingness was mixed with a feeling of helplessness. ng enrolled in an educational institution, pursuing a nal, semi-secluded college life seemed futile now.

In answer we harken back to President Roosevelt's plea the youth of our college to realize that we need, more than thing else, educated, enlightened citizens to direct the tinies of our democracy. We must defeat the enemy with gorous counter-attack, but at the same time we must not sight of our responsibility to the future by an abrupt sation of our education.

There will be a place and a part for all of us in this war. Northwestern student body can show its cooperation by a ere backing of the government in all its policies, by a ingness to serve in whatever way is necessary, by the tinuance of a rational, unemotional attitude. The North- Defense commission has already been set up to cor- ate student activities; it is to this body that the students uld now turn for vigorous action.

We must face and accept our challenge. We must realize t a college education today takes on added importance, for cated, intelligent youth will be our strongest asset for nocracy's future.

2nd 'War Special'

This edition is the second War Special edition of the Daily North- western today. The first came off the presses at 2 p.m. and was rushed to campus. This edition went to press at 7:45 p.m. and will be distributed at the Northwestern basketball game tonight at Evan- ston high school.

VE (Victory in Europe) Day was big news at Northwestern, which was called "Annapolis of the Midwest" because of extensive naval training on both campuses.

Northwestern University Information

VOLUME X   JANUARY 19, 1942   NUMBER 21

Double Service

with your Victory Dollars

Because Northwestern served as a major venue for naval training, the appeal to University donors was folded into a patriotic war bond drive. Funds raised by the University during World War II were used to purchase Defense Bonds; thus each dollar given to Northwestern did "double service."

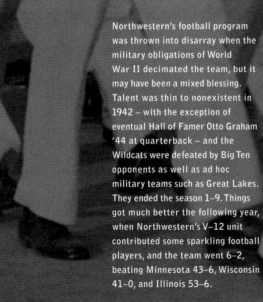

Northwestern's football program was thrown into disarray when the military obligations of World War II decimated the team, but it may have been a mixed blessing. Talent was thin to nonexistent in 1942 – with the exception of eventual Hall of Famer Otto Graham '44 at quarterback – and the Wildcats were defeated by Big Ten opponents as well as ad hoc military teams such as Great Lakes. They ended the season 1–9. Things got much better the following year, when Northwestern's V–12 unit contributed some sparkling football players, and the team went 6–2, beating Minnesota 43–6, Wisconsin 41–0, and Illinois 53–6.

After reading this Program mail it to a man in Service.

FOR VICTORY BUY UNITED STATES WAR BONDS AND STAMPS

GREAT LAKES ★ NORTHWESTERN
DYCHE STADIUM ★★★ NOVEMBER 26, 1942
TWENTY-FIVE CENTS   N. U. ARCHIVES

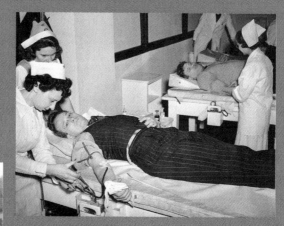

The Northwestern Blood Bank was another homefront activity of the University. Here, medical student Tom Feeny '40 (MD '44), gives blood.

Northwestern's V-7 Midshipmen's School produced "90-Day Wonders," transforming raw civilians into commissioned naval officers in three months of training, both in the classroom and on the freshwater sea by Evanston.

A Saturday afternoon inspection at the V-7 Naval Midshipmen's School on the field adjacent to the Chicago campus.

Housing was in constant shortage at Northwestern, but the military took the situation in hand. Quonset huts became a part of the architectural character of the Evanston campus during the war and afterward, when the influx of veterans pushed enrollment well past the University's normal capacity. One housing project at Ridge Avenue and Central Street (far right) was completed in 90 days and housed approximately 1,000 students and faculty members.

Abbott Hall midshipmen were a common sight on the Near North Side during the war. Here a unit marches past the Chicago Armory, next door to the Chicago campus.

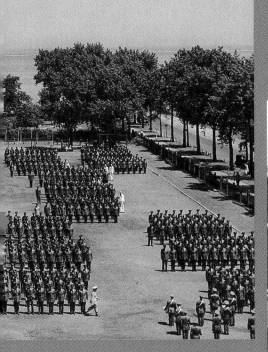

Hundreds of Northwestern students and graduates joined the military even before Pearl Harbor. In Pensacola, Florida, a group of aviation cadets, who were also Northwestern alums, assembled on the tarmac for a picture used by the University publicity office.

Following Pearl Harbor, however, the committee was renamed the Student War Council and quickly succeeded in mobilizing the campus. A Civilian Defense Organization was created to devise campus blackout plans. A Curriculum Committee helped develop dozens of courses ranging from ambulance driving and home nursing to an engineering course called "Camp Sanitation and Water Supply" and a journalism course entitled "Propaganda". These initiatives were just the tip of the iceberg, it turned out, for Northwestern was soon chosen as the site for a long list of military training programs. Mostly naval, these programs trained thousands of officer candidates, radiomen, pilots, and others who passed through the University en route to wartime duty.

Patriotism ran deep at Northwestern, and the campus was mostly of one mind in working toward victory. In 1942, however, a serious controversy arose when Snyder issued what he thought was a routine administrative order in line with the government policy of internment camps for Japanese Americans. Snyder's action was to bar students of Japanese descent from enrolling at Northwestern. It brought immediate negative reaction from the campus and the Chicago press.

Undergraduate Mary Ellen Munger '42 wrote in the *Daily* that "there is a delicate line to be drawn between the Japanese militaristic government...and an American student who may have the current misfortune to be of Japanese extraction."

A flood of similar views forced Snyder to revise the policy and accept Japanese American students who were both qualified and could show authorization to be free from the internment protocol.

But dissent of any kind was rare, due in part to the thousands of military personnel in an array of mostly naval training programs in Evanston and Chicago. With so many uniforms on campus, the gravity of the national emergency impressed everyone. An editorial in the *Daily* entitled "America Must Mobilize Her Artists for Action" went so far as to propose a National Bureau of Art to organize wartime activities for "a number one fighting man being kept out of this war – the American artist." The idea, never realized on such a scale, was for artists to be mobilized like people in other industries. "Billboards, cartoons, ceramics, letterheads, calendars, graphs, in fact almost everything that an artist can create could now be working for victory," the columnist wrote.

Northwestern men and women participated in World War II with distinction. Of some 11,000 Northwestern alumni, 274 died giving "the last full measure of devotion that America might emerge victorious in World War II," as a special edition of the alumni directory put it. Two were awarded the Congressional Medal of Honor: Army Major John L. Jerstad '40, who died piloting the lead plane during a raid on a Romanian oil field, and Army Lieutenant Walter E. Truemper '41, who died in a crash after he took the controls of a B-17 that was hit near Leipzig and stayed in the cockpit while the rest of his crew had time to bail out.

While the University could be proud of its war service, it was determined to distinguish itself in the postwar peace as well. This was a challenge, since the federal GI Bill program sent unprecedented thousands to college – well beyond the

Otto Graham '44 is widely regarded as
Northwestern's greatest athlete. From Waukegan,
Illinois, he led the Wildcat football team in
1941, 1942, and 1943, breaking nearly every Big
Ten passing record on the books, making the
All-America team twice, and being named the Big
Ten's most valuable player in his senior year.
His dominance can be measured by the 1943
Wisconsin game, when he scored three touch-
downs, passed for another, and kicked three
extra points. Graham's basketball and baseball
exploits were almost as dazzling; he was a
basketball All-American and the only two-sport
All-American in Northwestern history. Graham
went on to the NFL Hall of Fame after leading
the Cleveland Browns to several championships.

Home economics flourished at Northwestern
in a period when young women were expected to
attend college and then move into careers as
homemakers.

Course registration was often an adventure,
but it was businesslike at the School of
Commerce in Wieboldt Hall on the Chicago
campus.

FACULTY AUTHORS

An important element of Northwestern's prestige was earned by its faculty authors. Publishing was always a part of the scholar's work, as evidenced by the towering *Treatise on Evidence* first published in 1904 and authored by John Henry Wigmore, dean of the law school. After World War II, the book publishing industry grew considerably, and with it grew opportunities for members of the faculty to extend their reach. The fact that President Snyder had gained notoriety early in his career with his book on Scottish poet Robert Burns also stimulated emulation, and the president's eagerness to raise the stature of his faculty increased the flow of books by Northwestern professors.

Winifred Ward, *Theater for Children*, D. Appleton-Century Company, 1939. As creative dramatics was pioneered at Northwestern, Ward's book helped make it a national movement.

Cyrus Colter, *A Chocolate Soldier*, Thunder's Mouth Press, 1988. Colter had been a lawyer and member of the faculty of the Department of African American Studies when he wrote his fifth book, a novel about a restless student at a black college in Tennessee who devours military histories of all kinds as a way of feeding his vision of black liberation.

Leon Forrest, *There is a Tree More Ancient Than Eden*, Random House, 1973. Forrest was a journalist for African American newspapers when he became a novelist. This, his first novel, centered on the details of life in the black ghetto. Forrest joined the faculty in the Department of African American Studies in 1973. His later novel, *Divine Days*, was called by Henry Louis Gates "the *War and Peace* of African American literature."

Melville Herskovits, *The Myth of the Negro Past*, Harper & Brothers Publishers, 1941. Herskovits's explosive work proved true cultural links between African Americans and Africa.

Baker Brownell and Frank Lloyd Wright, *Architecture and Modern Life*, Harper & Brothers Publishers, 1937. Medill professor Brownell was a journalist, teacher, lecturer, minor poet, and in this case collaborator with Wright on the latter's ideas regarding language, politics, urbanism, and other aspects of the master builder's elaborate vision.

Charlotte Lee, *Oral Interpretation*, Houghton Mifflin Company, 1952. Lee joined the faculty of the School of Speech in 1945 and wrote what became a popular text for translating the written word to oral presentation.

Curtis D. MacDougall, *Interpretative Reporting*, MacMillan Company, 1938. Medill professor MacDougall wrote nearly a dozen books; his *Hoaxes* was an oft-cited compendium of gullible newspaper miscues. *Interpretative Reporting* was his first tome – a frequently updated textbook for journalism students. It included guidelines and terminology for reporting on local affairs, science news, and other areas of journalism.

Carl Condit, *The Chicago School of Architecture*, University of Chicago Press, 1964. Professor Carl Condit became one of the nation's leading architectural historians after he chronicled the Chicago architecture of Burnham, Sullivan, and their contemporaries. He showed how and why the Chicago School represented a central turning point in 20th-century architecture.

Ernest Samuels, *Henry Adams: The Middle Years*, Belknap Press of Harvard University Press, 1958. This book was the second installment of Samuels's three-part biography of historian and literary genius Henry Adams. English professor Samuels received the Pulitzer Prize for the third, *Henry Adams: The Major Phase*. He later wrote a two-volume biography of art critic Bernard Berenson.

John Henry Wigmore, *A Treatise on the Anglo-American System of Evidence*, Little, Brown, & Company, 1923. This treatise, in print since its introduction in 1904, made the dean of the Northwestern University School of Law a nationally recognized legal scholar.

preparedness of many colleges and universities. During the 1945–46 school year, the admissions office mailed out 28,000 applications for fewer than 2,000 places in the freshman class the following fall. It was a period of enormous growth, and by 1949 more than 9,000 students were enrolled on the Evanston campus alone.

While such growth pushed resources to the limit, it also gave Snyder satisfaction to select the best students from so large a pool of applicants.

"A few parents of children who were not admitted have been persistent in demanding a bill of particulars showing the precise reasons underlying our decisions," Snyder wrote in the President's Report in 1946.

"These it is usually undesirable to give. Many times they trace back to confidential statements by school principals; sometimes to physicians' reports; often to comments from members of our own staff who have interviewed the applicants. We do not violate these confidences."

Power of prestige

While postwar growth provided a range of opportunities for Northwestern, Snyder's attention was fixed on the stature of the College of Liberal Arts. For example, there were three vacancies in the history department, and the president made it his business to find eminent or extremely promising young scholars for these positions. Among them was Richard Leopold, a young PhD from Harvard, hired to teach American diplomatic history. Snyder insisted on approving all new members of the faculty, and Leopold remembered his interview with the president consisting mostly of Snyder's reminiscences of his own days at Harvard. Whatever the criteria, the president's instinct was right; Leopold remained an academic pillar of the college for nearly half a century.

It took longer to fill the two other history positions, since two or three candidates proposed by the department were rejected by Snyder. "We can do better," he said of one. "Been in the bush leagues too long," he said of another. Finally, a junior professor from Princeton was recommended by an acquaintance at the Institute for Advanced Studies. That scholar, Arthur Link, was already involved in groundbreaking work on Woodrow Wilson, and although 20th-century history was not then the department's most pressing need, Link was approached and hired. "Princeton was the magic touch in this case," Leopold remembered later.

Snyder and the School of Education

As Snyder raised Northwestern's academic stature through hiring, he was bound to clash with some established members of the faculty. The most serious case came when Ernest O. Melby, dean of the School of Education, sought support to expand its well-regarded program in teacher training. It was not to be. Snyder had long distrusted the rigor of the education school; he had even discontinued the master's degree in education when he was dean of the Graduate School. "Were the classes open only to properly prepared persons?" Snyder asked in a report at that time.

"Were those who attended them really interested in professional training or only in a diploma which could be exhibited to some school superintendent?"

Snyder's misgivings might have been unfair, but clearly a philosophical difference existed between his conception of the University and Melby's. Melby was a consummate democrat who hated elitist education. "Faith in the few – only in the highly endowed – will not suffice," Melby wrote. "Democracy rests on faith in the common man." In part because of Melby's popularity and nurturing style, the school's enrollment grew considerably in the 1930s. Many of the students were practicing teachers who attended part-time or in the summer. Whether they were as qualified as other Northwestern students was debatable; Snyder thought they were not and pulled the purse strings tight when Melby requested raises for his faculty.

The situation deteriorated until Melby resigned in 1941, an event that distressed many educators, particularly on the North Shore. Letters came in protesting that Melby's resignation represented a loss of "progressive leadership" in the school community. Snyder seemed unmoved by these complaints, however, and by the mid-1940s he achieved what he intended all along, which was to incorporate most of the teacher-training curriculum into the College of Liberal Arts, a move Melby had strenuously resisted.

The Medical Center grows

Snyder's grand plans for Northwestern were centered in Evanston, but they did not neglect the Chicago campus. In 1946 he announced Northwestern's vision for an expanded medical complex around the University's Medical and Dental Schools. It would be another generation before this plan was fully realized, but a major step soon came with the addition of Wesley Hospital adjacent to the Medical School in Streeterville. The hospital was a onetime partner and then a bitter antagonist of Northwestern.

Ties between Northwestern and Wesley dated back to 1888 when the hospital was founded, like Northwestern, by Methodists. A teaching relationship developed, and a few years later, the Medical School provided money and property for the hospital to relocate in a new facility next door to the school on Chicago's near South Side. In exchange for the site and $30,000 for construction, Wesley agreed to provide a setting for clinical training and staff positions for Northwestern faculty.

But the relationship grew hostile. Trouble began in 1914 when James Deering, a Northwestern trustee, provided a $1 million grant to Wesley primarily for the care of the poor; it came with the stipulation that

"Wesley shall become a teaching hospital and in both the charity work herein provided for, and everywhere else in the hospital, it shall give all proper teaching facilities consistent with the principle that the patient's welfare is the first consideration."

Deering's bequest was meant to strengthen ties between hospital and school, but they quickly broke down when students and faculty found themselves largely unwelcome in the hospital wards. This spirit of noncooperation lasted for years, during which time the Medical School successfully affiliated with other teaching hospitals. Most saw Wesley as the intractable party. When James Deering suggested, for example, that a single person be appointed to head both school and hospital, Wesley responded by reappointing its offending superintendent for another five years. By 1920 lawsuits were filed to force Wesley's compliance with the terms of the Deering gift.

Shortly thereafter, Northwestern established its new Chicago campus, and Passavant Hospital, located at Erie and Dearborn Streets, agreed to relocate on Superior Street near the Medical School and serve as a primary teaching hospital. Passavant had been experiencing hard economic times, and the opportunity to relocate came as a godsend to its board, which raised money for a stately new building that was dedicated in 1929.

These developments clearly isolated Wesley Hospital, which was in decline itself and had responded by closing some of its floors. Finally, the Wesley trustees began to come around vis-à-vis Northwestern. In 1936 a benefactor, George H. Jones, announced that he would contribute $1.2 million for a new Wesley building to be built on property contributed by Northwestern. Ground was broken the following year, but a deepening of the Depression brought work to a halt shortly thereafter. The Wesley-Northwestern marriage seemed cursed, but here again Jones saved the day, donating another $1.8 million to complete the new "Cathedral of Healing," as the Wesley building was called. It was dedicated in 1941.

School of Speech

Back on the Evanston campus, far-reaching developments were unfolding in the School of Speech. With roots in the old-fashioned discipline of elocution, its programs were producing leaders in theater, speech correction, and even radio and television. How the school developed in this way is the story of a succession of innovative professors who made Speech arguably Northwestern's most eclectic school.

In the 1940s the theatre department of the School of Speech trained students in the practical aspects of theater. Backstage at Annie May Swift Hall, students applied makeup. Other students designed sets, worked the lights, and created costumes for productions by the University Theatre and a variety of studio workshops.

In the 1940s, there was at least one dance studio in Evanston that had Northwestern students enrolled. Few photographs of college dances, however, exhibit the rug-cutting panache of this couple.

POSTWAR SOCIAL LIFE

By the postwar era, strict campus regulations separating the sexes had been lifted. The frenzy of the Jazz Age was past. By the 1930s and 1940s, a certain *savoir faire* infused Northwestern social life, which involved formals, smokers, coke dates, and late nights at the College Inn at the Sherman House Hotel downtown.

There was a party for every taste. The brothers of Phi Mu Alpha held their formal at the Edgewater Beach Hotel. Delta Upsilon gave its "Deep Sea Party," a winter romp in costumes reminiscent of buccaneers. This period was also the heyday of big dances for the whole University, and one of the biggest of them all was the Navy Ball, often held at the Stevens Hotel (now the Chicago Hilton and Towers Hotel on South Michigan Avenue).

There were plenty of photo bugs on hand to record the festivities of the era. The most ubiquitous was James L. Bixby '43, who toted his 4 x 5 Speed Graphic everywhere while a student at Northwestern. No one ever captured student life more vividly, which was not a constant pleasure to the University. Bixby was temporarily expelled when he sold a spread of photos on fraternity hazing to the *Chicago Tribune*.

The photographs on these pages were taken before Bixby dropped out of school to join United Press as a reporter and copyreader during World War II. He later worked in public relations, and after his retirement he donated his vast collection of photos of student life to the Northwestern University Archives.

"Coke dates," often in groups, were an important component of the dating scene.

Getting comfortable with members of the opposite sex was easier for some students than for others.

Despite the self-confident claims of Northwestern men, campus women were not always convinced that their social lives should revolve around Evanston. They sometimes packed their bags for greener pastures.

The Navy Ball in the early 1940s featured chiffon gowns, tuxedoes, and midshipmans' uniforms.

Jimmy Dorsey was big in the early 1940s, and so were campus venues. Here a group of coeds met him at the airport for a series of publicity photos.

Overseeing the growth was Ralph Dennis, Robert Cumnock's successor as dean in 1913. Dennis was eager to expand the school, and he built the faculty with teachers who could devise new courses and develop new specialties. Many were successful, and the School of Speech became increasingly popular with professors such as Winifred Ward '05, who joined the faculty in 1918 to teach storytelling. Ward's course, which might have been an innocuous elective for future teachers, was soon transformed into a pioneering new field, creative dramatics, which spawned the Evanston Children's Theater in the local schools and later many such programs around the United States.

"I take my cue from the kind of dramatic play that children use every day," Ward said in describing dramatics as a teaching tool. Her approach was to go "from a child's imaginative play to the very simple play involving movement, involving the senses." As Ward wrote on the subject, the children's theater movement grew nationally. Evanston remained the recognized leader, and its grade-school troupe even went to Washington, D. C., in the 1942–43 school year to perform *The Emperor's New Clothes*.

Two other later legends of the School of Speech joined the faculty in 1920. Lew Sarett arrived as a poet and former Chautauqua speaker with a law degree; his first course had the quaint title of "Prosody," which was the study of the metrical structures of verse and language. But Sarett was a dramatist as well. Students remembered that classes sometimes resembled performances; Sarett mesmerized them with voices such as that of a French-Canadian voyager hilariously discussing the behavior and habits of bears.

But as Sarett entertained, he taught. "He explained that if you mentioned a little boy, a dog, a cripple, the flag," remembered one former student, "the audience would promptly be with you.... It was really quite practical."

Also hired in 1920 was Clarence T. Simon, who several years later founded Northwestern's speech clinic. Simon came to Northwestern as a speech instructor fresh out of Ohio's Wittenberg College. He went on to get a master's degree in economics from Northwestern in 1922 and a PhD in psychology and speech from Iowa in 1925. Returning to Northwestern, Simon became convinced that the School of Speech should help not only talented speakers but also those who needed help speaking. "This is a talking civilization," Simon said. "It never occurs to us that there are men who are barred from business conferences because they cannot express an idea, and cannot even wish a friend a cheery good morning without enduring laughter and mockery."

Charlton Heston '45 (pictured here), a future Academy Award winner, arrived at Northwestern in the fall of 1941. He was a promising young actor from neighboring New Trier High School and involved himself in Northwestern's theater subculture along with other Hollywood-bound students such as Patricia Neal '47 and Ralph Meeker '43. In the two years he spent at Northwestern before he joined the service, Heston performed in a number of University Theatre productions, including this one, *Hedda Gabler*.

Voice and Diction class, here in the 1950s, established good habits of speech as students analyzed pronounciation and articulation in their own voices. This introductory course in the School of Speech formed the groundwork for further study in the curriculum, from public speaking and theatre to radio and television.

Radio became a logical extension of the School of Speech, especially after three alumnae appeared on an NBC program called *Clara, Lu 'n' Em*; they portrayed over-the-top town gossips and were a nationwide hit in the '30s. In the '40s, the radio department produced *The Reviewing Stand*, an important Chicago-based program of public affairs. On May 8, 1950, WNUR, the campus radio station, debuted with a 10-watt transmitter and control room (pictured) in Annie May Swift Hall. From the beginning, WNUR was the voice of Northwestern students — with world news, sports, music, and small acts of on-air rebellion.

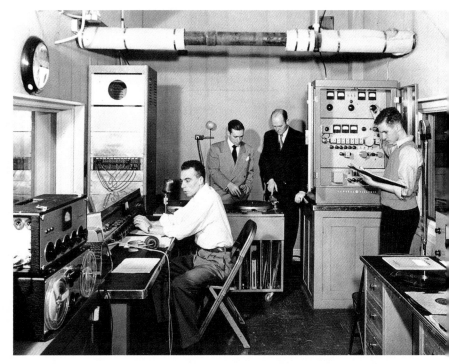

School of Speech professor Lew Sarett (left) was a well-loved figure on the Midwest literary scene, which made him a natural compatriot of Carl Sandburg (right), who favored Sarett with frequent visits to campus.

By the 1940s Simon had built a leading department of speech correction; its speech clinic served as a laboratory for this work and also assisted hundreds of people, initially Northwestern students and Evanstonians, in coping with speech problems. The first two PhD graduates under Simon, Paul Moore and Raymond Carhart, both class of 1936, were engaged in research on many kinds of speech pathology, the most common being stuttering. Stuttering, they learned, had a complex etiology. Both neurological and psychological causes were likely – the latter seemed quite poignant, as they observed that many stutterers stumbled on the word "mother."

A variety of early stuttering therapies were devised and practiced at the speech clinic in Annie May Swift Hall. One of them, the "two-room technique," placed a stutterer alone in a room to read or speak. The theory was that a listener's reaction to stuttering often aggravated the condition, perhaps because of past experiences with family members. In the case of a 24-year-old man, for example, it was discovered that his family had been classic "enablers" who finished sentences for him as a child. This patient "was obviously using his speech difficulty as a means of escaping responsibility," Carhart wrote in 1938. By isolating the stutterer and then bringing listeners gradually into his or her presence, the problem could be greatly, though not completely, reduced.

The speech pathology field produced a long line of distinguished scholars at Northwestern and new treatments for a wide range of disorders. Moore and his followers, some of whom were stutterers themselves, developed and used apparatuses such as a high-speed photographic equipment to study the larynx during speech production. They also devised "delayed auditory feedback," using earphones to play back a patient's speech at a 150-millisecond delay, which sometimes suppressed the stuttering reflex.

After World War II, the Department of Speech Correction, later renamed the Department of Communicative Disorders, entered the field in audiology. Carhart became the nation's recognized father of this field after his experience working with hearing-impaired veterans. This work involved a spectrum of techniques, from lip reading and signing (signing was limited at first) to measuring patients for hearing aids.

Melville Herskovits

Northwestern was moving ahead, sometimes with surprising brilliance. Among the brilliant was Professor Melville J. Herskovits, who brought the kind of academic prestige to Northwestern that President Snyder craved. Herskovits, a young anthropologist, had arrived in 1927 from Columbia University, where he had studied under the eminent Franz Boas. Along with Ruth Benedict and Margaret Mead, Herskovits was at the forefront of cultural anthropology, traveling to far-flung places to examine the complex threads of living cultures. With gargantuan ambition and with his wife, Frances, as an indispensable partner, Herskovits chose to specialize in an area rarely studied in depth – the cultures of Africa and of Africans in America.

Herskovits admitted that the field fooled him at first. In 1924 he wrote in a journal article that African Americans "have retained nothing in their African behavior." It was a judgment that he reversed a few years later, and he spent most of the rest of his career discovering fascinating cultural links between blacks in North and South America and their past in Africa. One of his first field trips, for example, took him to Dutch Guiana (now Suriname), a refuge for escaped slaves in the 1700s. There, Herskovits found elements of language and social structure strikingly similar to those of old African kingdoms in Dahomey, Nigeria, and the Gold Coast. Later, by recording indigenous music in North America and in Africa, he established links between the tones and rhythms of West African chants and Negro spirituals of the United States.

Understanding African culture enabled Herskovits to argue against the bitter assertion that African Americans were endowed with lower native intelligence than whites. Herskovits was one of the earliest social scientists to dismiss such theories.

In 1952, when a psychologist from Villanova University contended that tests showed blacks lacked the "educational capacity" of whites, Herskovits made quick work of disproving it. "What this man is talking about is an underprivileged social group – not a racial group," Herskovits told the *Chicago Daily News*. He added that "only about 15 percent of American Negroes do not have some white ancestry… and there is no relation that we can see between the amount of white ancestry and the achievements of those Negroes who have had educational opportunities."

Antidiscrimination

While Herskovits never led antidiscrimination fights at Northwestern, he participated in them. And there were definitely fights to be waged, as the conservative University and the town of Evanston bridled against any pressure to change traditional social practices. Pressure for change came from many directions. Among them was a women's counselor employed by the University, Ruth McCarn, who had been pressing for on-campus housing for black students since before World War II. By the late 1940s McCarn was floating such ideas as an African American sorority.

Ruth McCarn, a women's counselor at Northwestern from 1937 to 1947, gave lectures and counseled students on issues related to sex, marriage, and divorce. On most issues she was a moderate. But McCarn was out in front on the issue of racial integration, which eventually proved her undoing. She was dismissed from the University when President Snyder had heard enough on the integration issue and considered her to be one of the chief instigators of all the talk.

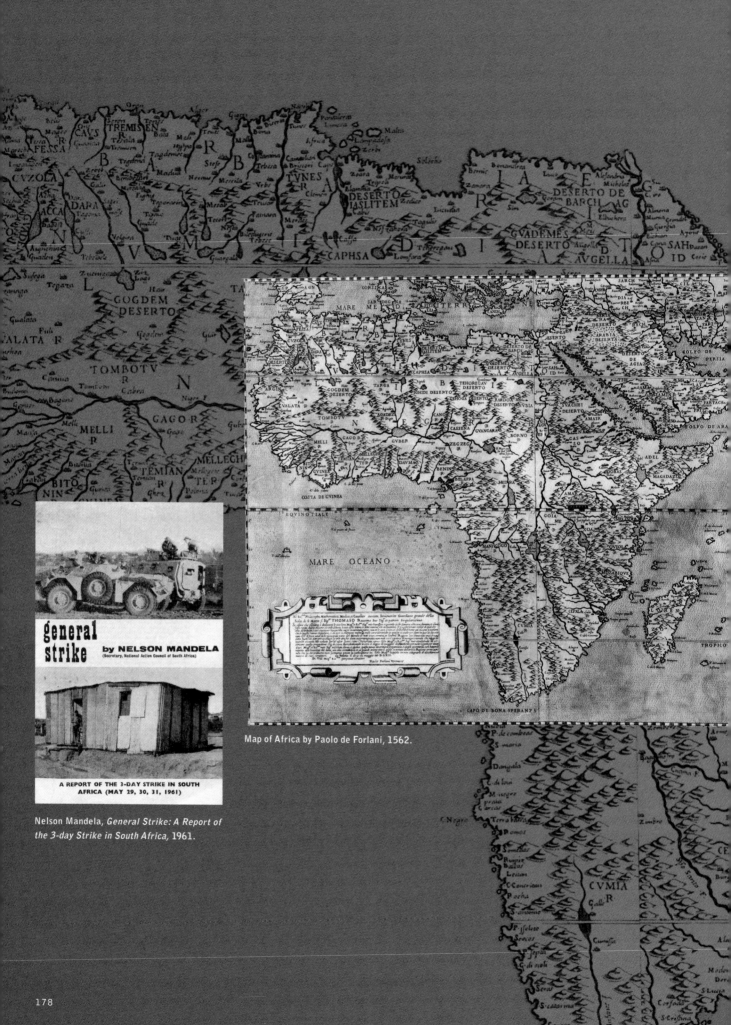

general
strike
by NELSON MANDELA
(Secretary, National Action Council of South Africa)

A REPORT OF THE 3-DAY STRIKE IN SOUTH
AFRICA (MAY 29, 30, 31, 1961)

Nelson Mandela, *General Strike: A Report of the 3-day Strike in South Africa*, 1961.

Map of Africa by Paolo de Forlani, 1562.

THE MELVILLE J. HERSKOVITS LIBRARY OF AFRICAN STUDIES

Anthropology professor Melville Herskovits and his wife, Frances, brought scholarly rigor to the study of Africa, changing perceptions of a greatly misunderstood continent.

Among Herskovits's major contributions to this field was the development of a library of Africana. Northwestern's Library of African Studies was formalized around the time that the Herskovits-inspired Program of African Studies was established in 1948. But well before that, Herskovits made clear that the message of African culture must be transmitted through the written word.

From the time Herskovits arrived at Northwestern in 1927, he encouraged University librarians to buy books on African history and ethnography. He dealt with rare-book dealers in search of volumes on slavery and

African American history. He even facilitated Northwestern's purchase of the private library of his mentor, Franz Boas, after the older anthropologist's death.

Today the Melville J. Herskovits Library of African Studies is the largest such collection in existence. It contains some 245,000 bound volumes, including more than 3,500 noncirculating rare books, such as early European accounts of African exploration. The collection includes artifacts from the Herskovitses' fieldwork, archives from noted Africanists, pamphlets and ephemera, and 2,500 current periodicals.

Melville Herskovits in 1929 with objects he acquired in Suriname.

19th century Ethiopian prayer scroll.

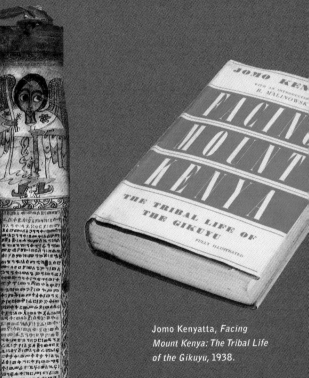

Jomo Kenyatta, *Facing Mount Kenya: The Tribal Life of the Gikuyu*, 1938.

(Blacks were still forced to rent rooms in Evanston if they could find them, and in Chicago if they could not.) McCarn was also involved in "mixed" social events, a subject that particularly riled President Snyder. In 1943, for example, the president was informed of an integrated beach party on the edge of campus. He shot off a memo without delay. "No such groups," he wrote, "should be admitted to a University building."

Black women finally got University housing when "International House," primarily a euphemism for a segregated black women's dorm, was created in 1947. The *Daily Northwestern* had been writing sometimes strident editorials in favor of open housing for at least a year and continued to do so even after editors were called to the office of the dean of students and ordered to soften their tone. In 1948 the paper reported on a questionnaire circulated on campus indicating that the majority of students were ready for integrated dorms (though they were not ready at this point for interracial roommates). Shortly thereafter a black men's social club called the Quibblers intensified its demand for University housing and finally pressured the administration to purchase a residence for African American men. Finally, the University purchased Asbury Hall, on the southwest edge of campus. Intended by the administration to be a black dormitory, it was immediately integrated by a group of liberal white students who moved in.

Asbury Hall soon became the cradle of civil rights at Northwestern, a university that still had a long way to go in this area. A year or so after settling in the new dorm, Asbury men took the next step, demanding to know why so few black students entered Northwestern (rarely more than five in a class) and asking why Jewish enrollment seemed to be restricted as well. The admissions office answered that the problem was the lack of qualified applicants, to which the Asbury group responded with a letter-writing and recruiting campaign directed at principals of predominantly black and Jewish high schools across the country. This outraged the administration, and the dean quickly threatened to expel the leader of the campaign, a white student named John McKnight '53. McKnight resisted the attempts to stifle him and went on to become a professor of communication studies and associate director of the Center for Urban Affairs.

The Progressive MacDougall

There were other progressives irritating the conservatives of Northwestern in the postwar era. One was Medill professor Curtis MacDougall, a journalist who ran several times for elective office on liberal or radical tickets. "Dr. Mac," as he was called by his students, had a varied past, working for newspapers in Wisconsin and Illinois and getting a master's degree at Medill ('26) and later a PhD in sociology from the University of Wisconsin. After he began teaching at Northwestern in the 1930s, MacDougall said his objective was "to carry on the tradition of [Medill's] founders, teaching journalism as a social science and not communications."

But he did not mention that he might also cause grief for the rock-ribbed Republican Northwestern brass. MacDougall later said that his political activity was in the interest of journalism. A political reporter who never ran for office, he said, is "like an aviation writer who has never flown." The University administration did not see it that way, especially in 1948, when MacDougall was enticed by the Illinois Progressive Party to run for the U.S. Senate. In the McCarthyite environment of the day, Progressive Henry Wallace, who headed the ticket for president that year, was frequently accused of being communistic. For that reason MacDougall was discouraged by Medill dean Kenneth Olson from carrying out what the dean regarded as a dangerous campaign. "I was only trying to save his neck," Olson told the *Daily News*. "I explained to him that I believed that every Wallace candidate is going to be smeared with a red brush."

For a while, MacDougall demurred and dropped out of the race. Then he thought twice and got back in. As the campaign got going, President Snyder grew impatient, but to his credit he tolerated MacDougall's foray in politics. "Much as I dislike the friendship which Henry Wallace seems to be showing for Russia," he wrote to an angry anticommunist who called for MacDougall to be fired, "I do not think you or I would recommend Russian methods of liquidating people who disagree with us."

MacDougall's senate campaign was eventful though futile. He was stoned in West Frankfort, Illinois, during a campaign swing with his family. He campaigned at Bughouse Square in Chicago, long a center of soap-box oratory. With a bit of hellfire he deplored "witch-hunting, intimidation, and red baiting." But it was soon clear that Illinois was not ready for Progressives. Despite a vigorous effort, MacDougall could not even get his name or those of other members of his party on the statewide ballot.

Though MacDougall grew bitter in later years, the popular professor always had an optimistic side. Much later, when a former Northwestern graduate student was running for office himself, MacDougall remembered the polite kid who ran his senate campaign on the Northwestern campus. He was George McGovern, who graduated with a PhD in history in 1953. McGovern, who later revived the Democratic party in South Dakota when he became a U.S. representative and a U.S. senator himself, received the Democratic nomination for president in 1972. Dr. Mac was delighted.

"I predict McGovern not only will win, it won't even be close," MacDougall said. "It's about time Northwestern had a crack at the White House. We've tried all those other punk schools, and they haven't done a bit of good."

The A Cappella Choir frequently performed at University events, bringing a sense of grandeur to any occasion. It gave recitals at Lutkin Hall, dedicated in 1941, a suitably stately place for the choir's timeless sound.

Running back Ed Tunnicliff '50 scores on the big play that gave the 'Cats a late fourth-quarter lead and a 20–14 win over California.

THE PURPLE ROSE BOWL

It wasn't that Northwestern was unfamiliar with gridiron glory. It had been helping national powerhouses like Notre Dame and Michigan achieve it for years. But the 1948 season was different. That year the Wildcats finally got their bid to the biggest football game in the nation at the time – the Rose Bowl.

When the Wildcats beat Illinois in the last game of the regular season, they clinched second place in the Big Nine. (Without the University of Chicago, which dropped football in 1939, and Michigan State, which was admitted in 1949, it was not then "Big Ten.") Since the conference champion normally went to the Rose Bowl but was not permitted to go two years in a row, repeat champs Michigan stayed home, and Northwestern got its first chance against the best of the Pacific Conference on New Year's Day 1949.

When the bid came, the campus was on cloud nine. A 24-hour celebration erupted, with undergrads prowling the streets and fraternity men serenading women in their dorms. President Snyder, always bookish and disciplined, also got a visit from happy songsters, who tacked a "no school" sign on his door. The Admiral even seemed to enjoy it.

On Monday a good-natured "strike" was called. Pledge classes were assigned to barricade the doors of classrooms, which was unnecessary, because no one went to class anyway. That night a Rose Bowl dance was followed with an announcement by Captain Alex "Sarkie" Sarkisian '49 that school was off the rest of the week.

Such a vacation from academic work seemed extreme to some, including students at the University of Chicago, who rushed out with a *Daily Northwestern* parody. The *Daily Country Club* had the headline "Onions!" mocking the *Daily's* "Roses!" And it purported to quote President Frank "Blissful" Snyder: "Other schools might suspend classes for a big thing like a bid to the Onion Bowl, but here at CCU [Country Club University], where we have no classes of importance anyway, we are not faced with this problem."

Hyde Park's jealousy aside, Coach Bob Voigts's tough Wildcat team was the real thing, led by Sarkisian at center and a front line that included tackle Steve Sawle '50, the following year's captain. Art Murakowski '51 and Frank Aschenbrenner '49 did most of the running chores. Everyone was ready on January 1, 1949, when the Purple team went up

against the Golden Bears of the University of California, headed by former Northwestern coach "Pappy" Waldorf. The game went down to the final minute, when
Northwestern's halfback Ed Tunnicliff '50 scored on a 45-yard end sweep. The 20–14
victory was sealed when Loran "Pee Wee" Day '50 intercepted a pass to stall Cal's
final drive.

It was a good thing for Evanston that the victory took place in Pasadena, or
Evanston might have collapsed under another celebration. Instead, Cheyenne,
Wyoming, bore the brunt of Northwestern's school spirit. That's where the "Wildcat
Special" Rose Bowl train was stranded for three days in a blinding Rocky Mountain
blizzard. The streets of Cheyenne were subjected to three days of spontaneous
Northwestern cheers before 275 students finally left town.

Tickets to the parade and the winning game.

The 1949 Rose Bowl Cup, the
most memorable trophy in the annals
of Northwestern sports.

As Wildcats (from left)
Frank Aschenbrenner, Ed
Tunnicliff, and Alex
Sarkisian boarded the
homebound train in
Pasadena, they were
slated for a southern route
back to Chicago. The band
and other fans took the
northern route and hit a
snowstorm that waylaid
them for three days in
Wyoming.

WESTERN UNION

After a few days in sunny southern California, the marching band
and other Northwestern fans were on their way home when their
train hit a blizzard in Cheyenne, Wyoming. While some lamented
not getting back to school, others whispered that three days in
Cheyenne with a trainload of Wildcat fans wasn't so bad.

CHICAGO DAILY
SUN TIMES
THE PICTURE NEWSPAPER

Wild day for Evanston
N.U. VS. CALI
IN ROSE BOW

Stories on page 3 and 74

ROSE BOWL FEVER HITS N.U. STUDENTS

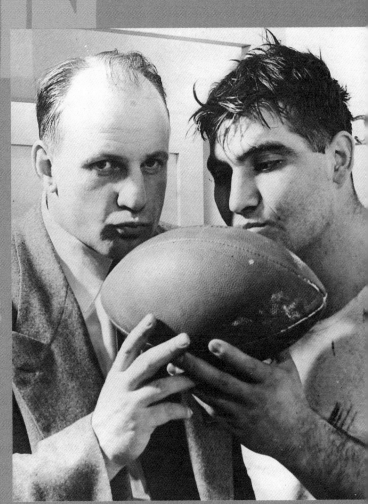

Coach Bob Voigts and Captain Alex "Sarky" Sarkisian buss the
game ball after the Rose Bowl win.

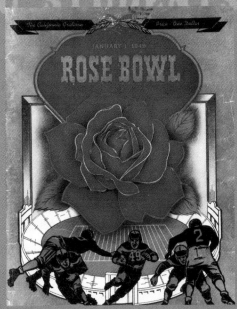

The official Rose Bowl program.

Getting to the Rose Bowl was a dream come true for Northwestern,
and all of Evanston was caught up in the excitement...whether it
liked it or not.

The *Sun-Times*, a
serious-minded tabloid
at the time, could not
contain its surprise and
delight at the news
from Evanston.

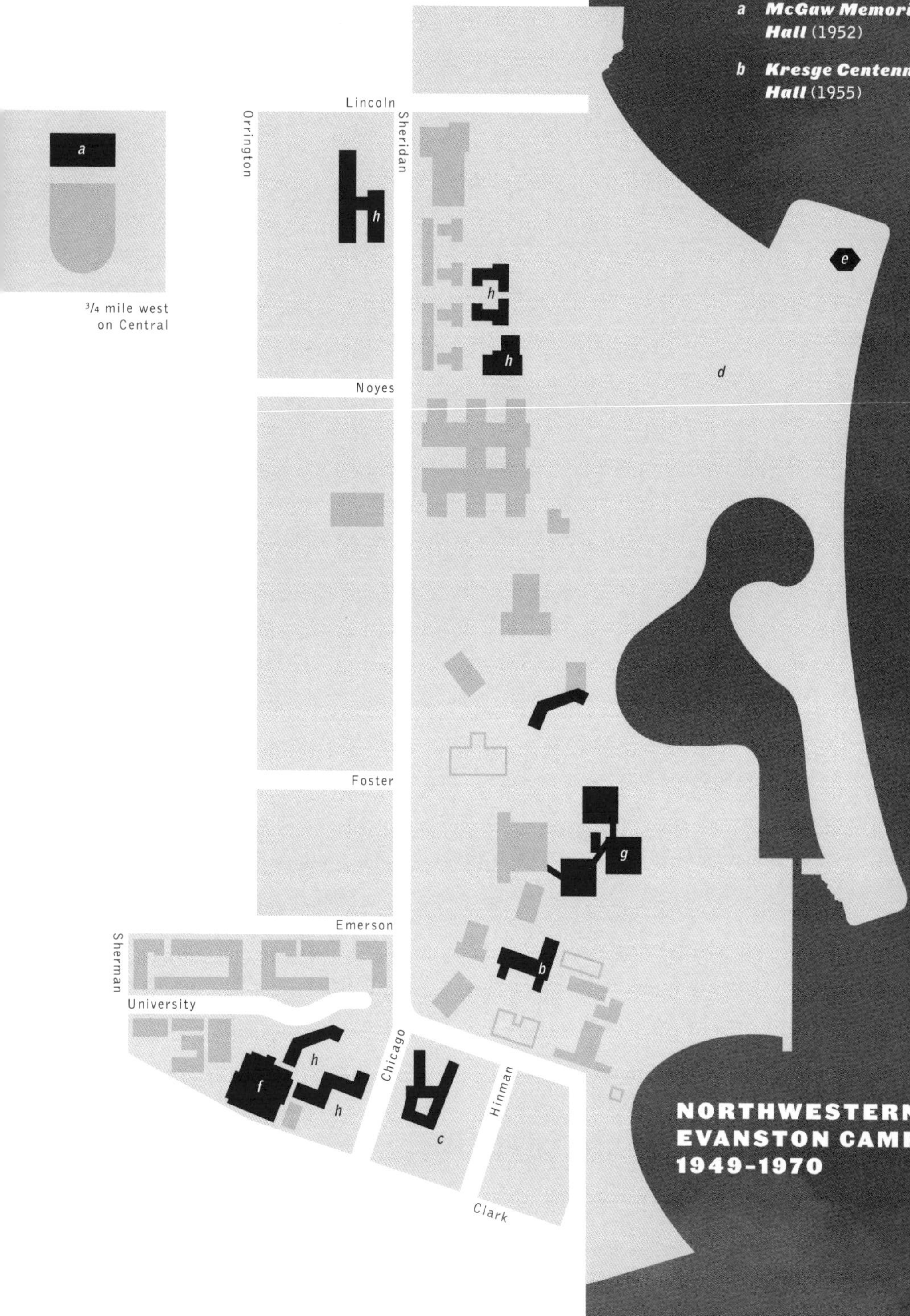

a
Lincoln
Orrington
Sheridan
h
h
h
h
3/4 mile west
on Central
e
d
Noyes
Foster
g
Emerson
Sherman
University
b
h
f
h
Chicago
c
Hinman
Clark

a ***McGaw Memorial Hall*** (1952)

b ***Kresge Centennial Hall*** (1955)

c ***Alice Millar Chapel*** (1963)

d ***J. Roscoe Miller Campus*** (lakefill, 1964)

e ***Lindheimer Astronomical Research Center*** (1966) Razed in 1995.

f ***Rebecca Crown Center*** (1968) Pictured.

g ***University Library*** (1970)

h ***Student Residences*** (1950–1970)

NORTHWESTERN'S EVANSTON CAMPUS 1949–1970

BUILT DURING THIS PERIOD

BUILT PREVIOUSLY

RAZED

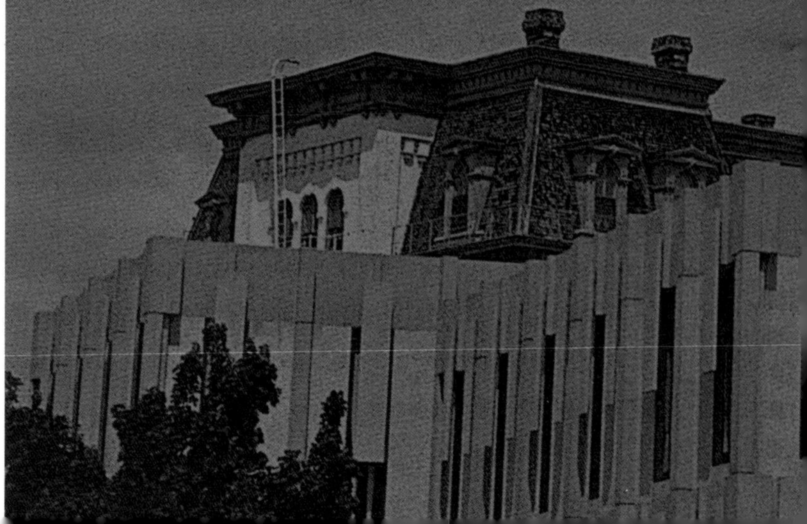

CHAPTER

i   ***Morton Medical Research Building***
    (1955)

j   ***McCormick Hall***
    (1962)

k   ***Searle Building***
    (1965)

NORTHWESTERN'S CHICAGO CAMPUS 1949–1970

Chicago

i   k   j

Superior

Huron

Fairbanks

McClurg

Lake Shore Drive

7

THE ROCKY MILLER ERA

J. Roscoe "Rocky" Miller was the right man for his time to preside over Northwestern, but he was not the obvious choice to succeed President Snyder. At least Miller didn't think so, as he related in the story of his selection. It began in 1948 when Snyder was preparing to retire and called Miller, then dean of the Medical School, to come to Evanston for a meeting. Meetings between the dean and the president were not uncommon, so Miller did not think twice about postponing it when he was unexpectedly called to Washington to meet with the office of the Surgeon General. Miller left word with Snyder's office that he would be back in a few days.

When Miller arrived in Washington, however, he learned that Snyder had been looking for him, and when the president got Miller on the phone, he told him that it wasn't a routine meeting at all. "Dammit, Rocky, the trustees want to meet with you so they can offer you the presidency of the University." They agreed to another meeting, and this time Miller kept the date. He was inaugurated as president in 1949.

Miller's legacy

The Miller years are remembered as an era of great change at the University, in the physical look of the campus and, more important, in its world view. When Miller became president, Northwestern was an institution slow to move and quick to muffle contrary views; even the old humor magazine, the *Purple Parrot*, was censored and finally discontinued in 1950. But a period of complacency was about to give way to a wave of entirely new issues – financial, academic, and increasingly political. While Rocky Miller instigated only a few of these changes, his leadership was also marked by great progress, due to his intuition and tolerance of outside pressures.

Miller's first deliberate move as president was to set the scene for a larger and more modern physical plant. He had unstinting pride in an institution with a fast-rising reputation, but as he walked the grounds of the Evanston campus, he noted with distress that the campus itself had been neglected. "Parts of it looked like a slum," he later said. "We were really run down." Miller's objective was to change this situation.

That would take fundraising, and Miller's first opportunity to promote the University to a broad audience came in 1951, when Northwestern turned 100 years old. Elaborate plans were made to celebrate the Northwestern Centennial, and tied to them was a well-publicized campaign to raise $8.5 million, primarily for capital improvements. Most people would remember the 1951 Centennial for a succession of scholarly conferences and learned visitors, but these were also conducted with a view toward reminding donors that Northwestern, despite its physical appearance, was a place of high academic standing. Contributions flowed in, and the campaign goal was exceeded.

The Centennial celebration

As an intellectual exercise, the Centennial provided a vivid snapshot of what leading academic minds were thinking at the time, and one thing on everyone's mind was the atom bomb. Among several major conferences that year, "Science, Technology, and the World's Resources" was opened by Gordon Dean, chair of the Atomic Energy Commission.

J. Roscoe Miller (1905–77) presided over the great postwar expansion of the University. Miller (left) is pictured with Robert H. Strotz (1922–94), who became president in 1970, sharing leadership of the University with Miller, who remained chancellor.

"We have a good idea where we are headed in atomic energy," Dean said in a panel discussion at the Technological Institute. **"But we don't have all the answers on what effects our achievement will have when we get there."**

In retrospect, the second part of Dean's statement was more true than the first, but Dean was challenged only mildly if at all.

The nuclear issue did not entirely escape debate. The *Reviewing Stand*, Northwestern's nationally syndicated radio program, took up the question in a show entitled "What Are the Social Responsibilities of Scientists?" One of the panelists, Dean Ovid Eshbach of the Technological Institute, opined that when you have nuclear energy, politics determine whether it is used for peaceful purposes or for war. "What I am saying is that the direct responsibility is political...the people are responsible."

While this sounded reasonable to some, it was completely unsatisfactory to another panelist, Purdue University physicist Karl Lark-Horovitz. "How can the people be responsible if they don't know what they are handling?" he snapped. "We have modern technology, very complicated and very sophisticated, superimposed on a rather primitive mind." This debate did not go much further, however, and it left the radio audience with the impression that the experts had everything well in hand.

The fraternity question

The 1950s were prosperous and complacent years both nationally and locally. Through most of this period Northwestern remained a staunchly conservative institution; even the student body appeared resistant to social change. Pundits from other colleges, notably the University of Chicago, nicknamed Northwestern "Country Club U" for its alleged emphasis on social life. And Northwestern's reputation for conservatism only hardened when in 1952 Northwestern's mock political convention organizers invited controversial Senator Joseph McCarthy to appear as the keynote speaker. A few students shouted insults at McCarthy during his speech, but the convention participants eventually endorsed his views, and several prominent faculty members later went on record applauding the senator's questionable anticommunist tactics.

Northwestern in the 1950s and early 1960s
was a staunch upholder of traditions.
Freshman beanies made their last appearance in this period, which was followed
by a wave of social change.

While fad-crazed students all over America were stuffing themselves into small cars, Northwestern students were sticking to the books. In 1959 these undergraduates crammed 1,155 textbooks into this Renault sedan – an apparent record that got their stunt in the newspapers.

Northwestern through the ages was the theme of most of the floats and decorations for the 1951 Homecoming parade. In this tableau, hemlines were shown to be gradually rising. What did not change over the years were Northwestern's football misfortunes, and the Homecoming game this year was no exception, with Wisconsin soundly trouncing the Wildcats.

Wooden nickels, which served as tickets to the Centennial Jubilee, a grand pageant that chronicled Evanston's and Northwestern's parallel histories, were sold door-to-door in Evanston. The popular show was the town's contribution to the University's Centennial and featured more than 1,000 people in a musical and dramatic spectacle at Dyche Stadium.

In the middle 1950s Alpha Epsilon Phi was one of the sororities to hold coed pajama parties.

Northwestern's Alpha Epsilon Phi chapter prided itself on its grade point average but still claimed that it was hard "squeezing the academic and social into a short nine weeks" each term.

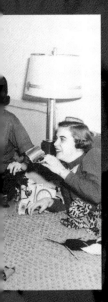

Gamma Phi Beta in the 1950s was not known for
violations of Evanston's dry laws but rather...
for its songbook. One of its published ditties went:

We're Gamma Phi Pirates,
We're gold diggers too.
We'll vamp the captain of the ship,
We'll vamp the mate, we'll vamp the crew...

GREEK LIFE IN YEARS OF CHANGE

Hardly ever did Northwestern's fraternities and sororities go about their business without being accused of a litany of misdemeanors. But they continued to flourish. As Greek
societies grew after World War II along with the University's fast-growing enrollment,
they were excoriated as never before for being discriminatory, anti-intellectual, and
sometimes even barbaric. But they still remained at the center of social life on campus
in this period and in the decades that followed.

Many factors favored the Greek lifestyle over that of "independents." One was the
shortage of campus housing that had plagued Northwestern for years; fraternities and
sororities solved that basic problem for their members. Another was that fraternities
and sometimes sororities threw the biggest and best parties – they had the money and
the organization to leave teetotaling Evanston and rent halls in the city for fancy-
dress affairs with appropriate beverages.

But they remained persistently under attack. Rush Week, which traditionally preceded
the fall term, was criticized "because it stresses the social side of the University before
the academic side even appears," wrote *Daily* editor (and later publisher of the *Chicago
Tribune*) Jack Fuller '68 in a series on fraternity life in 1966.

Reform was always difficult. Hell Week, a period of sometimes violent hazing for pledge-
class members, was outlawed in the 1950s by administration edict, but it reappeared
in some form almost every year. By 1963, all fraternities had removed or waived bylaws
of their national organizations that contained "bias clauses," or rules that narrowed
membership based on color or religion. Yet blackballing – exclusion by the vote of a single
member – effectively maintained homogeneity in many houses.

Fraternity and sorority membership began to shrink in the late 1960s, and by the end
of the decade only about 35 percent of the undergraduate student body were members.
Still, in a period when protest marches in Deering Meadow were more fashionable than
formals at the Edgewater Beach Hotel, Greeks survived and adapted to the times. In the
early 1970s Alpha Tau Omega had a coffeehouse with folk music in its basement. Acacia
sponsored a Christmas party for orphans. And, for the most part, fraternity paddles were
hung up on the wall and used only in secret if at all.

Chi Omega pledge class, 1949

Even though Greeks resisted the idea of stereotyping, they encouraged the fact that each house had an "image." By the early 1970s, Kappa Sigma was distinguished for its embrace of casual dress and relaxed customs.

Members of Delta Sigma Theta.

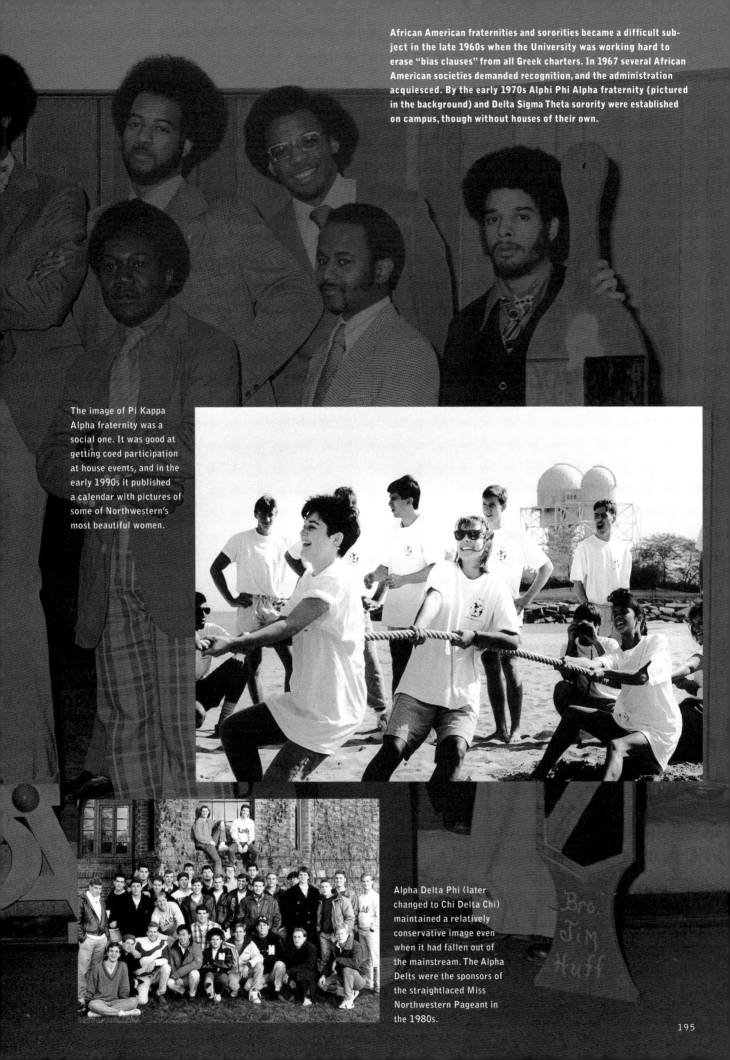

African American fraternities and sororities became a difficult subject in the late 1960s when the University was working hard to erase "bias clauses" from all Greek charters. In 1967 several African American societies demanded recognition, and the administration acquiesced. By the early 1970s Alphi Phi Alpha fraternity (pictured in the background) and Delta Sigma Theta sorority were established on campus, though without houses of their own.

The image of Pi Kappa Alpha fraternity was a social one. It was good at getting coed participation at house events, and in the early 1990s it published a calendar with pictures of some of Northwestern's most beautiful women.

Alpha Delta Phi (later changed to Chi Delta Chi) maintained a relatively conservative image even when it had fallen out of the mainstream. The Alpha Delts were the sponsors of the straightlaced Miss Northwestern Pageant in the 1980s.

Yet liberals on campus never fell entirely silent, especially on local issues. Civil rights in particular remained a topic of frequent discussion in *Daily* editorials — and the debate was effective enough to open University housing to black women in 1947 and black men in 1949. Yet progress was slow. If dormitories were nominally integrated, there were rarely more than 20 African American undergraduates at the University at the time, so integration made little impact. The admissions office, meanwhile, asserted that Northwestern was saddled by high admissions requirements — few qualified black or Jewish students applied, they insisted.

Such determined conservatism along with a measure of student apathy formed the backdrop for a group of liberal activist students who organized Constitutional Liberties Week in 1953, ostensibly to discuss the U.S. Constitution but also to initiate political action on campus. Among speakers invited for a series of programs was Walter White of the NAACP, who talked about the Civil Rights movement nationally and ended his remarks by listing five areas that needed work at Northwestern — admissions, housing, fraternities, part-time employment, and the Dental School (where a black veteran had recently been denied treatment at the clinic). White's list of transgressions seemed daunting.

Shortly after White's visit, members of a new student organization called the Human Relations Committee concluded that fraternities were one place where they could make inroads right away. The Greek system must have seemed like an easy target, as the houses were under fairly constant attack for sins ranging from anti-intellectualism to downright cruelty — Hell Week was a hard-to-abolish tradition of hazing freshman pledges before letting them join their secret societies.

Many fraternities also had bylaws barring blacks and Jews from membership. While these "bias clauses" were enforced by the national fraternities and sororities, the Human Relations Committee along with the editors of the *Daily Northwestern* believed they represented a good place for reform to start. So later in 1953, the group proposed a student referendum to abolish bias clauses in all Greek organizations and welcome students of all races and religions into membership.

As the referendum was debated, however, campus conservatism kicked in with unforeseen vigor. Many students, including fraternity members, campaigned against abolition of bias clauses and countered with a watered-down referendum of their own.

Thus, a strong statement against bias was defeated by the students, whereupon the powerful and conservative dean of students, James McLeod, declared that outlawing discrimination was not about to happen at Northwestern. "The process of education through individuals and groups will more readily achieve the desired goal than will any ultimatum," he said.

The referendum's defeat proved the power of the fraternities. This was not simply a matter of reactionary students barricading themselves against change. The amenities of fraternity life were considered good; many Greek houses had suites instead of the small rooms of most independent dorms. And they had support not only from fellow members but from conservative alums who helped with scholarships and jobs after graduation. Thus, fraternities were a force to be reckoned with, and only slight progress against discrimination was made in the next few years.

A turning point in fraternity politics came in 1956 with an event called the "Sherman Wu affair." It concerned a Chinese student, Wu '61, who was invited to pledge Psi Upsilon and was then blackballed when other freshmen threatened to back out because of his origin.

"Having an Oriental in the house," Psi U representatives admitted publicly, "would degrade them [the fraternity] in the eyes of other fraternities and make it more difficult to get dates from the sororities."

As the national press, which was generally antifraternity, picked up on the Sherman Wu affair, newspapers and magazines directed an unflattering spotlight on Northwestern. The long-term effect of the incident was the softening of discriminatory policies in many fraternities, though it was nearly a decade before racial and religious discrimination were entirely outlawed in Greek organizations at Northwestern.

Visions of growth

Fortunately for Roscoe Miller, the 1950s were mostly free from conflict; his major objective of capital improvement was moving along very nicely. With the success of the Centennial campaign, for example, the University met one of its most pressing needs – classroom space – by building Kresge Centennial Hall.

Jim Golliday '54 won the 1952 Big Ten 100-yard dash title with a time of 9.5 seconds. That year, quality and not quantity characterized the Wildcat track squad, which sent only four men to the conference championships but still took fourth place overall.

Football coach Ara Parseghian (left), is pictured with basketball coach Bill Rohr (center) and athletic director Stu Holcomb, circa 1959. Parseghian was named head football coach in 1956; he stayed until 1964 when he moved to rival Notre Dame where he coached two national championship teams.

Kresge Centennial Hall was the first major
building paid for by money raised during the
Centennial. Completed in 1955 and named
for the Kresge Foundation (which gave $500,000
of the building's $2.4 million cost), it provided
much needed classroom space.

As an auditorium and a fieldhouse, McGaw
Memorial Hall represented a major addition to
the Northwestern campus. The basketball team,
which had been playing most of its games at
Evanston High since 1940, finally had a proper
arena. It provided a venue for major convocations,
as McGaw Hall was the Chicago area's largest
auditorium north of the Loop. It also featured one
of the country's largest electronic organs, and
its lighting system, with 180 mercury vapor lights,
was said to approximate daylight.

Another major gift in this period – and one that foreshadowed many future gifts – came from Foster G. McGaw, founder of American Hospital Supply. McGaw had moved his company to Evanston some years before, and it grew phenomenally, due primarily to the expansion of hospital-based health care after World War II. Naturally enough, Miller developed a warm relationship with McGaw, who became a University trustee in 1950.

As Miller and McGaw socialized, often on the golf course, Miller produced his list of the University's many needs. Near the top was a gymnasium – the basketball team had been playing in rented quarters since 1940 when old Patten Gym was razed to make way for Tech. When McGaw admitted that athletics were not his burning passion, Miller added that Northwestern had recently agreed to host the quadrennial Assembly of the World Council of Churches in 1954 but lacked a proper auditorium for the purpose. That was certainly to McGaw's liking, and he quickly decided that his first major contribution to Northwestern would be McGaw Memorial Hall in honor of his father, the late Reverend Francis McGaw. It was a gymnasium but also the largest auditorium north of Chicago's Loop. McGaw Hall was dedicated in 1953, and the following year it served as venue for the church assembly. The ranking guest at those proceedings was President Dwight D. Eisenhower, who also received an honorary degree from Northwestern on the occasion.

The lakefill campus

Money and increasing prestige were not Northwestern's sole prerequisites for growth. In Evanston land itself was not only expensive, but also nobody wanted to disturb the tree-lined ambiance of the neighborhoods west of campus, which appeared to be the only direction for growth. Expansion anywhere in Evanston was touchy, moreover, because of the tax issue; Northwestern's property-tax exemption rankled townspeople regularly, as it did again in 1960 when the University purchased the Oak Crest Hotel on the edge of campus for graduate student housing, thus removing it from Evanston's tax rolls.

These difficulties led the University to propose an audacious plan to accommodate future growth.

In October 1960 business manager William Kerr announced that the University's biggest building boom ever would take place on land that did not yet exist, east of campus, on more than 70 acres reclaimed from Lake Michigan.

Kerr explained that the "lakefill," as it was called, would extend out 1,200 feet from the existing shoreline, to the point where the depth of the lake dropped off considerably. The project would require extensive engineering and several years to complete, but the advantage was a cost savings – it would cost $113,000 an acre to reclaim land from the lake compared to $300,000 an acre to buy it from Evanston property owners. This plan would also leave the town's tax base untouched.

THE POLITICS OF THE LAKEFILL

In a sign of political goodwill – recognition of Northwestern's staunch efforts during World War II – the University's proposal for the new lakefill campus sailed over every political obstacle it encountered. The Evanston City Council approved the plan in one meeting. Members voiced concern for the city's newly renovated Clark Street Beach, though that issue was overshadowed by a more serious worry: Evanstonians were frantic that the state might extend Chicago's Lake Shore Drive as far north as Wilmette. The lakefill, they hoped, would help prevent a new highway on the suburb's pleasant shoreline.

There were some dissenters to the lakefill plan, but not many. "One encroachment on the lake area can easily be used as justification for others," wrote Northwestern alumnus and Evanston resident W. J. Bruns '26. He added that the University's rationale that reclaimed land was cheaper than existing property "does not justify the taking of public assets by unilateral private action...." Bruns added that the lakefill would place many Evanston homes considerably farther from the shore than they were at present. "Should the University seek to compensate for such loss of property values, it is quite likely that the cost of a lakefill campus addition would exceed that of acquiring adjacent property on an equitable basis," he said. But Burns's argument got nowhere.

Good feelings between Northwestern and state government were categorical; in Springfield, both houses of the legislature approved the sale of 152 acres of Lake Michigan for $100 per acre without a single dissenting vote. University business manager William Kerr had spent considerable time in Springfield lobbying for the measure, and with Governor Otto Kerner and Speaker of the House William Redmond, both graduates of the law school in 1934, Northwestern had powerful friends in the state capital.

On the federal side, any alteration of waterways required the approval of the U.S. Army Corps of Engineers, which quickly issued a permit with a report that the lakefill was "sufficiently removed from established lake shipping routes...." A single unpleasant glitch came up, however, just as the $5.2 million project was to begin. Because sand for the lakefill was to come from the dredging of a controversial harbor in the Indiana Dunes, Senator Paul Douglas of Illinois, an ardent conservationist, accused the University of being complicit in an act of environmental vandalism.

Before long, Douglas's protest was overcome; Indiana got its harbor, and Northwestern got the fill. But in retrospect, the controversy foreshadowed what was obvious later – that the growing environmental movement would make any further lakefill projects politically difficult if not impossible.

The idea to build a lakefill campus began in the late 1900s, and it was revived again in the 1930s. But it wasn't until the 1960s that the University created 74 acres of usable land previously under water.

The engineering to build the lakefill was not complicated, but it was labor intensive. A seawall around the perimeter was reinforced with layers of gravel and limestone boulders, and the interior was filled with sand barged in from a dredging project near Michigan City, Indiana.

There was little dissent when it came to getting Evanston's approval for the lakefill. Most citizens of Evanston liked the idea because it meant that Northwestern's growth would not impinge on the city's tax base.

ANSTON, ILLINOIS, March 15, 1962 - Ev. Red.   15 Cents a Copy

Council Expected to Approve
N.U.'s Lake Project Monday

Plans Call for Smaller Lagoon;
Work Slated to Begin This Spring

Formal approval of the Northwestern lakefront expansion program to be started this spring is expected to be granted Monday night by the Evanston city council.

The council this week heard a summary of final construction details from two Northwestern representatives, J. C. Sanderson, Jr., director of plant properties, and Alban Weber, university counsel.

The council last year gave preliminary approval to the proposed project with the understanding that the university return with detailed plans for final approval before the construction work starts.

Weather a Factor

Mr. Sanderson said the construction will start as soon as weather permits.

He said the land-fill project will begin at the south end of the Evanston campus lakefront and continue northward.

Final plans for the 1,200 x 1,500-foot piece of land call for a smaller lagoon area. The area was reduced to 12 acres from 16 in order to improve circulation of water, Mr. Sanderson said.

The north and south sea walls will consist of steel piling and the east wall will be of rocks. The interior land part will be a base of sand to be barged in from the southernmost part of the lake.

8 Inches of Topsoil

The area will be covered by 8 inches of topsoil, Mr. Sanderson said.

Both Mr. Sanderson and William S. Kerr, vice president and business manager of Northwestern, gave the city assurance that engineering problems and any damage to city property will be open for negotiation.

Mr. Kerr, in a letter to City Manager Bert W. Johnson, said, "With regard to the two specific problems which you have raised—the possible pollution of the Clark street beach by any outflow from the lagoon area and the possible silting up of the waterworks intake located north of the north grant line—I wish to emphasize that our various engineering consultants have assured us that neither of these contingencies is likely to occur.

Give Guarantee

"However, we hereby give the City of Evanston our fullest assurance that if either of these two contingencies occur and they directly result from and are attributable to the lakefront expansion, the university guarantees to take steps by mutual agreement with the city which will cure the problem, and we will completely defray the expense of such steps."

When asked why the university is planning a lagoon in the middle of the reclaimed land, Mr. Sander-
(Continued on page 94)

This is architect's concept of the outline of the Northwestern lakefront expansion. Main change since plan was announced in 1960 is reduction in the size of the lagoon.

(Continued from page 5)
son said it is mainly for esthetic values.

Mr. Weber said that there was no question but what the university will request the land be annexed to the City of Evanston.

He said 1,000-car parking plazas are planned for the landfill area east of Deering Library and near the technological institute.

Ald. Quaife M. Ward (2nd) asked if the university would permit perch fishermen to fish from the landfill. Mr. Weber said the university will not permit this. "It represents a public access with a lot of problems," he said.

Northwestern announced its plans for the $6,500,000 lakefront expansion in October, 1960, and won approval of the Illinois General Assembly when the legislators passed a bill to sell underwater land to the university last year.

Last week the university awarded a contract for the extension to the Missouri Valley Dredging Company, Omaha, and Mary Construction Company of Cape Girardeau, Mo. Completion is scheduled Jan. 1, 1964.

The lakefill proposal received broad support from the politicians empowered to approve it and from the engineers who would have to design it. Most of all, it received enthusiastic reviews where they were certainly needed – from donors. First to step up to the plate was John G. Searle, president of the pharmaceutical manufacturer G. D. Searle & Company. On Christmas Eve 1961 President Miller received a call from Searle, who asked that what he was about to say remain confidential: his Christmas present to Northwestern was a $2.5 million gift, the amount needed for Miller to get started on the lakefill.

The lakefill project took two and a half years to complete. Construction began with a limestone dike – or retaining wall – around the perimeter of the 74-acre lakefill area (another 10 acres were added to the south end in 1968), after which the sandy fill came in on barges from Indiana. By early 1964 enough solid land existed for a first modest building on the new campus: Vogelback Computing Center, named for Chicago industrial engineer William E. Vogelback. This modern concrete building, sited beneath what was a low bluff overlooking Lake Michigan, would open in February 1965 (it was demolished in 2000). But before the opening, Vogelback's flat roof served as the speaker's platform for ceremonies to dedicate the newly reclaimed land, named the J. Roscoe Miller Campus.

The ceremony was well attended; 4,000 sat facing the dais.

Former Illinois Governor Adlai E. Stevenson, a 1926 graduate of the School of Law, was the principal speaker, and his remarks were memorable mostly because they were abbreviated – a gust of wind off the lake had blown several pages of his prepared speech out of his hands a moment after he started. "That's a break for you," he told his audience.

Stevenson congratulated the burgeoning University for what it had accomplished in recent years, and he encouraged Northwestern to get on with what was next: a building phase tagged at $70 million.

The new library

The faculty regarded the lakefill campus as a positive development, but many professors also expressed concern that the land and even new buildings were only a start. New facilities were certainly needed, yet there was little idea, or at least

Pageboys, bobby socks, and bold-patterned fabrics were still the style among Northwestern women in the early 1960s, pictured here in the commons room of Allison Hall.

When the new University Library was opened in 1970, it reflected an innovative approach to library layout. Each of three "research towers" were designed to have collections arranged to encourage multidisciplinary exploration. Near the books are seminar rooms, carrels, and reading areas suitable for concentrated study and interaction between students and faculty.

consensus, of how they would improve education at Northwestern. This may have been because of Miller's style — he was good at making plans and financing them, but he was not good at outlining his vision in front of groups. While the president may have had academic priorities in mind, he was not sharing them with the Northwestern community at large.

Among those who recognized the new campus as an opportunity was Clarence Ver Steeg, a professor of history with a specialty in colonial America. Arriving at Northwestern in 1950, Ver Steeg had distinguished himself with a number of publications early in his career and for several years had entertained offers from institutions on the East Coast. But he stayed at Northwestern, he said, because he saw a bright future and the possibility that he could have a personal impact on it.

In 1961 Ver Steeg wrote Provost Payson Wild a frank letter. He said that Northwestern's building plans were encouraging, but the University was falling behind academically in some areas. In fact, Ver Steeg and many of his colleagues in the College of Arts and Sciences saw one overriding symptom of Northwestern's troubles. "The main problem was the library," said Ver Steeg. "It was a cork in the bottle." Deering Library at this time was overcrowded and ill-suited to advanced scholarship. For Northwestern to flourish, Ver Steeg said, a new library was needed.

Ver Steeg's appeal resulted in the creation of a new library planning committee, headed by him and including economist Robert Strotz, English professor Richard Ellmann, and dean Moody Prior '23 of the Graduate School. The committee began by asking what a new library should accomplish.

"The physical plant should reflect the intellectual relationships," said Ver Steeg in the *Daily*. "Intellectual relationships are the underlying cohesive force of the University."

Among many other things, the committee imagined a new library as a force to unify seven often-disconnected schools and colleges on the Evanston campus.

To blend this objective with a major new building, the University engaged Walter Netsch of the architectural firm Skidmore, Owings and Merrill. After several proposals, the committee settled on a design of three interconnected "towers," and an interior plan that would feature open stacks arranged radially from the center. This scheme, said Netsch, would facilitate research, permitting "the search from a single point of 125,000 volumes" on those floors allocated to book storage.

Professor Clarence L. Ver Steeg came to North-western in 1950 and distinguished himself as a scholar of American history. In the 1960s he assumed roles on faculty committees that made him one of the intellectual leaders of the University.

Each research tower – dedicated to history, humanities, and social sciences – would include faculty studies, seminar rooms, and other areas where professors, graduate students, and undergraduates could interact.

When plans for the new library were published, the committee girded itself for resistance, which came initially in a barrage from campus librarians, who preferred a classical and rectilinear approach. But as the money quickly came in for the project – including $2.5 million from Grover Hermann of the Martin-Marietta Corporation – criticism was muted.

When the library opened in 1970, there was some trepidation. "Most librarians are not going to like Northwestern University's new $12 million library that sits on stilts on a thrust of landfill edging Lake Michigan," wrote *American Libraries* magazine. But the new library achieved its goals. In 1971, the *Daily* wrote that one lounge "was filled with bodies sprawled about every available chair, corner, and piece of floor. Barefoot or shoeless students talked about Soviet history or socialization, or more often just rapped about any topic at hand."

"First Plan for the Seventies"

As the committee planned the new library to house "a community of scholars," it became clear to a large part of the faculty that Northwestern needed more than a new building to reach its goals; it needed an increased level of intellectual inquiry.

"There was a fundamental change in the way American universities functioned in this time," said Jeremy Wilson '55, the University's director of planning through this period. "More than ever they were being defined as places for research."

Led by Coach Parseghian, the 1962 Wildcats were a national power and were ranked first in the nation at midseason. Alums were making plans for Pasadena that fall until the 'Cats were declawed by the Wisconsin Badgers.

Marty Riessen '64, Big Ten singles tennis champ from 1962 to 1964 was one of a long line of Northwestern athletes who excelled in individual sports. Riessen later made a name for himself on the U.S. Davis Cup team in the era of Chuck McKinley and Arthur Ashe.

While its native soil
was rarely the focus or
preoccupation of
TriQuarterly – some of
its greatest literary
coups have come from
abroad – the spring
1984 issue was a liter-
ary examination of
Chicago. It began with
an interview of Nobel
laureate Saul Bellow '37.

The fall 1966 issue of
TriQuarterly dealt with
the work of poet Sylvia
Plath. Much of it was an
excerpt from a book by
the magazine's editor at
that time, Charles Newman.

TRIQUARTERLY MAGAZINE

TriQuarterly magazine is like other journals whose purpose is literary experimentation.
But *TriQuarterly* is unique in that it has not only flourished, but it has survived for more
than 40 years. This is a credit to the University that supports it, a succession of editors
who uphold it, and readers and critics such as a writer in the *New York Times* who have
called it "perhaps the pre-eminent journal of literary fiction."

TriQuarterly was founded in 1958. Since then it has been responsible for giving early
exposure to writers who went on to win the National Book Award and the Pulitzer and
Nobel Prizes.

Like all "little magazines," as they're called, *TriQuarterly* attempts to push the boundaries
of literary art both with big names and with writers who are otherwise little known. It
is published three times annually (there are occasional "supplements"), and sometimes as
thematic issues – the "Womanly" issue, for example, or the "Zen" issue – which emerge
from the cream of over 10,000 submissions that come in each year.

The publication has overcome a variety of obstacles, such as offending an important
Northwestern trustee with frontal nudity on the cover of one issue. It also survived a
fascination with postmodern fiction in the 1960s and 1970s when novelists like Robert
Coover and John Hawkes filled its pages with nonplot, noncharacter-development, highly
intellectualized fiction. And it breezed past a challenge in the 1980s by a former editor
who attempted to start a rival publication.

Finally, *TriQuarterly* has overcome the extreme difficulty of a magazine like this to
remain solvent. Lately, that's due largely to Reginald Gibbons of the English department,
editor from 1981 to 1999, and current editor Susan Hahn '63, a highly regarded poet.

This meant that graduate programs were at the core of leading academic institutions, and there was broad concern among faculty members that in too many areas Northwestern was not among these leading universities.

While this issue went beyond the scope of the library committee, provost Payson Wild believed that its work contained the seeds of a broad-based academic plan. So, in 1962 Wild asked Ver Steeg to expand the work that his committee was already doing. This resulted in the Faculty Planning Committee, a much larger body that began the most extensive process of academic planning ever undertaken at Northwestern. The committee began by interviewing members of every academic department. Members then talked to people at peer universities. Ultimately they judged Northwestern against the standard in each field, and they made frank appraisals — which departments were on track to succeed and which were not. "We were determined to change the University from being a regional institution to one of national and international distinction," Ver Steeg said.

Naturally enough, they ruffled feathers. "No university in this day and age can achieve distinction without being distinguished in the basic sciences and engineering," stated the committee's 1964 interim report. And while Northwestern had an extensive engineering curriculum, the report suggested a sea change was needed in the basic sciences. Chemistry, biology, and physics were too long the neglected stepsisters of technology.

In the social sciences, the committee's report recommended the expansion of research centers for "advanced training and dissertation research of graduate students.... These functions of course are already being carried on under traditional departmental organizations, but the research center can facilitate bringing together people of related interests into joint or related research activities and can provide a programmatic basis for the raising and distribution of outside research and instructional funds."

For some people, the work of Ver Steeg's committee was past due. But for others, it was meddlesome in the extreme. Particularly vocal was James McBurney, longtime dean of the School of Speech — he objected to the committee's proposal

The Koster Site, center of the Northwestern archaeological field school, has been called the "capital of the archaeological universe." In Kampsville, Illinois, near the confluence of the Illinois and Mississippi Rivers, the site was discovered by Northwestern anthropologist Stuart Struever when he passed the Koster family farm in 1958 and noticed a local amateur digging for artifacts. Since then Struever and the anthropology department have directed the work of thousands of undergraduate, graduate, and continuing education students on a site where 14 successive Native American communities date back some 12,000 years.

to separate the communication disorders department from theater facilities in its scheme to divide the campus into zones corresponding to science, social science, and the arts. "What do you think you know about this," McBurney snarled at a meeting. There were other discouraging responses as well, but the administration supported the committee, which went on to produce the "First Plan for the Seventies," an academic road map for the future.

Science for the future

Planning committees were not the only people gazing into the future. Among others with their eyes on change were faculty members in the sciences, especially in the chemistry department, which for years had resisted the current trend in the discipline to subdivide itself into specialties — organic chemistry, inorganic chemistry, physical chemistry, and others.

While the old guard in chemistry still believed that the unified approach to the discipline was the best way to turn out well-rounded PhDs, a growing number of biochemists felt differently. Creating an entirely new department would be no easy matter, but a first move in this direction came in the mid-1960s, when the eminent biochemist David Shemin was brought to Northwestern. The hope was that Shemin would broaden the department's horizons, and in large measure he succeeded, helping colleagues gain increased exposure for their research and new sources of funding.

In 1955 when the Morton Medical Research Building (in front) was dedicated, the Northwestern University Medical School had been expanding its research functions. Laboratories and offices were used by the departments of pathology, radiology, urology, psychiatry, and others. The facilities accommodated larger numbers of faculty members conducting research on a full- or part-time basis.

As a result, Northwestern biochemists made considerable progress in the late 1960s, primarily in research on protein structure and cell activity, which underlay many of the medical advances of the decades that followed. Several of these scholars were elected to the National Academy of Sciences on the recommendation of Shemin, who was already a member. Then in 1970 the new O. T. Hogan Biological Sciences Building was opened on the lakefill campus, and the biochemists took up residence there as part of a program in molecular biology and biochemistry.

"We saw where the future was," said Laszlo Lorand, one of the biochemists involved in the transition. Others saw it, too, and in 1974 the Department of Biochemistry and Molecular Biology was established as a new, separate department at the University. This move recognized the growing importance of cellular and DNA research in addressing common ailments such as cancer, cardiovascular disease, and diabetes. The new department advanced the cause of research; it also enabled freshmen and sophomores to take courses in biochemistry, which had not been permitted to that point.

Transition at the Medical School

On the Chicago campus, the medical complex that Miller and Snyder envisioned in the 1940s took shape with new hospitals – the Rehabilitation Institute and the Veterans Administration Hospital, both opened in 1954. These and other hospitals on Northwestern's Chicago campus were linked under the new McGaw Medical Center of Northwestern University in 1966. This development was prompted in part by a U.S. Department of Health, Education, and Welfare study on a new concern in health care – the cost-effectiveness of hospitals. Northwestern was not the single focus of this study, but members of the advisory committee had particular influence locally, as it was chaired by the dean of the Northwestern School of Business, John A. Barr.

As the medical center evolved, its benefits were not just economic; it developed enhanced capabilities in medical specialties and research as well. Wesley Memorial Hospital developed an adult cardiac unit in this period. Passavant Memorial Hospital established itself as a leader in dialysis treatment, which was relatively new at the time. The affiliated nursing schools at Wesley and Passavant were also more rigorous than ever, with students taking Northwestern courses in microbiology, pharmacology, psychology, and a number of other life sciences.

Not forgotten amid all the other activity was the Medical School's primary mission of training practicing physicians. Prominent in every medical student's education, for example, was work in the Chicago Maternity Center. For decades the center had operated from an old brick and stone clinic on Maxwell Street, a picturesque if forlorn building later used as the police station in television's *Hill Street Blues*. This clinic did yeoman's work in prenatal care – rare in poor communities – performing hundreds of home deliveries all over Chicago. A two-week stint at the center was still required of all Medical School seniors at this time, and for many it was one of the eye-opening experiences of their education. Most students at the time were middle-class males who had never seen tough neighborhoods, and service at the center often meant ungodly hours performing as many as ten deliveries a day.

It taught at least one medical student "that I didn't want to go into obstetrics," but it motivated others to go into public medicine, a field in which many Northwestern graduates distinguished themselves.

The Chicago Maternity Center left another legacy in these years when some mothers, too overwrought by birth to name their children, left that duty to the students responsible for filling out birth certificates. In doing so, a few students remembered their imperious and intimidating professor of surgery back at Passavant. Thus in Chicago there was born a cohort of male babies named Loyal, in honor of famous neurosurgeon (and stepfather of future First Lady Nancy Reagan) Dr. Loyal Davis (MD '18).

Alvina Krause and her stars

Among the strongest departments at Northwestern at the time was theater, and among its godmothers was Alvina Krause '28, one of the legendary acting teachers for more than a generation of American performers. At least three of Krause's students won Academy Awards – including Charlton Heston '45, Patricia Neal '47, and Jennifer Jones '40. That distinction was only the most obvious sign of her skill as a director and acting coach.

Krause was not involved in acting for the glitter and celebrity. Born in New Lisbon, Wisconsin, she enrolled at Northwestern's School of Oratory in 1914 and taught high school after graduation. She returned to Northwestern for a bachelor's degree, then took a position at Hamline University in St. Paul, Minnesota. The drama department at Hamline was in decline, but Krause whipped it into shape and brought a one-act play to a theater competition at Northwestern and won. Dean Ralph Dennis could not help but notice her talent and in 1930 hired her as an instructor in voice and interpretation.

Few educators had such an impact on the acting profession as Alvina Krause. As an acting teacher at Northwestern, she had a way of eliciting both emotion and discipline from students, who became stars of the stage and screen.

Krause was soon directing productions at the University Theatre. Her first play, *Anna Christie*, earned praise in the *Daily* for its emotion and "sincere effect." And for decades she coaxed good actors into great performances, according to Bill Kuehl '52, who remembered her "help" while getting ready to go on stage in the title role of *Uncle Vanya*.

Krause approached him backstage, and Kuehl expected a word of encouragement. Instead she slapped him in the face as hard as she could. Kuehl was shocked, and his face was stinging, but almost instantly he knew what Alvina Krause was doing. The blow "made me hurt and confused and unhappy, so that I would take those feelings with me on stage" and use them as Uncle Vanya, he said.

Less in need of an emotional jump start was Paula Ragusa '59, later screen actress Paula Prentiss, who came to Northwestern with abundant talent but, some said, little discipline. Krause could provide this and more, as she did for Ragusa one summer at the Eagles Mere Playhouse in Pennsylvania, a summer theater directed by Krause and featuring mostly Northwestern student actors. Ragusa, playing Queen Margaret in *Richard III*, was throwing curses at the court in dress rehearsal when Krause yelled, "Make them stronger, Paula; make them real." Perhaps frustrated at herself, Ragusa's response was to snap. She pulled half her dress off and snarled, "If you think you can do it better, you wear the dress."

Krause stayed calm. "*Now* say the Queen's curses," she said, which Ragusa did, and the scene was transformed. Also on stage at the time was another future film actor, Tony Roberts '61, who had the next line. "My hair doth stand on end to hear her curse," Roberts said with added resonance that was not lost when the play opened to a live audience.

Famed English scholars

As many academic departments in the University were improving, a model for excellence was in English, where the work of several individuals brought considerable prestige to Northwestern. First among them was Richard Ellmann, who arrived in 1951 and became the nation's, if not the world's, leading literary biographer. Ellmann's first important book was on William Butler Yeats, published in 1948,

Richard Ellmann's reputation as one of Northwestern's most eminent scholars was secured with the publication of his award-winning *James Joyce*. He went on to write the definitive literary biography of Oscar Wilde.

which not only made his early reputation but also led the professor to his great masterwork, *James Joyce*.

Ellmann's interest in Joyce was triggered when he found an unpublished essay by Yeats about the poet's attempt to move toward a more vigorous and earthy style. In doing so, Yeats was introduced to Joyce, already known for his realistic prose about life in the streets and pubs of Dublin. In the account of their meeting, Joyce said to Yeats, "I am 20. How old are you?" Yeats said he was in his late 30s. "I thought as much," Joyce said. "I have met you too late. You are too old."

This kind of literary dissection became Ellmann's stock in trade, especially in the Joyce biography, which won the National Book Award in 1960 and was called "the greatest literary biography of the century" by novelist Anthony Burgess.

The book consumed Ellmann for seven years as he traveled to Ireland, Great Britain, and the European continent in search of living witnesses to Joyce's life. Ellmann's sympathetic ear and utter lack of pretense earned him the respect of those he interviewed, though one of Joyce's sisters rebuffed him. "I know we are an extraordinary family, and I wish to God we weren't," she told Ellmann.

Ellmann did find and make friends with Joyce's brother Stanislaus, younger by three years than the novelist. Stan had provided a lifeline for James when the novelist left Ireland and moved to Trieste in 1904. Stan wrote elaborate letters to James about goings-on in and around Dublin. Many of these events were used in James's later stories, and through this correspondence Ellmann discerned a pattern throughout the novelist's career. "James's gift was for transforming material, not originating it," Ellmann wrote, "and Stanislaus was the first of a series of people on whom he leaned for ideas."

Another road to fame was taken by English professor Bergen Evans, hired in the 1930s and renowned for his "Introduction to Literature," one of the most popular lecture courses of the era. Teaching it for years in the Tech auditorium, Evans held hundreds of students rapt while describing the Bible, for example, as "the greatest single book I know of... also the most stolen book." Whereupon Evans noted that most booksellers put their Bibles in the back of their stores so religious shoplifters would have a harder time of it.

The skills that made Evans shine in the lecture hall also made him a natural for television. He was first tapped by the new medium in 1949 as permanent panelist on a talk show called *Majority Rules*. He had been recommended for it, Evans insisted, by the office of University of Chicago President Robert Maynard Hutchins after Evans had written an article in *The Atlantic* that insulted Hutchins in print.

In any event, Evans definitely took to television. In 1951, he created and hosted a nationally broadcast quiz show called *Down You Go*, featuring a panel of minor celebrities in semiformal attire. As panelists guessed letters making up a well-known phrase, Evans provided witty clues. In his high-pitched, half-English accent, Evans might say, "A lying position in which one is prone to tell the truth." The correct phrase was "On the psychiatrist's couch."

Evans's career was punctuated by an array of books. *The Natural History of Nonsense* was published in 1946 about myths and superstitions (among which

English professor Bergen Evans was easily Northwestern's most famous personality in the 1950's. His "Introduction to Literature" one of the University's most popular courses. He adapted his lecture style to the small screen and hosted a popular early game show called *Down You Go*.

religion was included). *A Dictionary of Contemporary American Usage*, a compendium of slang, was coauthored with his sister Cornelia Evans in 1957. "At Northwestern University," they said, "a *Mickey Mouse* was a notoriously easy course, a *four-wheel friend* was one devoted to your car, a *clootch* a girl and a *brain* a serious-minded and possibly intelligent student."

Whatever envy his popularity incited among colleagues, Evans received overwhelming support on campus when faced with one of the toughest situations of his career — charges that he was a conspirator in the quiz-show scandals of 1959.

Evans was then the writer of questions for the *$64,000 Question*, a program exposed as faked by disgruntled contestants. As the U.S. Congress raised the scandal to operatic proportions, Illinois Congressman Peter F. Mack tried to make political hay locally by calling for Evans's resignation from Northwestern.

He got nowhere, as President Miller stated that he believed Evans was innocent of any wrongdoing. Students in Evans's popular literature course went one better — they hung Rep. Mack in effigy on the stage of the Tech auditorium.

Change in admissions

While leading scholars in many fields were making Northwestern a more worldly place, progress in the arena of civil rights remained slow until a series of events that occurred in the 1963–64 school year. In October 1963 liberal students of the Human Relations Committee embarked, along with editors of the *Daily Northwestern,* on an investigation of the Undergraduate Admission Office, which had been headed for years by William Reilly. Reilly had denied repeatedly that quotas for African American and Jewish students had ever existed, but the accusations were definitely more highly charged this time. Many faculty members were pushing for a more heterogeneous student body, and the *Daily* was more aggressive than ever. The issue came to a head the following February when Reilly lost his patience at a meeting with student leaders on the subject. The next day he blew up again at a *Daily* reporter who questioned him, and he even threatened to have the student's scholarship revoked.

When Robert R. McCormick Hall was completed in 1960, the law school gained additional classrooms and doubled the size of the law library. Of the $1.8 million cost of the building, $400,000 came from the McCormick Charitable Trust, created by the late owner of the *Chicago Tribune,* Colonel Robert R. McCormick, a member of the law school Class of 1906. Pictured at the cornerstone ceremony are, left to right: Dean John Ritchie III, Mayor Richard J. Daley, U.S. Supreme Court Justice John Harlan, President J. Roscoe Miller, Governor William Stratton, charitable trust chairman Stewart Owen, law alumni president Harold Smith, and board chairman Kenneth Burgess.

Reilly's behavior was fully reported, and he ended up making a public apology. But, more important, the silence that had always shrouded University admissions policies was cracking. Soon after this incident, a former admissions office clerical worker admitted that she had been instructed to code all applications by race and religion, marking those of Jews and African Americans in red. While the administration did not act immediately on this story, Reilly was soon moved to a less sensitive post.

To succeed Reilly, the position of director of admissions was filled in 1966 by Roland J. Hinz, who was later made vice president for student affairs, and then in 1967 by William Ihlanfeldt, who moved up from director of financial aid. Together, Hinz and Ihlanfeldt ushered in a period of great demographic change at Northwestern. In the fall of 1966, for example, an inner-city recruiting effort aided by additional money for scholarships, more than doubled African American undergraduate enrollment with 52 black students in the freshman class. Another turning point came in 1968 with a sweeping expansion of financial aid to undergraduates, which was regarded as a way to broaden the pool of potential applicants to Northwestern, thus increasing the quality of the student body.

The financial-aid proposal would cost well over $2 million a year from the beginning, but the administration and the faculty, particularly deans such as Robert Strotz of the College of Arts and Sciences, saw more scholarship money as a clear path to greater academic stature. By the fall of 1968, therefore, undergraduates on financial aid increased to 30 percent from 14 percent the previous year and rose to 50 percent by the early 1970's. "Feedback from the faculty was that the quality of the student body changed dramatically," said Ihlanfeldt. While the Vietnam era also triggered a new seriousness on campus, many believed the aggressive recruiting of smart middle-class and ethnic minority students led to a campus environment that was more intellectually inclined than ever before.

Dawn Clark Netsch at the School of Law

In another arena, progress came slowly but less rancorously. The Northwestern University School of Law was relatively insulated from campus activism and had never been a hotbed of politics of any kind. While Dean Leon Green had written articles in support of FDR's effort years earlier to pack the U.S. Supreme Court, the tradition at Northwestern was conservative and workmanlike. Green was succeeded by Harold Havighurst, whose major contribution to the profession was his book on contracts. Havighurst was succeeded in 1957 by John Ritchie III, whose métier was estates.

The law school remained, moreover, a bastion of white males. But Dawn Clark Netsch, a graduate of the College of Liberal Arts in 1948 and of the School of Law in 1952, became the first woman on the faculty in 1965, despite the relative lack of pressure to open the faculty to minorities and women. While Netsch was by her own admission a liberal activist in her youth, she was hired primarily for

When the Lindheimer Astronomical Research Laboratory was completed in 1966 it housed a pair of telescopes, automatic star-tracking equipment, and remote video monitors. In the years that followed advanced telescope technology made Lindheimer obsolete. In 1995 the telescopes were moved to Arizona, where the atmosphere is clearer. Lindheimer was razed later that year, though its demolition was a difficult chore; a single charge of dynamite barely moved the rock-solid structure.

Styles were in flux in 1968, a decade defined by change. Folk music and bathing suits were signs of students' increasing sense of freedom and self-expression.

Yet another sign of change was the first African American Homecoming Queen, Daphne Maxwell '70, who was crowned in 1967. President Miller assists in her coronation.

Founded in 1971, the Northwestern Community Ensemble became one of the University's most visible student organizations. Gospel music was not well known on campuses at that time, and ensemble concerts were a hit in Evanston. Their credo was "The Banner of Blackness, the Vessel of Soul, and the Epitome of Spirit."

her record as an antitrust attorney. Being female was neither an asset nor a particular liability early in her career, Netsch recalled, though she perplexed the partners where she worked. "That Dawn Clark thinks just like a man," they would say, and they meant it as high praise.

Netsch's political instincts made her grin and bear this type of comment. Politics of the electoral kind had her leaving the law practice for periods of time to work on the presidential campaign of Adlai Stevenson in 1956, on the gubernatorial campaign of Otto Kerner in 1960, and then on Kerner's staff.

In all of these positions, Netsch was accustomed to working almost entirely with men, and at Northwestern she did not play the part of gender pioneer. Instead, she allowed things to move naturally, watching as more females applied and were admitted to the law school, and in 1972 helping the dean recruit a second woman for the faculty. This was not a simple matter, as female professors were few and far between. But in time she identified and helped hire Joyce Hughes from the University of Minnesota, who arrived in 1974.

Despite (or because of) her gentleness on the subject of feminism, Dawn Clark Netsch emerged naturally as a mentor and spokesperson for the rising number of female students in the law school. In 1976, for example, she was asked to speak on the subject to the school's Law Alumni Association.

Entitled "76 Girls 76" (a takeoff on an old-time burlesque marquee), Netsch's speech pointed out that women made up 14 percent of enrollment in the law school and that their quality was at least as high as that of the males.

She also punctured the myth that while women might be good students, they ran the risk of getting pregnant and dropping their careers. Statistics showed that among young associates, females stayed with their firms longer than men, Netsch said. Her message was clear: if you wanted the best lawyers working for you, you needed to hire women as well as men.

It was a well-received speech, and her comments were reinforced moments later by a sharp bit of irony when the president of the alumni association thanked Professor Netsch for her talk. "We just can't wait to see all those pretty young things who are going to be working for us soon," he said. While some may have chuckled, most were aghast at the comment. Several came up to Netsch after the lunch. "No one could have helped make your point better," one of them told her.

The Bursar's Office sit-in

Racial progress at Northwestern, never particularly smooth or steady, had reached a sharp turning point by the 1967–68 school year, when the African American enrollment on the Evanston campus had risen to 160. Until 1966 it had been almost always less than 50. The University's accomplishments in recruiting and admitting more African Americans were positive, but the immediate result was that difficult racial issues were bubbling up with more force than ever.

Among these issues was the strict segregation of housing in Evanston and the resulting lack of decent apartments for African American undergraduates and graduate students near campus. This situation had been difficult for several years, although the University had long refused to impose sanctions against local landlords who discriminated. Eventually the University came around and wrote letters to all landlords expressing their intolerance of such practices. This was too little, too late for many African American students, who were already forming organizations on campus.

In the spring of 1968 Martin Luther King Jr. was assassinated, and race riots tore open many American cities, including Chicago. Very quickly, several African American organizations at Northwestern grew militant and expressed starkly separatists views.

The black undergraduate group For Members Only called for the organization of black-only fraternities, an idea that was widely resisted by white students. "I can't see that we're doing anything but encouraging campus segregation," said one student in the *Daily*. But, despite the controversy, the idea was soon endorsed by the administration.

Racial strains did not abate. Later that spring, African American students made additional demands related to recruiting, admissions, and curriculum matters. When the administration balked, the students took their most radical step to date. On May 3, more than 100 members of For Members Only and the graduate student organization called the Afro-American Student Union marched to the administration complex and occupied the Bursar's Office in the first major sit-in experienced at Northwestern. The students delivered an expanded list of demands and threatened to keep the financial nerve center of the University closed until they were satisfied. For 36 hours, the occupation of the Bursar's Office was a peaceful though tense confrontation. "Closed for Business 'til Racism at NU Is Ended," read a sign on the door. The press gathering outside was told by the protesters' spokespeople that nothing would be damaged as long as police didn't move against them.

Police did not. Instead, Roland Hinz, who was then vice president of student affairs, opened negotiations with James Turner '68, the leader of the Afro-American Student Union. Mindful of angrier student protests at Columbia and Berkeley that spring, the administration carefully considered the student ultimatum. And so they came to terms. On a number of matters, the administration promised student involvement, though they drew the line when it came to admissions and financial aid decisions. Importantly, the administration drafted a concise and largely acquiescent

By the early 1970s, counterculture styles were ubiquitous: bell bottoms, India prints, Kurt Vonnegut novels, and abundant hair were standard issue. Psychedelic decor took many forms, and footwear was optional.

ANTIWAR PROTESTS AT NORTHWESTERN

In 1965 the Student Senate passed a resolution in support of President Johnson's policy of full-scale bombing of North Vietnam. In response to this conservative expression, a group of liberal and left-leaning students created a local chapter of the Students for a Democratic Society (SDS).

SDS at Northwestern grew in the years that followed, but it rarely included more than 50 or so active members, and its influence on campus was hardly galvanizing. The group had an intellectual cast, led by Steven Lubet '70, later a professor at the School of Law, and it had sympathetic faculty members with whom members debated Weberian and Marxist political theory in class.

The organization held weekly meetings and tried to generate political excitement by picketing and demonstrating against various targets, such as recruiters on campus from Dow Chemical Company, the maker of napalm. Results of this protest were tepid, but a later series of "teach-ins" were more successful. The first was in 1967, attracting more than 1,000 people over a weekend of lectures, discussions, and music.

In one of the most effective student protests of the 1960s — not just at Northwestern but anywhere in the country — students occupied the Bursar's Office. This event in 1968 proved to antiwar activists that student political action could be effective.

Eva Jefferson was the Associated Student Government president, a relatively innocuous role until it thrust her into the leadership of the student strike against the Vietnam War in 1970. She became well known not just at Northwestern but throughout the nation for promoting a strong but nonviolent protest in the wake of U.S. bombing in Cambodia and the killings at Kent State University.

In 1969 the nationwide Vietnam moratorium led to a cessation of normal academic business and a rally in Deering Meadow.

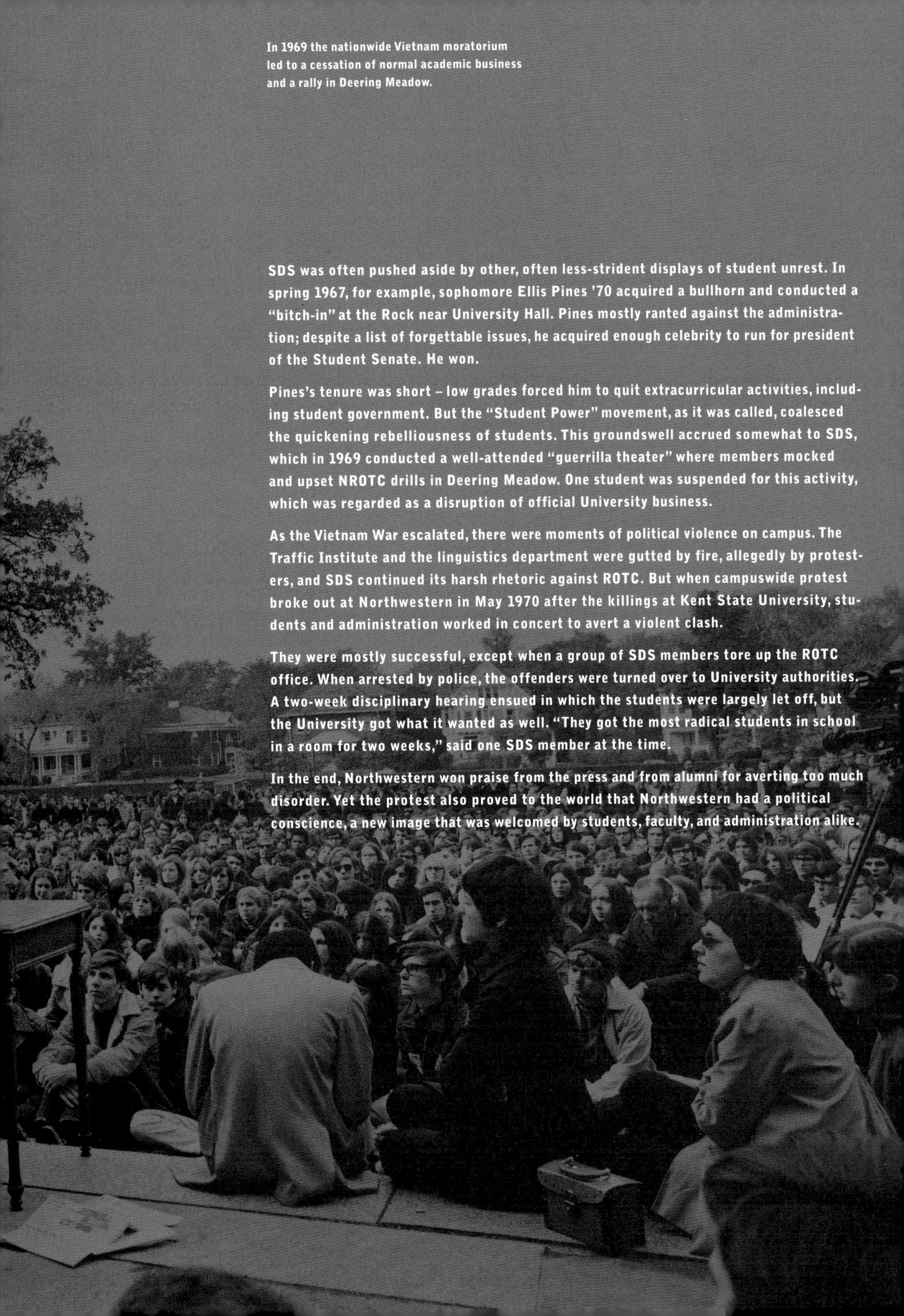

SDS was often pushed aside by other, often less-strident displays of student unrest. In spring 1967, for example, sophomore Ellis Pines '70 acquired a bullhorn and conducted a "bitch-in" at the Rock near University Hall. Pines mostly ranted against the administration; despite a list of forgettable issues, he acquired enough celebrity to run for president of the Student Senate. He won.

Pines's tenure was short – low grades forced him to quit extracurricular activities, including student government. But the "Student Power" movement, as it was called, coalesced the quickening rebelliousness of students. This groundswell accrued somewhat to SDS, which in 1969 conducted a well-attended "guerrilla theater" where members mocked and upset NROTC drills in Deering Meadow. One student was suspended for this activity, which was regarded as a disruption of official University business.

As the Vietnam War escalated, there were moments of political violence on campus. The Traffic Institute and the linguistics department were gutted by fire, allegedly by protesters, and SDS continued its harsh rhetoric against ROTC. But when campuswide protest broke out at Northwestern in May 1970 after the killings at Kent State University, students and administration worked in concert to avert a violent clash.

They were mostly successful, except when a group of SDS members tore up the ROTC office. When arrested by police, the offenders were turned over to University authorities. A two-week disciplinary hearing ensued in which the students were largely let off, but the University got what it wanted as well. "They got the most radical students in school in a room for two weeks," said one SDS member at the time.

In the end, Northwestern won praise from the press and from alumni for averting too much disorder. Yet the protest also proved to the world that Northwestern had a political conscience, a new image that was welcomed by students, faculty, and administration alike.

The Vietnam moratorium in October 1969 was a day of orderly rallies and intensive teach-ins. The *Daily* described the weather forecast for the day as "peaceful."

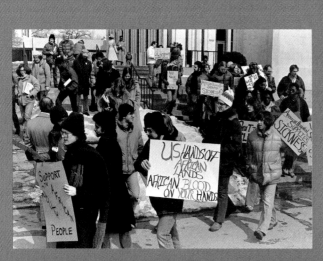

In this period of protest, there were many targets. Corporate America was one of the biggest, and activist students demanded that the University open its investment portfolio to expose unethical investments. Here, a 1988 demonstration protests the South African holdings of the Evanston-based American Hospital Supply Corporation.

N. U. ARCHIVES

Published
by and for
Northwestern
Students
Vol. 1, No. 1   Evanston, Ill.

SPARTACUS
"WE ARE ALL SPARTACUS"

TODAY'S WEATHER
Good for protestin'
Bad for studyin'

May 27, 1969

STRIKE SCHEDULE ANNOUNCED

NO MORE BULLSHIT

In their continued struggle for a more humane society, hundreds of NU students have joined together in an attempt to remove the NROTC from their campus. Disgusted by the university's complacent support of the U.S. war effort in Vietnam (NROTC provides the Navy with 15 per cent of its newly commissioned officers) and angered by the university's blatant suppression of campus dissent (four demonstrators were punished by the UDC for their participation in a non-violent, anti-ROTC protest on May 15), students are now willing to employ disruptive tactics until the university meets their demands.

The actual demands, as articulated in an SDS leaflet, are threefold:

1. AN END TO ALL UNIVERSITY TIES WITH NROTC.
2. AN END TO ALL POLITICAL REPRESSION, which includes dropping all charges, past and forthcoming, surrounding the demonstration against NROTC.
3. Since our protest is directed against the University's complicity and the NROTC program and not the cadets enrolled, when the University severs the NROTC contracts it should REPLACE ALL NROTC SCHOLARSHIPS WITH UNIVERSITY SCHOLARSHIPS.

Until the university officially removes NROTC from campus, NU students have apparently decided to do so unofficially by disrupting NROTC activities. On May 22, over 600 students entered two NROTC classes shouting "ROTC MUST GO!" Both classes were immediately dismissed.

(Continued p. 2, col. 2)

The schedule for NU's first student strike is (more or less) as follows:
8:30-10:30 am - Breakfast in Deering Meadow
1 pm - Mass rally in Tech Auditorium
afternoon - discussion in Deering Meadow
8 p.m. - Street dance in University Circle

During the day, there will be pickets around major building entrances.

PISSING IN THE OCEAN

A one-day strike is fine as far as it goes, but if we stop there, it's like pissing in the ocean: it makes your bladder feel good, but it doesn't change the current.

Sure, it's finals, and strikes take a hell of a lot of time. But there are other actions that can be taken. Among them are:

Picketing the NROTC circle jerk on Thursday.

Calling Rocky and Rollin' Jack and letting them know what you think about the whole mess.

Letting your parents know the truth about the NU situation.

Telling your high school buddies about NU.

Keeping in touch for further developments.

OK, I've told you a few; why don't you think of some?

THIS DAY IN HISTORY

May 27, 1960 -- Turkish students and (can you believe it?) liberal military men overthrow the right-wing dictatorship of Adnan Menderes and Celal Bayar. It can't happen here, can it?

Student protests trailed off after the Vietnam War, but by the end of the Reagan years, University-based groups such as the Latin American Committee and the South African Solidarity Organization were able to generate new waves of political activism. In November 1988 students tried to disrupt a recruiting visit of the Central Intelligence Agency. Sixteen students were arrested by University and Evanston police in the scuffles that ensued.

It wasn't only the left that focused on the Vietnam War. The Naval ROTC unit on campus brought a variety of professorial speakers to discuss the impact that military engagement had on foreign affairs.

Steve Lubet '70 (on car) was a leader of Students for a Democratic Society (SDS), which attempted to gain control of the student strike of May 1970. When emotional students barricaded Sheridan Road, SDS was on the front lines and later went on to tear up the offices of the Naval ROTC unit. All along, National Guard troops were nearby and ready to intervene, but the Northwestern administration convinced the guard and the police to stay away and thus minimized the potential for violence.

Arm bands signified solidarity for a cause that started with students and percolated into the conservative precincts of the Evanston and Northwestern communities.

response to the student demands. One of the most enduring concessions was the development of a Department of **Afro-American** Studies.

When the crisis was over and the Bursar's Office vacated, the press gave mixed reviews. The *Chicago Tribune*, still a strongly conservative newspaper, wrote a harsh editorial criticizing the University for giving in to "Black Power." But other papers, including the *Daily Northwestern*, endorsed the agreement between the African American students and the Miller administration. "It again places 'old, conservative Northwestern' among the leading institutions in attempting to understand Negro needs," the *Daily* editorialized.

The rise of Eva Jefferson

Another important effect of the 1968 protest was the rise of one of the most celebrated Northwestern students of the era, Eva Jefferson '71. A middle-class African American, Jefferson was a freshman when she participated in the occupation of the Bursar's Office. In the years that followed she was involved in campus politics on many levels until she was elected in April 1970 as the Associated Student Government's president, the highest student office at the University.

**While Jefferson was not a separatist, her platform had a radical edge. "The quality of education is poor,"
she said. "The quality of social life is poor, and the quality of student services is poor." She blamed these
problems on a lack of student participation and vowed to encourage change.**

Initially, student apathy looked like it would be hard to crack. In Jefferson's election campaign, most student forums had more candidates in attendance than other students. While Jefferson defeated the fraternity-endorsed candidate (who was also black) by a comfortable margin, little was expected of her or her office at

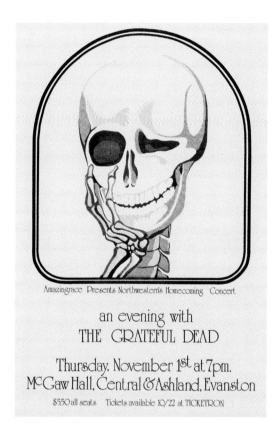

Amazingrace Presents Northwestern's Homecoming Concert.

an evening with
THE GRATEFUL DEAD

Thursday, November 1st at 7pm.
McGaw Hall, Central & Ashland, Evanston

$5.50 all seats   Tickets available 10/22 at TICKETRON

STEVE GOODMAN

8:00 FRIDAY OCTOBER 4TH
IN CAHN AUDITORIUM
AMAZINGRACE AND A & O PRESENT AN EVENING
IN EVANSTON WITH STEVE GOODMAN AND FRIENDS
TICKETS $3.00 · IN ADVANCE AT NORRIS CENTER AND
WHOLE EARTH · FOR INFORMATION CALL 492-5400

O
R
G
Y
of
the
A
R
T
S

ALLEN GINSBERG
Reading His Poetry

Friday, February 24, 1967   Tech Auditorium
8:30 P.M.   2145 Sheridan Road, Evanston
Admission: $1.50   Northwestern University
Tickets Available: Scott Hall Student Activities
And at the Door

As the youth culture of the 1960s and 1970s became widespread, Northwestern was a frequent stop for bands and "counterculture" performers on tour. While the Kingston Trio was from a more tranquil era, on-campus music traditionally promoted by the student-run Activities and Organizations (A & O) Board changed with the times. So did the promoters. In 1970, a "student collective" called Amazing Grace started a commune and coffeehouse, first located in Shanley Hall on campus. Before long, this group encountered problems with Evanston liquor laws, and while the administration owned the building it occupied and generally supported its efforts, President Robert Strotz worried about "a situation that would lead to the place being busted." Its concerts were sponsored by the University until 1975 when it became clear that its members were no longer Northwestern students. Amazingrace, as it was later spelled, continued as a concert venue at the Main Building at Chicago Avenue and Main Street until 1978.

Radio newswriting was introduced at the Medill School of Journalism in 1931, after which the broadcast program expanded steadily. By the 1970s Medill students in newspaper, radio, and television were working in the modern Urban Journalism Center in downtown Chicago — covering newsmakers such as Congressman Abner Mikva, pictured here giving a radio interview.

While Medill students were expected to develop interests in the liberal arts, their curriculum always placed an emphasis on the practical skills of newspaper work. Drills included describing a building entirely from memory or explaining in writing how to tie a shoe. Successful Medill students tackled such assignments with gusto amid the clatter of other people's typewriters.

Art, like politics, was a highly regarded form of self-expression in the 1960s and 1970s.

Getting a good tan and typing a serious paper were not at all contradictory undertakings in the 1970s.

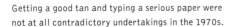

first. Political activism on campus was rising, but it was mostly focused on national issues – the environment and Vietnam – not Jefferson's campaign issues, which had more to do with the conduct of fraternity and sorority rush.

But Eva Jefferson quickly showed herself to be bigger than the relatively toothless student government. Her moment came in early May 1970 after the Ohio National Guard shot and killed four student protesters at Kent State University, igniting one of the largest national student protests in history. The next day, a nationwide "student strike" was called, and 5,000 Northwestern students responded by attending a rally in Deering Meadow. Eva Jefferson rose to lead it.

Northwestern's strike was eventful. It was supported by the faculty and won the endorsement of the administration. Classes were called off for the remainder of the week. In a spontaneous act of rebellion, students barricaded Sheridan Road and passed out leaflets to drivers. Accompanying these peaceful events were the more violent arson burnings of the Department of Linguistics, suspected (wrongly) of engaging in military research, and the Traffic Institute, regarded as a police bastion in a time when police were broadly regarded as political enemies of anti-war students. But compared to many other campuses, Northwestern's strike was orderly, and the person most credited for that was Jefferson. When a contingent of radical students started a night-time raid on the NROTC building, Jefferson got on the loudspeakers: "I can see torches out there," she said. "I don't know what they are, but they remind me of other torches on other nights." Her allusion was to the Ku Klux Klan, and these words from a black woman had the moral authority to end what might have been an ugly conflagration.

There was a moderate tone to Jefferson's leadership of the strike, but she was never accused of weakness. And over the summer and school year that followed, she became a celebrity and nationally recognized student spokesperson. A high point came when she appeared with three other students to debate Vice President Spiro Agnew on *The David Frost Show*. Jefferson was the lightning rod of this 90-minute exchange, especially when the vice president accused her repeatedly of advocating violence.

"I wish you would listen to what I am saying, because I have said two or three times that I am not in favor of violence," she snapped at Agnew. "I have never participated in a violent act except at the Chicago 'police convention,' called the Democratic Convention, in which I was tear gassed."

Jefferson did not persuade Agnew to change his views, but she got fan mail for weeks after her appearance with him. And she succeeded in influencing some other notable conservative Republicans, namely those on the Northwestern Board of Trustees. During the strike, she even cajoled board chairman John G. Searle to wear a red antiwar armband at a meeting she had with board members and senior administrators. In the strike's aftermath, Eva Jefferson convinced many other conservatives at Northwestern that the student protest movement was an intelligent force to be reckoned with.

NORTHWESTERN'S
EVANSTON CAMPUS
1970–PRESENT

a   **Norris University Center** (1972)

b   **Frances Searle Building** (1972)

c   **Arthur Andersen Hall/Leverone Hall** (1972)

d   **Blomquist Recreation Center** (1974)

e   **Pick-Staiger Concert Hall** (1975)

f   **Regenstein Music Building** (1977)

g   **Seeley G. Mudd Science Library** (1977)

h   **James L. Allen Center** (1979)
Original building; additions later.

i   **Theater and Interpretation Center** (1980)
Original building; additions later.

j   **Block Museum of Art** (1980)
Original building; additions later.

k   **Henry Crown Sports Pavilion and Norris Aquatics Center** (1987)

l   **Annenberg Hall** (1993)

m   **Materials and Life Sciences Building** (1993)

n   **Student Residences** (1970–1999)

o   **Transportation Center** (1999)

¾ mile west on Central

Lincoln

Orrington

Sheridan

Noyes

Foster

Emerson

Sherman

University

Chicago

Hinman

Clark

BUILT DURING THIS PERIOD

BUILT PREVIOUSLY

RAZED

The Medical School's Tarry Research and Education Center on the Chicago campus was completed in 1990. Architecturally it transcended the modern style that had prevailed for 30 years and revealed a new reverence for the University's neo-Gothic style of the 1920s and 1930s.

CHAPTER

p   *Health Sciences Building* (1979)

q   *Arthur Rubloff Building* (1984)

r   *Tarry Research and Education Center* (1990) Pictured.

NORTHWESTERN'S CHICAGO CAMPUS 1970-PRESENT

Chicago

Superior

Huron

Fairbanks

McClurg

Lake Shore Drive

8

TOWARD THE UNIVERSITY
OF THE FUTURE

Through most of its 150-year history, Northwestern's objectives
were clear, and its path to achieve them was well defined. In the
1850s, the fledgling University acquired land and established a
campus. Forty years later, it transformed a disparate collection of
schools into a recognized center for classical, scientific, and professional learning. Eventually the University assembled a faculty
of distinction and later built impressive new buildings to house
them. Step by step, Northwestern had come up in the world, and by
the end of J. Roscoe Miller's mostly happy tenure, Northwestern
had accomplished all this and much more.

But the milestone of Miller's retirement in 1970 in no way
signaled that Northwestern had achieved all of its goals. The
successes of the postwar years instead raised expectations yet
another notch. By the end of the Miller era, Northwestern no
longer judged itself against schools it lost to in football but rather
against the institutions that had, with some regularity, lured
away its best professors.

Yet as Northwestern moved toward the upper ranks of higher
education, it did so without a precise road map. In the rare air

of elite colleges and universities, stature and prestige were elusive objectives. A school that had been safely homogeneous until the 1960s was now demographically and ideologically diverse. A school that had been an ivory tower in the past could no longer ignore social conflict, technological change, or especially its own student body, which was brimming over with smart and impatient people.

In fact, Northwestern had begun to reflect many signs that its efforts, especially lately, were being repaid with a fast-rising reputation. The Medical School was expanding and increasingly recognized for its powerful combination of clinical teaching and research. The economics department boasted well-known scholars who could influence public policy at the highest levels. The business and engineering schools, too, had evolved from average status to positions of true prestige. All of these accomplishments brought satisfaction to the University and its alumni but also highlighted the fact that Northwestern's ambition depended upon a multiplicity of interests working toward a common goal. The path was not always smooth nor linear, but the objectives established by the Miller adminstration were now clear — a broadened role as a major research institution while maintaining its commitment to the highest quality undergraduate education. This path was not always smooth and linear, but the goal of excellence was clear.

Strotz takes over

Professor Robert H. Strotz, dean of the College of Arts and Sciences, became the early front runner to succeed Miller as president, primarily because the increasingly powerful faculty favored him. Strotz was an esteemed econometrician with a scholarly outlook that his professorial colleagues trusted. He could, they hoped, understand the academic needs of the University, nourish them, and encourage their growth.

Robert H. Strotz (1922–94) began his Northwestern career as a professor of economics. He was later dean of the College of Arts and Sciences before serving as president of the University from 1970 to 1985.

Blackbeat, the paper of the black student alliance, For Members Only, covered current affairs on campus and beyond – from African American fraternity news to the largely successful campaign to force University divestment of holdings in South African–related businesses.

The *Northwestern Review* was founded in 1982 as a conservative voice. In its early issues it covered gun control and protested a $3,500 fee paid to Abbie Hoffman to speak at Northwestern. The *Review* published for more than 11 years; then, after a short hiatus, its ideological spirit was revived in the *Northwestern Chronicle*. The *Chronicle* was also pugnacious and ran afoul of Associated Student Government in 1997, which moved to derecognize the weekly – even though the paper's funding came not from the University but from private donations. ASG's action drew protest from people across the political spectrum, and the decision was reversed the following year.

THE POWER OF THE PRESS

Campus journalism at Northwestern has been robust since shortly after the University was founded, but in the 1970s – with the rise of offset printing – the "alternative press" flourished even if it did not prosper. Politics inspired many a new paper to be launched amid evanescent passions and short-lived crusades. Satire tended to be more enduring, insofar as campus publishing was concerned. Humor magazines such as the *Purple Parrot* (1921–50) and *Rubber Teeth* (1979–93 and 1997–98) had the staying power that ideological organs did not.

But longevity has never been a central feature of American journalism, nor of Northwestern's alternative press. What writers and editors care about is being heard. And what history values in the archives of defunct campus newspapers is the record of diversity, rebellion, wilting anger, twisted humor, and the endless stream of ideas that has always animated student life at Northwestern.

The humor magazine *Rubber Teeth* lampooned all the usual suspects. It published a parody of the *Daily Northwestern* in 1981 ("Libes closing leaves thousands homeless," cried one headline). Flourishing in the middle 1980s, the magazine went after President Strotz ("Whatsoever things are obtuse," it rhapsodized in his honor). *Rubber Teeth* experienced a brief revival in 1998.

The Real Press had the psychedelic graphics of a true alternative newspaper In its heyday in 1968, the paper railed against the University administration. "We must assert our right to live as free people," it editorialized, opposing both the war in Vietnam and dormitory regulations. By 1974 *Albatross* was more sophisticated both graphically and politically.

A short-lived journal of the Women's Center, *Mountain Moving*, carried articles about home birth, the women's collection in the library, and the nature of dating at Northwestern. "If you're picky, forget it," said one woman in reference to the latter.

The Board of Trustees was not so sure. They were emotionally tied to Rocky Miller's successful presidency, and they were dubious of any candidate whose résumé suggested abstract thinking. It was 1970, and several trustees, unsettled by campus unrest, were searching for an authority figure – preferably one from the outside. Such a candidate did not emerge, however, and after a protracted selection process, Strotz was selected as Northwestern's 13th president.

In the interests of a smooth transition, the trustees took the additional step of creating the post of chancellor, which Miller would occupy for four years in a power-sharing arrangement. If Strotz distrusted such a scheme, he concealed his feelings and exhibited extreme optimism in his first address to the faculty as president. Northwestern was "dedicated to learning and to teaching, but beyond that it is dedicated to discovery," he declared. "It is an institution that must do some things because of the general social and cultural advantages they bring, whether those things pay off in the marketplace or not."

To the faculty, these were words from heaven, though Strotz did not work the magic that particularly the College of Arts and Sciences was waiting for. Inevitably, Miller's close focus on a balanced budget prevailed as long as he was chancellor and still influencing the Board of Trustees. Strotz was restrained, therefore, from embarking on his own plans to enhance Northwestern's "distinction and prestige," as he described his objectives for the institution. The Miller-Strotz interregnum meant that ambitions for a more powerful academic and research institution were delayed.

The life sciences

Some change was inevitable and already in progress, such as the remarkable advances already taking place in the "life sciences," a newly coined term that emphasized the interdependence of once-separate disciplines such as biology, biochemistry, and medicine. A decade before, the Faculty Planning Committee had predicted great strides in this fast-developing area, and in 1974 a new department was created that embraced cellular biology, biochemistry, and related laboratory sciences. The new department, under the leadership of David Shemin, represented an emphatic response to a revolution in the field known as "molecular genetics."

In this rapidly advancing subject, researchers were beginning to isolate individual genes and were learning how to read them. And as these insights often touched on the relationship between genetic structure and disease, the work created

Neurobiology and physiology professor Neena Schwartz distinguished herself by reaching out to other disciplines in her research as well as to undergraduate students in the classroom.

232

closer ties between basic science and clinical research. More than ever before scientists from different departments – from both the Evanston and Chicago campuses – were seeking each other out and interacting.

In some ways, this collaboration happened naturally. "You don't drive this subject; you are driven by it," said biochemist Emanuel Margoliash, whose work on the structure and function of protein cells was one of several projects bringing widespread recognition to Northwestern.

While his was basic research without clinical applications in mind, Margoliash and his closest colleagues found themselves increasingly called upon by the Medical School to explain new discoveries in chemistry which so directly influenced biomedical science.

In other cases, collaboration among the life sciences required deliberate and repeated effort, as well as growing assistance from the National Institutes of Health and other federal funding sources. In 1974, for example, the Medical School hired physiologist Neena Schwartz, a 1953 PhD graduate of the school and a rising star in cellular research. Support was still lacking in the Medical School for serious and sustained research, however, which discouraged Schwartz and led her to consider leaving the University before her first year was complete. Fortunately, she was offered the chair of the department of biological sciences in Evanston, which she accepted. The appointment kept Schwartz at Northwestern and began a period of heightened collaboration in these fields.

With the increase of interdisciplinary work and a $10 million gift from the Chicago Community Trust in 1980, Northwestern went on to create major research centers in the life sciences. These "centers without walls," as they were called, offered high-level interaction among faculty members and researchers from both campuses in reproductive science, cancer, neuroscience, and other areas.

Computers at Northwestern

Another signpost of the modern University was the rise of academic computing at Northwestern, first introduced in 1949 when a bulky IBM was installed in a spare room in Dearborn Observatory. Computers at this time were arcane and clumsy,

When the faculty became politicized in the 1970s and 1980s, the old guard was represented by history professor Richard W. Leopold. He held his classes early in the morning and had little patience for any activity, including protests, that kept students from maintaining perfect attendance in his class.

The IBM 709, located in the basement of the Technological Institute, was used mainly by engineers and scientists, though faster machines were on the horizon. Social scientists, among others in nontechnical fields, also took an early interest in the computer's hitherto unimaginable potential for number crunching.

WIRING THE CAMPUS

Northwestern installed a University-wide network in 1994. At the time, departments were connected to each other and all dorm rooms were equipped with high-speed Internet access.

Technology had come a long way since the mid-1980s, when the few users of desktop computers on campus – notably in the math department – could send messages around the country through an online network called Usenet. When the Internet emerged, it evolved with unimagined rapidity.

In 1993, when vice president for information technology Morteza Rahimi designed Northwestern's fiber-optic network, he wanted to connect heavy users as well as those who rarely worked with computers. His theory was that "people who create technology are usually wrong when they try to predict how other people will use it."

He was right. While faculty and students in the sciences had been first to make use of computers, those in the humanities soon caught up and surpassed everyone else as the most creative and frequent users of the network. Language teachers created Web sites with teaching videos. Music classes made use of powerful software that ran keyboards.

The computer injected itself into student life as well. E-mail created new and sometimes rich dialogue in seminars and student organizations. In 1999 University course registration was brought online. By then, computing continued to advance in countless directions, but for most people on campus, it had become less a dazzling new technology than an essential part of academic life.

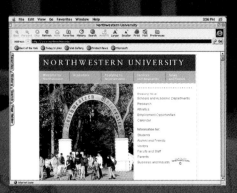

The Northwestern home page is a familiar site to all who log on.

Widespread use by students of computing and networking first took place in the library in the middle 1980s. Initially the library terminals were connected to the Vogelback mainframe with an online catalogue system and an early e-mail network.

but the technology progressed rapidly. In the 1950s a succession of new machines was introduced, and in 1965 Vogelback Computing Center opened on the new lakefill campus with a CDC 3400, which was five times faster than the computer it replaced.

The early mainframes, which used stacks of punch cards to input data, were employed mainly by chemists and physicists to process information and, as they took to saying, "crunch" numbers. Before long, scholars from other fields also were attracted to the power of computing. In the late 1960s, for example, a PhD candidate in industrial engineering, O. George Kennedy '71, wrote his dissertation on the use of computers in designing the new Rehabilitation Institute at the medical center. Kennedy and undergraduate Bruce Foster '70 used "queuing theory" to understand the daily movement of patients and identify potential traffic jams, which helped architects create the ideal design for a modern facility.

Computers also led to less worldly pastimes, such as computer chess. Among the enthusiasts in this area was Larry Atkin '69 (MS '75), who was an undergraduate when he wrote Northwestern's earliest chess program, a relatively simple system that assigned values to each piece on the board and selected each move to protect or attack the piece with the greatest value. Computer chess grew more sophisticated, however, and in 1970 a Northwestern team won the first of a long string of national championships. Success brought more people to Vogelback to try their skill at chess, and many came from unexpected fields, such as psychologist Peter Frey, who later edited a book on the subject, *Chess Skill in Man and Machine*.

Other faculty members also took to computers in innovative ways. By the early 1970s, political scientist Kenneth Janda was using the mainframe to apply detailed statistics to his discipline, which was traditionally much more subjective and philosophical.

Unfazed by the machine's complexity, Janda and a succession of student assistants embarked on a decade-long project that used the Vogelback computers and resulted in the 1980 book *Political Parties*. In it, Janda quantified the nature of political change, proving that centralized political parties change less than fragmented ones, for example, and that political parties in poor countries are more centralized than those in rich ones.

Mee-Ow, Northwestern's satirical comedy theater group, was founded in 1974 and named to mock Waa-Mu, the University's sacred cow of musical theater. In 1980, for example, the Mee-Ow show *Ten Against the Empire* was loosely based on the premise that an evil force was breeding apathy at Northwestern.

Norris University Center, dedicated in 1972, filled a longtime need to accommodate University-wide social activities. Replacing the much smaller Scott Hall, it instantly became the vibrant center of activity among the many new buildings on the lakefill campus.

THE EVANSTON CAMPUS

By 1970 Northwestern had grown largely according to the "First Plan for the Seventies," written in 1966 by the Faculty Planning Committee. The plan called for the reorientation of Evanston campus buildings into "three major intellectual complexes or zones." North would be science and engineering. Central would be the social sciences. South would be arts and humanities.

Other buildings in the scheme would serve the campus at large, such as the library, dedicated in 1970, and Norris University Center, opened in 1972 – both centrally located and a short stroll from one another. "We wanted a walking campus," said Jeremy Wilson, planning coordinator and a key administrator during the two decades of growth.

By the time the lakefill was created, architect Walter Netsch had become the master builder of Northwestern, receiving the commissions for the Rebecca Crown Center, the library, and Hogan Hall. Netsch was an award-winning and highly theoretical designer, but his work did not always please clients who used these buildings, so University planners also brought in the firm of Loebel, Schlossman, Bennett and Dart, best known for shopping centers such as Old Orchard and Water Tower Place. They designed Norris, Pick-Staiger, Leverone, and other buildings largely from the inside out. These were less than elegant to the eye but functional for years to come.

New residence halls of this period presented a different architectural challenge. Housing was a priority as soon as the "First Plan for the Seventies" increased undergraduate enrollment to 6,500, but luxurious dormitories were beyond the budget. The Foster-Walker complex, with single rooms and air conditioning, was an improvement over previous dorms. But it wasn't until later, with residential colleges on the rise, that dormitory design piqued real interest in University planners and the architects they hired.

On the south campus, three residential colleges plus the 1835 Hinman dormitory went up by the early 1980s – designed in brick and scaled for residential use, they featured luxuries such as suites, commons rooms, and other amenities suitable for Northwestern's "community of scholars."

The 1987 dedication of the Henry Crown Sports Pavilion and Norris Aquatics Center represented a major step in the University's campaign to improve athletic and recreational facilities. The pavilion included courts for basketball, volleyball, and racquet sports. The aquatics center was designed with modern features to accommodate several different water-sport activities at the same time.

Pick-Staiger Concert Hall was completed in 1975, funded primarily through a gift of hotelier Albert Pick. The auditorium boasted an expansive interior space, near-perfect acoustics, and a seating capacity of 1,003.

Leverone Hall (top right) was dedicated in 1972 to house Northwestern's business school. It was connected to Arthur Andersen Hall (left). Andersen had been built for the School of Education, which later moved to the new Annenberg Hall (top of page), leaving Andersen to the burgeoning Kellogg Graduate School of Management.

Northwestern and the American city

The academic world was undertaking new research in many different fields, one of which was urban America. Inner cities throughout the country were deteriorating in the late 1960s, and to encourage scholarship to address this challenge, the Ford Foundation chose Northwestern as one of 40 colleges and universities to receive major grants for new professorships and teaching facilities.

Northwestern received Ford money in 1969 and used it to create the Center for Urban Affairs, a research center with funds for more than 20 professors. Each faculty member had a joint appointment in another department, but all shared an interest in the economics, politics, race relations, and other aspects of the American city. Sociologist Raymond Mack, who was charged with developing the project, naturally was concerned with bringing serious scholarship to the endeavor, but Mack also was determined to have its work reach beyond the ivory tower.

While many members of the new center were already on the Northwestern faculty, Mack went outside the University for several new appointments. One was John McKnight '53, who was entirely new to the academic-research environment. Years before, McKnight had been one of Northwestern's campus activists and later worked as regional director of the United States Civil Rights Commission. McKnight lacked an advanced degree, but he knew the American city and sensed where hard research could make a difference. One such area was police brutality, and as McKnight and his colleagues collected data on this subject, they quickly revealed something not widely known: that Chicago led all major American cities in killings by police and alleged instances of police brutality.

The faculty at the center believed that serious study of urban problems was the first step toward solving them, but when the headlines of the brutality study appeared on the front pages of Chicago newspapers, the first reaction was ill will.

Hardly had Mayor Richard J. Daley read these stories before he was on the phone to President Strotz, threatening to end the longtime friendship between the city of Chicago and Northwestern. To Strotz's credit, he moved not an inch. Research was research, the president replied, and it would never be altered by the inconvenience it caused the mayor of Chicago.

The rise of Kellogg

Another early effort to move beyond the ivory tower came when John A. Barr, former president of Montgomery Ward, was made dean of the School of Business. Barr arrived in 1966 with a mandate to strengthen ties with the business community. He accomplished this goal initially by forming an advisory committee of senior executives in Chicago that included John deButts, president of Illinois Bell, and James Allen '29, chairman of Booz, Allen and Hamilton, a leading consulting firm.

Raymond W. Mack was a highly regarded
sociology professor whose courses on
race and society represented the first
exposure many students had to the subject
of inequality. Mack was later provost
under Strotz and is credited with keeping
the academic programs on an upward
trajectory in the hardest economic times
at Northwestern since the Depression.

One reason for the longtime national influence of Northwestern's
economics department was Professor Robert Eisner. In the
1980s and early 1990s his Keynesian views were heard in the
halls of Congress where he testified and read on the op-ed
pages of major newspapers to which he contributed. His position
was that the fiscal conservatives were choking the economy
and creating needless unemployment. A teacher at Northwestern
for 42 years, who was deservedly famous for his introductory economics course, Eisner died in 1998.

At the Kellogg Graduate School of Management, emphasis was placed
on technology and team-building well before they became obvious
keynotes of American management. By the time computers had transformed American enterprise and as old autocrats gave way to new
entrepreneurs, Northwestern was ranked No. 1 among business schools
in the United States.

This committee was not shy in recommending a wide range of changes in the business program, including renaming it the School of Management, which reflected a focus on the work of not-for-profit organizations and government as well as business. A less modest proposal was to abolish the undergraduate business program altogether and concentrate entirely on graduate studies. Employers were convinced, the committee declared, that executives benefited most from a full liberal arts education followed by training in the science of management.

Barr agreed with the proposals, as did President Miller, though the transformation of the School of Business met with resistance from students. Momentum was on Barr's side, however. The market for MBA graduates was growing, he pointed out, and when the new program started in 1967, he promised that Northwestern would soon have "one of the few truly great business schools in the nation."

But greatness was not on the horizon when Barr retired in 1975, and it seemed even less so when the school's first three choices to succeed him turned the job down. Fourth choice was Donald Jacobs, then a professor of banking in the school and a member of the search committee. Jacobs agreed to act as dean "until you can find someone better," he said.

Jacobs believed, though, that Northwestern could realize Barr's goal of greatness. With a keen sense of the future, Jacobs and other members of the faculty saw that American management was in a state of rapid flux.

"We knew that the world was globalizing," Jacobs said, "and as the world became more competitive, it was going to have to change more rapidly than ever before." This assumption led directly to changes in management education.

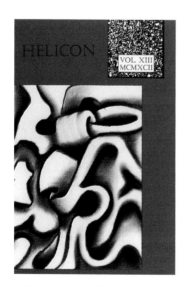

Helicon was launched by the Humanities Residential College in 1980. With campuswide submissions, its first issue included a short story of young love, an essay on Robert Browning, and many poems. By 1992 art and photography had become prominent in the yearly literary magazine.

A fireside in the College of Community Studies, one of the oldest residential colleges on campus.

Jacobs had worked with early computers at Northwestern and knew the power of change in that area. He also discerned that management was becoming less hierarchical and more team-oriented.

With change in mind, Jacobs began to hire young professors (the school could not afford established ones) who were engaged in research on "the frontiers of knowledge," he said. Among them were proponents of "game theory," a fast-evolving area in business analysis. He created a unique Department of Managerial Economics and Decision Sciences and also developed a highly regarded curriculum in "organizational management and change" to prepare students for rapid evolution in the business environment. But Jacobs also went beyond theory, bringing real-world business executives to the school. To this end he also raised money for an executive conference center where scholars and students could interact with managers. The James L. Allen Center (named for consultant James Allen) opened on a prime lakefill location in 1979.

For years, Jacobs and his school had garnered little respect among the faculty on campus or from other graduate business schools. His colleagues saw business as somewhat suspect from a scholarly viewpoint, and other schools saw Northwestern as a newcomer. But in 1979 the Graduate School of Management received a $10 million gift from the family of J. L. and Helen Kellogg. The sum was large enough to bring additional faculty to the school, and it also enabled Jacobs and the faculty to expand successful programs that were preparing real-world managers. By the time Kellogg graduates had been in the workplace just a few years, Jacobs could show that the school's ideas were breeding success.

They were building recognition as well, which culminated in 1985 when, in a poll of corporate recruiters, a respected business magazine survey shocked the MBA world by ranking Kellogg No. 1. And then, before Jacobs could find a modest way to explain Kellogg's good fortune, a *Business Week* survey produced the same result. "Dark horse" Northwestern, it said, suddenly had the best B-school in the country.

Residential colleges and the ideal university

In 1969 the Faculty Planning Committee, chaired by English professor Jean Hagstrum '38, issued a report entitled "A Community of Scholars." It was a largely philosophical tract, quoting lavishly from Shakespeare and other sources, and it recommended many changes in the educational environment. Many did come to pass – interdisciplinary programs, for example, and increased interaction between graduate and undergraduate education. It also made a strong call for "civility," as Hagstrum termed the rich collegiality that could be cultivated in an academic community.

WILDCAT WOMEN

Success breeds success in athletics, and the women of Northwestern have emphasized this point on numerous occasions. The women's athletic tradition at Northwestern goes back to 1876, when the University's first gymnasium was used by women as well as men. In 1911 the Women's Athletic Association (WAA) was organized for instruction in field hockey, basketball, and other sports and to establish codes for on-field conduct.

Competition for women was strictly intramural until the late 1950s when Northwestern teams scheduled games with other schools. They lacked the money to travel far but found plenty of willing opponents in the Chicago area.

By the early 1970s Northwestern had become a leader in intercollegiate sports for women. While many other schools awaited court decisions to enforce Title IX, the federal law that mandated equal resources for men and women,

Northwestern saw equality as an opportunity: A women's athletic director was hired in 1975, and many club teams were promoted to varsity status that year.

By the 1980s Northwestern had nine varsity sports for women, and seven of them have competed in NCAA championship events to date. Full scholarships have attracted serious athletes in all varsity sports. As Wildcat coaches recruited top prospects for Northwestern's women's teams, many created something that money could not buy – a winning tradition.

In 1994 Kathleen Sullivan '95 was one of the senior stars on a field hockey team that made it to the Final Four in the NCAA national championships.

Diane Donnelly '87 and Katrina Adams '89 (far court) battle a team from the University of Southern California in a benefit match at Welsh-Ryan Arena in 1986. The following year the pair won the NCAA doubles title as Northwestern's women's tennis finished in a tie for fifth in the nation.

It took time for Northwestern to catch up to the pack in cross country. When this photo was taken on the lakefill course in 1980, most opponents were local, and the Wildcat women weren't up to tough Big Ten competition. Several good years for cross country began in 1983 when Northwestern took a surprising fifth place in the conference and Coach Dee Todd was named Big Ten Coach of the Year.

Northwestern was a regional powerhouse in women's basketball in 1977 with a 17–4 record. By 1984 it had a tougher schedule of opponents from around the country and fought to a 14–13 record with a team that included Big Ten Player of the Year Anucha Browne '85.

Courtney Allen '00 led the 1999 swim team to ninth place in the NCAA championships. She took second in the 50-meter freestyle.

Big Ten officials sometimes joked that Northwestern's athletic director Douglas Single – an early enthusiast of women's sports – was diverting the University's football budget to build a volleyball empire. Wildcat volleyball was one of the best in the Midwest in the mid-1980s.

Northwestern softball was the undisputed powerhouse of the Big Ten in the mid-1980s, winning four straight conference titles between 1984 and 1987. Lisa Ishikawa '88 led those teams on the mound. A pitcher from Stockton, California, Ishikawa was later named Northwestern's Woman Athlete of the Decade.

The Hagstrum report offered few specifics, but one of them was adopted right away — residential colleges designed to "help connect curricular with extra-curricular experiences by extending the intellectual atmosphere to residences." The first five residential colleges were opened in the fall of 1972 as a relatively small but viable alternative to the fraternity system. Two were "thematic" — one focused on philosophy and religion and the other on urban affairs (called "community studies"). Three were not connected to a particular field of learning.

In time, more residential colleges were opened, and many established distinct identities, although not always as places where "new personal alliances are formed and where the self is discovered," in the words of a later faculty study on the subject. Willard Residential College became known, at least in the *Daily,* for "rowdy partygoers," a reputation its members did little to thwart. Willard was named for Frances Willard, Northwestern's first dean of women and later president of the Women's Christian Temperance Union. Ironically, her birthday, September 28, was used to host one of the biggest annual beer parties on campus.

Happily, the intellectual aims of the residential colleges evolved as well. The Philosophy and Religion Residential College, for example, conducted "firesides" and other cerebral events, including a 1974 debate between professors Ray Mack and Harrison Hayford on the relationship between cutting-edge research and good teaching. The debate was an earnest one even though Mack, who argued that research was vital to teaching, amused himself afterward by admitting that he could have debated the opposite side with equal ardor.

Additional "res colleges" were created during the next few years, although one or two came before Northwestern apparently was ready for them. The Women's Studies Residential College suffered initially because some members felt stigmatized as "feminists." But when the college moved to Hobart House, the Women's Residential College, as it was renamed, became a congenial alternative to coeducational dorms. As the idea of women's studies took hold academically, so did the college, which developed a diverse membership known for precisely what residential colleges were trying to achieve — "civility."

William McKinney '77, here against Indiana, was the backcourt spark of a team that in 1976 won 12 games, Northwestern's best season in seven years. The Wildcats' problem that year was that the Big Ten was loaded — two conference teams, Michigan and Indiana, played in the final for the national championship, which Indiana won.

The budget crisis

The building boom on the lakefill and Northwestern's rising national reputation were sources of pride to the University community. They were also a source of exasperation, because developing both was expensive, especially during the mid-1970s when the nation hit its hardest economic times since the Depression. Inflation was raging, real economic growth was frozen, and financial trouble was fast approaching.

In 1980 the University posted its first budget deficit in years — almost $1 million. That figure was shocking, but it was only the beginning; within two years the deficit had ballooned to almost $9 million. In response, Strotz announced a pay freeze for faculty and staff in the spring of 1982. The faculty saw this as a major reversal in policy since the administration had previously promised a series of increases that would bring Northwestern faculty salaries to the top ten among U.S. colleges and universities.

As a result, the pay freeze triggered the most serious faculty revolt in the history of the University. Some predicted disaster. Northwestern ran "a serious chance of losing major professors to industry and engineering," said Sia Nemat-Nasser, an engineering professor who headed the faculty budget committee. There was also anger.

"I feel the faculty has tried earnestly for at least a half-dozen years to work with the administration," said a professor in the psychology department. "I feel that Northwestern University needs new leadership."

The Arthur Rubloff Building at the Northwestern University School of Law was completed in 1984 — a tower of glass, steel, and granite standing beside the stately neo-Gothic architecture next door. The old and the new are joined by a six-story glass atrium, where students gather in the courtyard of Levy Mayer Hall as they have done for a half-century.

By the end of the school year the College of Arts and Sciences faculty passed a vote of no confidence in Strotz. This clearly got the attention of the trustees, who moderated the salary freeze but did not placate the faculty. Nor did pressure for more bricks and mortar abate. On the Chicago campus in particular, increased federal research funding was problematic, since more research demanded more laboratories. The School of Law needed new quarters as well, and despite budget constraints, it completed the Arthur Rubloff Building in 1984. The building came with a maintenance endowment and a major new tenant, the American Bar Association. Nevertheless, the School of Law seemed particularly resistant to fiscal conservatism in the waning years of the Strotz administration.

The administration, meanwhile, struggled with the pressures of balancing the University budget while maintaining the mission of building educational quality. When challenged to make changes in his administration, the president said publicly that at his age (he was in his early 60s), he was not about to change his staff. Instead, he announced that he would retire, which he did in 1984.

The firm hand of Arnold Weber

As the Board of Trustees sought a successor to Strotz, the quest looked like a tall order: they needed a budget disciplinarian to solve the fiscal crisis as well as a strong academic leader who could also raise the academic stature of the University. By mid-1984 the list of presidential candidates was pared down to two, at which point an important member of the search committee, Lester Crown, happened to be in Washington, D.C., meeting with Secretary of State George Shultz on other business. As the meeting ended, Crown mentioned to Shultz that one finalist for the

Arnold R. Weber, president of the University from 1985 to 1995, employed strong leadership to balance the budget and move academic programs ahead at the same time — no mean trick, as Northwestern was growing larger, more diverse, and increasingly more difficult to govern.

By 1988 many Northwestern students saw the CIA as a legitimate career choice, but others disagreed, and recruiters from the intelligence agency were met by protesters, smaller in number than those of the Vietnam era but tenacious in opposing CIA-backed Contra rebels in Nicaragua.

Mayfest 1988. For decades May festivals were a way to shed the stresses and strains of winter, and beginning in the early 1970s, Armadillo (or 'Dillo) Day was its climactic celebration of sunshine and music. "Armadillo Day is the one time many future-minded, career-conscious yuppies-in-training throw caution (and the results of future drug tests) to the wind and live for the moment," wrote *Daily* columnist Kathy Cantillon '88.

MAYFEST AND 'DILLO DAY

Celebration of spring at Northwestern goes back to the 1890s, when a queen was selected and white-gowned girls danced around the May pole. May Week was then a decorous occasion that also included induction ceremonies for honor societies accompanied by the sweet strains of violins in Deering Meadow.

The rites of spring took a different turn in the 1970s, and Armadillo Day (named for a nonindigenous armored mammal) became its climax. 'Dillo Day was an exultation of music and art, a moment "when the freaks come out and mingle with the preppies," as the *Daily* put it. Freedom from authority was key: The chief of the Northwestern police force was the star attraction in a dunking booth in 1974.

By the 1980s Mayfest (as it was then called) featured semiathletic feats (such as water balloon contests). The "Chug for Charity" even allowed men and women to raise money for the American Cancer Society in proportion to their capacity to rapidly consume malt beverages. And 'Dillo Day entertainment ranged from the ridiculous to the sublime. Bluegrass, reggae, poetry, "The Best of Mee-Ow," and "eviscerated Shakespeare" were a typical mix.

In Northwestern's post-'60s era, Mayfest became a time to toss the books aside and enjoy music, sunshine, and other pleasures of spring. "It might be too enjoyable," said a Mayfest promoter some years ago. "People should be shocked a little."

The annual One-Ton Sundae at Norris Center was a happy but short-lived event, beginning in 1981 and ending after this boatload of ice cream was consumed outside Norris in March 1982. The weather kept the ice cream frozen, and the price was right (sundaes were free), but perhaps due to the season, the event did not become a permanent tradition.

Sponsored by the School of Speech, WNUR acquired a 7.2-kilowatt transmitter in 1976 that reached well into Chicago. As most other music stations in this market were commercialized, homogenized, and otherwise unadventurous about music, WNUR (pictured here in 1993) made itself an early proponent of the latest styles — such as new wave, hip-hop, and acid jazz — well before they became common fare on other stations' play lists.

Among many volunteer activities on campus, Special Olympics began in 1978 when the athletic department and a group of dedicated students organized the event at Dyche Stadium for children and adults with mental handicaps.

Northwestern presidency was a former Shultz protégé, Arnold Weber, who was then president of the University of Colorado. Shultz knew Weber when both were professors at the University of Chicago business school in the 1960s. Shultz later served as Secretary of Labor under President Nixon and brought Weber with him as assistant secretary.

When Shultz heard Weber's name he became dead serious. "Get Weber. Don't lose him. Do it this afternoon," he told Crown. Shultz insisted that he knew no one with more energy and acuity than Arnold Weber. Crown reported back to the trustees, and the Northwestern board took Shultz's advice.

As the University's 14th president, Weber's first order of business in early 1985 was to resolve the University's out-of-control finances. This was not complicated for Weber. He first established a new staff for planning and finance, then announced that budgets were neither elastic nor fictional and stated clearly that deficits would not be tolerated. But he also did the deans a favor: he installed computers in the finance office that would throw up red flags when any department appeared on a budget-breaking trajectory. "Weber scares the hell out of me," said one longtime dean during Weber's first year. "You cannot con him."

Weber derived some satisfaction from the positive impact he had on University finances, but he pointed out that money was only a means to an end. "I don't want to go down in history as the University's greatest accountant," he said more than once. He insisted that budgets made it possible to "go about the main chore of the University with a sense of choice and comfort." That chore was to elevate educational quality, and to advance that goal, Weber instituted another administrative invention. "Program review," as it was called, was the regular and formal examination of each academic and administrative unit in the University on a seven-year cycle.

The reviews were painstaking, with evaluators from both inside and outside the University, who determined departmental strengths and weaknesses, looked to the future, and helped to allocate resources. The process had an impact: In one

As new sports were introduced at Northwestern, some of them caught on. Ultimate Frisbee became a club sport in the 1980s. Other seasonal contests, such as snow football in Deering Meadow, were less organized but required a measure, or at least a moment, of dedication.

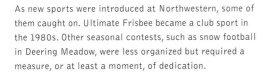

case an entire PhD program was abolished after a withering review. In another, the Department of Slavic Languages and Literatures was revealed to be unexpectedly strong despite its small size, and the review led to several new positions in the department. Slavic languages hired judiciously and became even stronger as a result.

As was true with increased budget discipline, program review was likewise a means to an end. And that end, in Weber's words, "was the transformation of Northwestern from what had been a more regional, socially oriented university to a national institution of academic distinction – without losing the soul of the place."

Weber, who had a PhD from MIT and had spent years on the faculty at the University of Chicago, saw clearly what made Northwestern unique. It was the first place he had ever worked "where you had to tell people how good they were. The last thing we wanted was to be just like the Ivy League," Weber said. "Our goal was to raise Northwestern's aspirations as a national university and to elevate its academic performance while retaining the strong values in its Midwestern roots."

Focus on the undergraduate

The importance of undergraduate education became a particular preoccupation of Weber's, and in 1987 history professor T. William Heyck was asked to head a new Task Force on the Undergraduate Experience. This turned out to be an ambitious and timely undertaking, partly inspired by a recent bestseller, *The Closing of the American Mind*, by the University of Chicago's Allan Bloom, in which Bloom argued that "relevance" had made tatters of a well-rounded college education.

While Heyck avoided the polemics of Bloom's book, his task force studied the undergraduate experience in great detail and proposed a wide range of specific recommendations on what a Northwestern education should include. Science and language requirements should be stiffened, the report said. Rigorous "junior tutorials" should be required to promote mastery in the undergraduate major; senior projects should demonstrate true achievement. The Heyck report generated enthusiasm in some quarters. Its proposals were adopted in many departments, and the deans of the undergraduate colleges – coaxed by the promise of additional financial resources – added several new interdisciplinary programs.

Jerome Cohen served as dean of the Robert R. McCormick School of Engineering and Applied Science from 1986 to 1999, during which time he oversaw a major renovation and expansion of the school. From the time he arrived at Northwestern in 1959 with a PhD in metallurgy, Cohen assumed a central role in the development of the materials science program, helping bring it to national prominence.

Dancers in 1980 dressed for comfort.

There are many theories about what keeps Dance Marathoners going for 30 hours. What really works, evidently, is taking a load off your feet when they feel like a pair of smoked hams.

DANCE MARATHON

Rarely does a university come together like Northwestern does for the biggest bash of the winter's end – Dance Marathon. One of the largest student-run charity events in the United States, Dance Marathon brings some 500 dancers and thousands of spectators to Norris University Center in a sometimes star-studded, completely exhausting, and always enriching 30-hour marathon on the dance floor.

It's a formula that raises nearly half a million dollars a year, with each dancer raising his or her entry fee, and the rest of the University paying to watch and enjoy a weekend's worth of entertainment.

Dance Marathon began in 1975, when Alpha Tau Omega fraternity filled Blomquist Gym with several local bands and a few female disc jockeys and convinced 21 couples to dance for 52 straight hours. Not all the marathoners made it, but the event raised an impressive $9,100 for charity.

Two years later, Dance Marathon was moved to Norris, raising $22,000 with a bigger venue and more dancers. A few years later, celebrity appearances added to the excitement – with Sha Na Na in 1981, Second City in 1984, model Cindy Crawford '88, who had briefly attended Northwestern, and Chicago Bears quarterback Mike Tomczak in 1990, among many others.

Always prominent at Dance Marathon is the beneficiary of the event – changing every year and ranging from Easter Seals to the Les Turner ALS Foundation to the Howard Brown Memorial AIDS Clinic. Dance Marathon gives a major boost to charity, and it does plenty for the participants as well. It's a grueling ordeal as the hours grind by, but that final hour, everyone claims, provides an exhilarating sense of commitment that endures for many years to come.

Contributions come from everywhere for Dance Marathon, one of the biggest student-organized charitable events in the country. Students pay to dance, and sponsors contribute money, food, and other services – all in the interests of keeping the 30-hour event going and raising half a million dollars for a charity each year.

Developments in engineering and medicine

While the Heyck report stressed undergraduate studies, other efforts were underway to strengthen the research side of University as well. This became especially important at the Technological Institute, where undergraduates had long enjoyed a high priority but where graduate students and leading-edge research were becoming increasingly important as well.

Opened in 1942 with the stated mission to train working engineers, Tech did not then encourage high-powered graduate students. But at Northwestern, as in other institutions, scientific inquiry could not be suppressed, and by the early 1960s, advanced work by a number of faculty members resulted in the development of two major new areas. In one, the Materials Research Center employed the combined efforts of science and engineering to develop a range of innovative materials, such as specialized polymers. In another interdisciplinary undertaking, engineering faculty and life scientists worked to create the Biomedical Research Center. These centers were meaningful to the University because they attracted infusions of federal money and because they moved engineering into exciting new fields.

Under Dean Jerome Cohen, Tech became a rising star among engineering schools in the 1980s, increasing its research endeavors significantly during that decade. Soon the most pressing problem became the need for new laboratories and more space. With cutting-edge research in progress, Tech had the stature to solve this problem with a $100 million-plus fundraising campaign. The successful campaign culminated in 1989 with a $30 million contribution from the McCormick Tribune Foundation, which resulted in the renaming of Tech as the Robert R. McCormick School of Engineering and Applied Science. The funds also provided the launching pad for a $125 million renovation of the Tech building, the largest project in the University's history, which was completed in 1999.

Joe Girardi '86 was an outstanding catcher who went on to a successful career with the Rockies, Cubs, and Yankees.

Todd Martin '92 was yet another Wildcat who brought Northwestern tennis to national prominence. Martin left school and turned pro in 1990, and by 1994 he was in the top ten in the world, making his mark in the late rounds of grand slam tournaments and advancing to the finals of the 1999 U.S. Open.

At the same time, the Medical School's growing interest in the laboratory was paying dividends. Long known as a school that produced first-rate physicians, the Medical School began to accelerate its research efforts as well. In 1990 the construction of the Tarry Research and Education Building, a large research facility in Chicago, aided its expanded mission to excel in research, as did the development of a substantial medical practice connected to the school to help support a first-rate clinical faculty.

The Bienen years commence

When Arnold Weber retired as president in 1995, he left the University in strong financial shape and with a growing academic reputation. Northwestern's faculty was highly regarded and among the best paid in the nation, and admissions were very selective. In searching for a new president, however, the trustees expressed no satisfaction with the status quo.

"We were looking for someone to take a successful university and move it to higher levels," said Patrick Ryan '59, a trustee and head of the presidential search committee. Their choice was Henry S. Bienen, who was dean of the Woodrow Wilson School of Public and International Affairs at Princeton.

Henry Bienen, who became Northwestern's 15th president in 1995, shared the trustees' ambition to elevate the University financially, academically, and athletically. A political scientist who had spent a portion of his career abroad, Bienen also focused on "raising the profile of the University internationally."

Crew at Northwestern goes back to 1981, when rowers organized themselves as a club. Self-aggrandizement meant little to these athletes, whose motto was "Sweet is pleasure after pain," a line of verse from John Dryden.

A distinguished political scientist and author of numerous books, Bienen had successfully crossed over into administration at Princeton. Northwestern's trustees believed Bienen's accomplishments as dean, plus his scholarly grasp of foreign policy and economic development issues, gave him an excellent background to master the infinitely complex task of governing Northwestern.

From the outset, Bienen was anything but complacent. In his inaugural address, he acknowledged Northwestern's deeply held traditions and its place among the finest universities of the land. But he also noted characteristics that impressed him even more – its "values of hard work and straightforwardness, and a striving for excellence."

A return to the Roses

In his first year as president, Bienen, along with thousands of Northwestern alumni and fans, enjoyed a "dream season" in football. The Wildcats stunned the Big Ten and surprised the entire country by winning the conference championship and going to the Rose Bowl for the first time in nearly 50 years. The ensuing national publicity, coupled with another Big Ten title the following year, highlighted not only Northwestern's return to football glory but also its insistence on recruiting scholar-athletes.

NO PARKING On The Dance Floor Feb. 7-8, 1986

The Gathering Place

1999

HAT @ N

SENIORS NU'85

Whatever Gets You Through The Night...

NU HOMECOMING 84

GO WILD Northwestern CATS

"CLICK" SYLLABUS 101

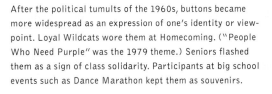

PWNP* NORTHWESTERN HOMECOMING 1979

M

After the political tumults of the 1960s, buttons became more widespread as an expression of one's identity or viewpoint. Loyal Wildcats wore them at Homecoming. ("People Who Need Purple" was the 1979 theme.) Seniors flashed them as a sign of class solidarity. Participants at big school events such as Dance Marathon kept them as souvenirs.

P.A.R.T.Y

NORTHWESTERN UNIVERSITY MAYFEST '92

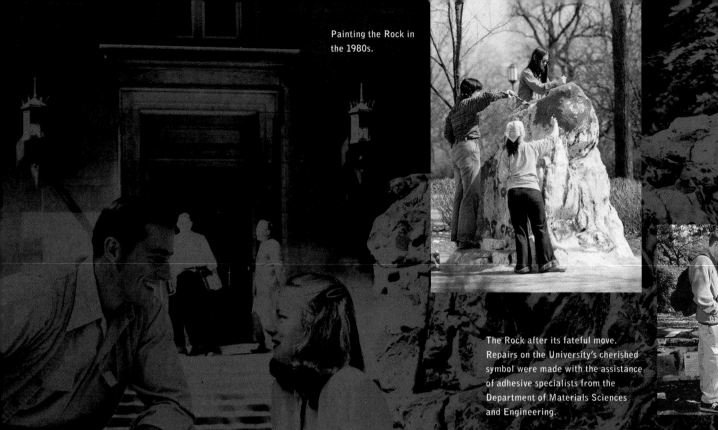

Painting the Rock in the 1980s.

The Rock after its fateful move. Repairs on the University's cherished symbol were made with the assistance of adhesive specialists from the Department of Materials Sciences and Engineering.

THE ROCK

It was once an attractive and even romantic landmark, a place where sorority women met lettermen, a hallowed icon that embodied the "spirit of alma mater." That was how the Class of 1902 envisioned it when they brought a six-foot-high quartzite boulder from Wisconsin and used it to create a drinking fountain and soothing oasis between Harris and University Halls.

In the 1940s, however, the Rock became a target for mild vandalism, as fraternity and sorority members made midnight visits and wantonly whitewashed the venerable symbol. Initially, the administration regarded such incidents as a sacrilege, but investigations and punishment were futile. By the 1950s, painting the Rock (by then its fountain was long defunct) became an accepted tradition.

The Rock witnessed other rebellions as well. In 1966 the Student Power movement began when undergraduate Ellis Pines '70 found a bullhorn and successfully campaigned by the Rock for Student Senate president. Over the years, protests of other kinds found their way to the old boulder, which lost its picturesque charm to much paint but retained its stalwart symbolism.

In 1989 the administration moved the Rock 30 feet to the east in an effort to keep people from tracking wet paint into nearby buildings. Unfortunately, the movers cracked the sacred stone, an embarrassment to the administration, which incurred the wrath of tradition-minded students. "The Rock was the one enduring symbol of student autonomy," said one. "And like the goddess of liberty in Tiananmen Square, the oppressive authorities chose to attack it."

The Rock was mortared back together — technical assistance in this matter came from the materials science and engineering departments — and it was none the worse for the wear, the administration declared. In any case, some things did not change. Students still paint it. Some faculty still think it's an eyesore. It's always hard to explain to outsiders. "It's a mystical sort of abstract presence on campus," said Patrick M. Quinn, University archivist, noting that its true meaning is as fluid as it is imprecise.

The Rock in 1947.

Sailing is a natural sport for Northwestern, and the Sailing Club grew to some 300 members in the 1970s, when it raced a fleet of six 12-foot Flying Juniors in Evanston, and a pair of 30-foot Shields Class racing sloops out of Monroe Harbor in Chicago.

Another opportunity to highlight Northwestern's excellence came when Bienen invited Diana, Princess of Wales, to visit Chicago and Evanston to open Northwestern's 1996 Symposium on Breast Cancer. This was a glittering event not just for Northwestern but for the city as well. Beyond the royal charm and news photos, Diana's visit brought valuable attention to The Robert H. Lurie Comprehensive Cancer Center. As never before, the festivities provided an opportunity to describe the spectrum of work, from cellular research to psychiatric counseling, in undertaking what was recognized as an enormous social objective.

While glamour was not viewed a substitute for knowledge, it could and often did support learning. While scholars seldom seek publicity, college presidents are less resistant to it, and Bienen seemed to have a knack for making sure that the glitter served scholarship and not vice versa.

"We want to use all this publicity," Bienen candidly told the *Chicago Tribune*. "The question is whether we can translate it into the long-run strength of the University."

Focusing resources

Northwestern was "a very good place that had the potential to be great," Bienen told the trustees. But to move ahead, it required resources, as education was an increasingly expensive investment. The board began discussing the usual methods for raising more money. A tuition hike was one; a large fundraising campaign was another.

It was a measure of Northwestern's ambition that it chose to embrace both methods. First came a sharp tuition hike to be used for improving undergraduate education. Then came fundraising, a subject not taken lightly by the trustees. While recent campaigns on behalf of specific schools – McCormick and Kellogg, for example – had been successful, a major University-wide effort had not been undertaken in two decades. Such a campaign would be ambitious and arduous: it would begin by asking each trustee to contribute to a nucleus fund, generating momentum that would then demand a major portion of the president's time.

New Year's Day 1996 in Pasadena, California.

Quarterback Steve Schnur '96 on the run as the Wildcats came back to take a short-lived fourth-quarter lead in the Rose Bowl.

Brian Musso '98, star wide receiver for the Rose Bowl Wildcats.

COMING UP ROSES

It had been almost a half century since the "Mildcats," as they were known in the 1980s, rose up and made it back to Pasadena. Then in 1995 Northwestern football took just about everyone by surprise — everyone except coach Gary Barnett and the team. In the season's first game, the Wildcats upset Notre Dame and took the win in such stride that fans wondered if the players had more surprises up their sleeves.

They did. After stumbling against Miami of Ohio, they rolled up wins — each game more exciting than the one before. At Ann Arbor, kicker Sam Valenzisi '95 hit four big field goals in the 'Cats' triumph at Michigan's Big House. In the Penn State game, running back Darnell Autry '98 scored three touchdowns in a win that lifted Northwestern to No. 5 nationally in the A.P. poll.

Winning football changed the tone of campus life. Cars sprouted purple flags all over the North Shore. Admissions applications jumped. Even fundraising was a bit easier that year. After the Wildcats finished 10–1 and Michigan beat Ohio State, Northwestern won the Big Ten title, and there was dancing in the streets of Evanston.

The Wildcats got off to a slow start in the Rose Bowl game against the University of Southern California. Regrouping at halftime, they came back strong in the third and fourth quarters. Unfortunately, late turnovers did Northwestern in. But the score, 41–32, was a good indication of the kind of game it was — fast-paced and exciting till the end.

A win in the Rose Bowl would have been a nice cap to a great season, said Coach Barnett. But the long-term effect was more important. A second Big Ten championship followed the next year along with a trip to the Citrus Bowl.

259

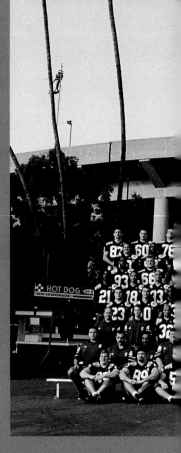

The 1995 Wildcats had a regular season record of 10–1. "Expect Victory" was their understated war cry.

Commemorative Edition

The Daily Northwestern

Friday, January 5, 1996

ROSES
A year to remember

Forty seven years after their last Rose Bowl game,
the Wildcats step into history again
on the heels of an astounding season.

Few football venues are so fabled as the Rose Bowl, and few games
have been so memorable as the Wildcats in 1996.

82nd Rose Bowl Game

$10.00

USC VS. NORTHWESTERN
January 1 1996 Pasadena California
1996 Official Souvenir Rose Bowl Game® Program

The 1996 Rose Bowl between Northwestern and the University of Southern California took place in the 50th year of the Big Ten and Pac Ten's pairing as New Year's Day rivals.

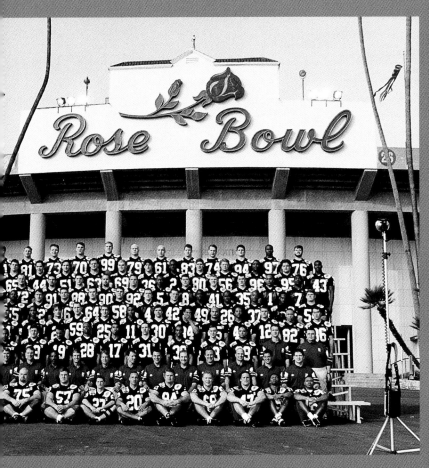

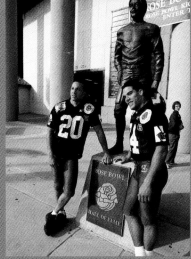

Running back Darnell Autry and free safety William Bennett '96 enjoy the attention and adulation of pregame media coverage.

After tying for the Big Ten title in 1996, the 9–2 Wildcats went to the Citrus Bowl in Orlando, Florida. They had a tough day against Peyton Manning and the Tennessee Volunteers, who won 48–28.

It seemed like a fantasy – the marching band entertained and the team was entertained at Disneyland before the big game.

Coach Gary Barnett with team members at Disneyland.

With little dissent, the board approved Campaign Northwestern with the formidable goal of $1 billion. Such a figure was not unprecedented in academic circles, but it required unity throughout an institution that sometimes seemed lacking an overarching vision. Yet such a vision was key to the success of the campaign, and to capture it the University turned to the early ambition of its founders. Evans, Lunt, Goodrich, and the others desired a university of "the highest order of excellence complete in all its parts." These words still resonated almost 150 years later and set a convincing tone for the campaign, which rapidly proved successful. Among the early gifts was one from an alumnus for a staggering $56.5 million for unrestricted purposes as well as a significant gift from the Weinberg family that resulted in the naming of the College of Arts and Sciences for Judd A. and Marjorie Weinberg. By the start of the year 2000, three years before Campaign Northwestern was scheduled to end, nearly $900 million had been raised, and the administration was ready to increase the goal.

While fundraising emphasized Northwestern's lofty objectives, a university with visions of the highest order required an assessment of its weaknesses as well as its strengths. Early on, for example, Bienen noted that Northwestern continued to lose many of its best faculty and strongest students to other institutions, primarily Stanford and those in the Ivy League. Fixing this problem was an imprecise science, he indicated, but increased resources were crucial.

At the same time, University leaders felt the need to focus resources on those areas where Northwestern best could provide an education of distinction. As a result, in 1997 the University decided to close the Dental School, after the Class of 2001 graduated. That decision was painful one, but it reinforced the administration's determination to use resources wisely.

Intangible assets

"Our most important qualities are that we are an unusually diverse and highly collaborative institution," said Lawrence Dumas in 1999, several years after assuming the office of provost, the chief academic officer of the University.

Dumas's description was characteristically straightforward. Nevertheless, it meant that Northwestern was staking its reputation on a "compulsively interdisciplinary approach and an unusually broad base of enterprise," as he put it.

This emphasis on interdisciplinary research and teaching was seen in many of the expected places. The Department of Materials Science and Engineering, for example, maintained its cutting-edge reputation by developing a range of materials of molecular precision designed for surgery and bioengineering. Materials science advanced on the classic path to excellence at Northwestern, crossing disciplines, encouraging direct involvement of industry, and actively seeking new problems to solve.

In less typical places the interdisciplinary approach also showed remarkable results. Northwestern's research on capital punishment, for example, represented not only a steadfast commitment to social justice but a meaningful collaboration between the law and journalism schools as well. Initially, the work of the Legal Clinic and law school professor Larry Marshall (JL '85) resulted in the freeing of a number of death row prisoners. Later came an investigative journalism course for undergraduates taught by Medill professor David Protess, in which students pursued a number of specific cases where a verdict and subsequent death sentence appeared to merit a second look, at the very least.

The most dramatic outcome of this endeavor came in 1999 with the case of Anthony Porter, an inmate who had been on death row for 17 years for a 1982 double murder committed on Chicago's South Side.

The students investigating the Porter case were assiduous and painstaking. By interviewing people connected to the case, the class eventually uncovered proof that another person committed the crime. Porter's conviction was reversed, and the case made four Northwestern undergraduates among the most celebrated capital-punishment opponents in America. A year later this work of the law and journalism schools led to a moratorium on executions in Illinois, the first state in the nation to take such action.

Yet another example of academic enterprise was the creation of the Northwestern University Institute for Neuroscience in 1989. For decades, life sciences had been studying the incalculably complex area of the nervous system and the brain. The institute formalized what had been taking place on a more informal basis – the sharing of results among individuals from a diversity of disciplines.

In 1996 the investigative journalism class of Professor David Protess had a major success in getting the "Ford Heights Four" freed after many years in prison (two of them were on death row) for a murder they did not commit. Three Medill undergraduates did the bulk of the legwork on a case that was clinched with DNA testing. In 1999 another death row inmate, Anthony Porter, was released due to the work of students in the Medill course.

One breakthrough connected to the Institute for Neuroscience was the discovery in 1997 that the "circadian clock," the internal regulator of life's daily rhythms, is governed by a single identifiable gene. On a more clinical level, the Northwestern Alzheimer's Disease Center was created in 1996, enlisting not only physicians but also basic scientists to study multiple aspects of this disease, including the relationships between physiology and cognition. The institute also drew in computer scientists from the McCormick School of Engineering and Applied Science, who work on prostheses that will function in close interaction with the nervous system.

Similar developments occurred as the result of the work of researchers associated with The Robert H. Lurie Comprehensive Cancer Center, the Feinberg Clinical Neuroscience Research Institute, and the Feinberg Cardiovascular Research Institute.

The power of random collisions

More informally, the spirit of interdisciplinary scholarship inspired another development in the late '90s: "domain dinners." These dinners featured speakers, occasionally from outside the University, and attracted a cross-section of faculty members to broad subjects of current interest. Intellectual "domains" were established in areas such as communications and "management and policy studies." The dinners encouraged good-natured and sometimes pointed conversation on subjects that tended to the speculative. A scientist at a performing and creative arts dinner, for example, was gleefully derided when he complained that artists, unlike scientists, lacked a standard for "truth."

Through such discourse, the University sought to create "random collisions," as Provost Lawrence Dumas called them, that might lead to new ideas. A collision might occur between a biochemist and a psychologist who could share insights on Alzheimer's disease. Or a philosopher and an economist might find a new approach to the issues of social inequality.

Journalist Garry Wills was appointed Henry Luce Professor of American Culture and Public Policy in 1980. The College of Arts and Sciences was then building a more interdisciplinary faculty, and Wills had written on Nixon and Jefferson by then and had books on Lincoln, Reagan, John Wayne, and St. Augustine still to come.

A role in the world

Another of Northwestern's longtime strengths was its engagement with the outside world. This spirit frequently directed academic programs, but it sometimes activated students almost spontaneously. One such instance occurred in 1996 with "alternative spring break" – an opportunity to volunteer in social work and community development projects around the country. It was created, said organizer Rob Donahue '97, as "a substance-free alternative" to wild spring break vacations.

But crossing the borders of Evanston was not always easy. In one early project to help rebuild an African American church in Alabama after an arson fire, a dozen white Northwestern students were initially downhearted by the enormity of the crime they were trying to redress. "Burning someone's church is like trying to destroy their faith," Donahue said. But eventually the students helped build a roof in one week's time, and they left with new understandings that would last a lifetime.

The highest order of excellence

At the start of the 21st century, Northwestern University's goals are as ambitious as of those of its founders 150 years ago. What Northwestern exhibited then and continues to demonstrate with vigor is a determination to strive for ever higher levels of excellence. Breaking down walls of perception, refining new ideas to make them useful – these are abilities that cannot be legislated or superimposed. But at Northwestern they are core values and in many ways are a legacy of the founders who imagined a great university before they had enrolled even a single student.

Even today, amid the successes of the past 25 years, Northwestern expresses a healthy dissatisfaction with the status quo that is not so different in quality from the eagerness of its founders for change, innovation, and the realization of greater destiny. President Bienen, in his State of the University address in 2000, stated those goals clearly.

"As we reflect upon Northwestern's remarkable heritage, we now enter the 21st century renewed in our purpose of making the University an institution of the 'highest order of excellence,' not just for the 'Northwest Territory,' but for the entire world. It is the entire world we want to reach, influence, and contribute to with our vitality and creativity."

Charter

An Act To Incorporate The Northwestern University
Approved January 28, 1851

Section I

Be it enacted by the people of the State of Illinois, represented in the General Assembly: That Richard Henry, Philo Judson, S. P. Keys, and A. E. Phelps, and such persons as shall be appointed by the Rock River Annual Conference of the Methodist Episcopal Church to succeed them in said office; Henry Summers, Elihu Springer, David Brooks, and Elmore Yocum, and such persons as shall be appointed by the Wisconsin Annual Conference of said church to succeed them; four individuals, if chosen, and such persons as shall be appointed to succeed them by the Michigan Annual Conference of said church; four individuals, if chosen, and such persons as shall be appointed to succeed them by the North Indiana Annual Conference of said Church; H. W. Reed, I. I. Steward, D. N. Smith, and George M. Geas, and such persons as shall be appointed to succeed them by the Iowa Annual Conference of said church; four individuals, if chosen, and such persons as shall be appointed to succeed them by the Illinois Annual Conference of said church; A. S. Sherman, Grant Goodrich, Andrew J. Brown, John Evans, Orrington Lunt, J. K. Botsford, Joseph Kitterstring, George F. Foster, Eri Reynolds, John M. Arnold, Absalom Funk, and E. B. Kingsley, and such persons, citizens of Chicago or its vicinity, as shall be appointed by the Board of Trustees hereby constituted to succeed them, be, and they are hereby, created and constituted a body politic and corporate, under the name and style of the *Trustees of the Northwestern University*, and henceforth shall be styled and known by that name, and by that name and style to remain and have perpetual succession, with power to sue and be sued, plead and be impleaded, to acquire, hold and convey property, real, personal, or mixed, in all lawful ways, to have and use a common seal, and to alter the same at pleasure, to make and alter from time to time such by-laws as they may deem necessary for the government of said institution, its officers and servants, provided such by-laws are not inconsistent with the constitution and laws of this State and of the United States, and to confer on such persons as may be considered worthy of such academical or honorary degrees as are usually conferred by similar institutions.

Section II

The term of the office of said Trustees shall be four years, but that of one member of the Board for each conference enjoying the appointing power by this act, and [the] term of three of the members whose successors are to be appointed by the Board hereby constituted, shall expire annually, the term of each member of the Board herein named to be fixed by lot at the first meeting of said Board, which Board shall, in manner above specified have perpetual succession, and shall hold the property of said institution solely for the purposes of education, and not as a stock for the individual benefit of themselves or any contributor to the endowment of the same; and no particular religious faith shall be required of those who become students of the institution. Nine members shall constitute a quorum for the transaction of any business of the Board, except the appointment of President or Professor, or the establishment of chairs in said institution, and the enactment of by-laws for its government, for which the presence of a majority of the Board shall be necessary.

Section III

Said annual conferences of the Methodist Episcopal Church, under whose control and patronage said university is placed, shall each also have the right to appoint annually two suitable persons, members of their own body, visitors to said university, who shall attend the examination of students, and be entitled to participate in the deliberations of the Board of Trustees and enjoy all the privileges of the members of said board except the right to vote.

Section IV

Said institution shall remain located in or near the City of Chicago, Cook County, and the corporators and their successors shall be competent in law or equity to take to themselves, in their said corporate name, real, personal, or mixed estate, by gift, grant, bargain and sale, conveyance, will, devise or bequest of any person or persons whomsoever and the same estate, whether real, personal, or mixed, to grant, bargain, sell, convey, devise, let, place out at interest, or otherwise dispose of the same for the use of said institution in such manner as to them shall seem most beneficial to said institution. Said corporation shall faithfully apply all the funds collected or the proceeds of the property belongings to the said institution, according to their best judgement, in erecting and completing suitable buildings, supporting necessary officers, instructors, and servants, and procuring books, maps, charts, globes, and philosophical, chemical, and other apparatus necessary to the success of the institution, and do all other acts usually performed by similar institutions, that may be deemed necessary or useful to the success of said institution, under the restrictions, herein imposed: Provided, nevertheless, that in case any donation, devise, or bequest shall be made for particular purposes accordant with the design of the institution, and the corporation shall accept the same, every such donation, devise, or bequest shall be applied in conformity with express conditions of the donor or devisor: Provided further, that said corporation shall not be allowed to hold more than two thousand acres of land at any one time unless the said corporation shall have received the same gift, grant, or devise; and in such case they shall be required to sell or dispose of the same within ten years from the time they shall acquire such title; and by failure to do so, such land over and above the beforenamed two thousand acres, shall revert to the original donor, grantor, devisor, or their heirs.

Section V

The treasurer of the institution and all other agents when required, before entering upon the duties of their appointment, shall give bond for the security of the corporation in such penal sums, and with such securities as the corporation shall approve, and all process against the corporation shall be by summons, and the service of the same shall be by leaving an attested copy thereof with the treasurer at least sixty days before the return day thereof.

Section VI

The corporation shall have power to employ and appoint a President or Principal for said institution, and all such professors or teachers, and all such servants as may be necessary, and shall have power to displace any or such of them, as the interest of the institution may require, to fill vacancies which may happen, by death, resignation, or otherwise, among said officers and servants, and to prescribe and direct the course of studies to be pursued in said institution.

Section VII

The corporation shall have power to establish departments for the study of any and all the learned and liberal professions in the same; to confer the degree of doctor in the learned arts and sciences and belles-lettres, and to confer such other academical degrees as are usually conferred by the most learned institutions.

Section VIII

Said corporation shall have power to institute a board of competent persons, always including the faculty, who shall examine such individuals as may apply, and if such applicants are found to possess such knowledge pursued in said institution, as in the judgement of said board renders them worthy, they may be considered graduates in course, and shall be entitled to diplomas according on paying such fee as the corporation shall affix, which fee, however, shall in no case exceed the tuition bills of the full course of studies in said institution; said examination board may not exceed the number of ten, three of whom may transact business, provided one be of the faculty.

Section IX

Should the corporation at any time act contrary to the provisions of this charter, or fail to comply with the same, upon complaint being made to the Circuit Court of Cook County, a *scire facias* shall issue, and the circuit attorney shall prosecute in behalf of the People of this State for forfeiture of this charter. This act shall be a public act, and shall be construed liberally in all courts, for the purposes herein expressed.

Sydney Breese,
*Speaker of
the House of
Representatives*

William McMurtey,
*Speaker of the
Senate*

*Approved
January 28, 1851,*
A. C. French,
Governor

*Attest: A true copy,
March 22, 1851,*
David L. Gregg,
Secretary of State

First Amendment

An Act To Amend An Act Entitled "An Act To Incorporate The Northwestern University"
Approved February 14, 1855

Section I

Be it enacted by the People of the State of Illinois, represented in the General Assembly:
That John L. Smith, Aaron Wood, Luther Taylor, and Wm. Graham, and such persons as shall be elected to succeed them by the Northwestern Indiana Conference of the Methodist Episcopal Church, be, and they are hereby, constituted members of the Board of Trustees of the Northwestern University.

Section II

No spirituous, vinous, or fermented liquors shall be sold under license, or otherwise, within four miles of the location of said University, except for medicinal, mechanical, or sacramental purposes, under a penalty of twenty-five dollars for each offense, to be recovered before any Justice of the Peace of said County in an action of debt in the name of the County of Cook: Provided, that so much of this act as relates to the sale of intoxicating drinks within four miles, may be repealed by the General Assembly whenever they may think proper.

Section III

The said corporation shall have power to take, hold, use and manage, lease and dispose of all such property, as may in any manner come to said corporation charged with any trust or trusts, in conformity with trusts and direction, and so execute all such trusts as may be confided to it.

Section IV

That all property of whatever kind or description, belonging to or owned by said corporation, shall be forever free from taxation for any and all purposes.

Section V

This act shall be a public act, and take effect from and after its passage.

Thomas P. Turner,
Speaker of the
House of
Representatives

G. Koerner, *Speaker*
of the Senate

Approved
Feb. 14th, 1855,
J. A. Matteson,
Governor

United States of
America, State of
Illinois

I, Alexander Stearm, Secretary of State for the State of Illinois, do hereby certify that the foregoing is a true and correct copy of an Enrolled Law now on file at my office.

In testimony whereof, I have hereunto set my hand and caused the great seal of State to be affixed. Done at the City of Springfield, at this 21st day of March 1855.

Alexander Stearm,
Secretary of State

Second Amendment

An Act To Amend An Act Entitled "An Act To Incorporate The Northwestern University"
Approved February 16, 1861

Section I

Be in enacted by the People of the State of Illinois, represented in the General Assembly: That the annual conferences of the Methodist Episcopal Church, which now are or may hereafter be authorized to elect or appoint Trustees of said University, shall hereafter elect only two Trustees each, who shall also be and perform the duties of the visitors to said institution, and the place of the two Trustees last appointed by each conference is hereby vacated. The trustees elected by such conferences shall hereafter hold their office for two years, and until their successors are chosen, the term of one elected by each of them expiring annually. In case any conference having authority to elect Trustees shall now or hereafter be divided into two or more annual conferences, they shall have authority to elect Trustees. On the request of the Board of Trustees made at a regular meeting, any such annual conference may elect Trustees as herein provided.

Section II

Any annual conference electing Trustees as herein provided, having at any time refused to elect successors thereto, or resolved to discontinue or refuse its patronage to said institution, shall authorize the Board of Trustees, by a vote of a majority thereof at any regular meeting, to declare vacant the place of all Trustees appointed by such conference, and its right to appoint Trustees shall thereupon cease.

Section III

Any chartered institution of learning may become a department of this University by agreement between the Board of Trustees of the two institutions.

Section IV

This act shall take effect and be in force from and after its passage.

Shelby M. Cullom,
Speaker of the
House of
Representatives

Francis A. Hoffman,
Speaker of the
Senate

Approved Feb. 16th,
1861, Richard Yates,
Governor

A true copy-Attest:
Feb. 16th, 1861,
O. M. Hatch,
Secretary of State

Third Amendment

An Act To Amend An Act Entitled "An Act To Incorporate The Northwestern University"
and The Several Acts Amendatory Thereof
Approved February 19, 1867

Section I

Be it enacted by the People of the State of Illinois, represented in the General Assembly: That the name of that corporation created by act of the General Assembly of the State of Illinois, approved on the 28th day of January, A. D. 1851, under the name of the "Trustees of the Northwestern University," be, and the same is, hereby changed to "Northwestern University," and by that name shall hereafter be known, and in and by such name shall have and exercise all the powers and immunities conferred on said corporation by said act of incorporation, and all acts amendatory thereof.

Section II

In addition to the number of Trustees heretofore provided for by law, the Board may elect any number, not exceeding twenty-four, and without reference to their several places of residence; and a majority of the whole Board shall be members of the Methodist Episcopal Church.

Section III

No greater number shall be required to constitute a quorum than has been heretofore required by law; *Provided,* that in all called meetings of the Board, the object of the meeting shall be particularly specified in the notice to be previously given to each Trustee.

Section IV

This act shall be a public act, and in force from and after its passage.

F. Corwin, *Speaker of the House of Representatives*

William Breese, *Speaker of the Senate*

Approved Feb. 19, 1867, P. J. Oglesby, *Governor*

A true copy-Attest: February 23, 1867, Sharon Tyndale, *Secretary of State*

Northwestern University Presidents

Clark T. Hinman, DD
1853–54

Henry S. Noyes, MA
1854–56+

Randolph S. Foster, DD, LLD
1856–60

Henry S. Noyes, MA
1860–67+

David H. Wheeler, DD
1867–69+

Erastus O. Haven, DD, LLD
1869–72

Charles H. Fowler, DD, LLD
1872–76

Oliver Marcy, LLD
1876–81+

Joseph Cummings, DD, LLD
1881–90

Henry Wade Rogers, LLD
1890–1900

Daniel Bonbright, MA, LLD
1900–02+

Edmund J. James, PhD, LLD
1902–04

Thomas F. Holgate, PhD, LLD
1904–06+

Abram W. Harris, ScD, LLD
1906–16

Thomas F. Holgate, PhD, LLD
1916–19+

Lynn H. Hough, DD
1919–20

Walter Dill Scott, PhD, LLD
1920–39

Franklyn Bliss Snyder, PhD, LLD
1939–49

J. Roscoe Miller, MD, LLD, ScD
1949–70

Robert H. Strotz, PhD, LLD
1970–84

Arnold R. Weber, PhD
1984–94

Henry S. Bienen, PhD
1995–

+ Interim

Bibliography

About the Northwestern University Archives

This history is largely based upon and grounded in the rich treasure-trove that constitutes the holdings of the Northwestern University Archives. The archives' holdings include over 20,000 cubic feet of records, papers, publications, photographs, and audio-visual materials with enduring value that greatly amplify and illuminate the history of the University. Especially valuable in researching and writing this history were the records of Northwestern's presidents and of other administrators, the personal papers of distinguished faculty members, thousands of serial publications issued by the University over the years, faculty biographical files, and general files relating to each college, school, department, or other unit of the University, including buildings past and present. The photographs that appear in this history were selected from the University Archives' photographic collection, which includes over 600,000 images of individuals, buildings, events, and organizations.

Further reading

Arey, Leslie B. *Northwestern University Medical School, 1859–1979.* Evanston and Chicago: Northwestern University, 1979.

Dummett, Clifton O., and Lois Doyle Dummett. *Culture and Education in Dentistry at Northwestern University, 1891–1993.* [Chicago]: Northwestern University Dental School, 1993.

Fine, Morris E., ed. *Tech, The Early Years: An Anthology of the History of the Technological Institute at Northwestern University from 1939 to 1969.* Evanston: McCormick School of Engineering and Applied Science, Northwestern University, [1995].

Morledge, Kirk W. *To the Memories: A History of the Northwestern University Waa-Mu Show, 1929–1980.* Evanston: Northwestern University, 1980.

Paulison, Walter. *The Tale of the Wildcats: A Centennial History of Northwestern University Athletics.* [Evanston]: N Men's Club, Northwestern University Club of Chicago, Northwestern University Alumni Association, 1951.

A Pictorial History of Northwestern University, 1851–1951. Evanston/Chicago: Northwestern University Press and Northwestern University *Syllabus,* 1951.

Rahl, James A., and Kurt Schwerin. *Northwestern University School of Law – A Short History.* Chicago: Northwestern University School of Law, 1960.

Rein, Lynn Miller. *Northwestern University School of Speech: A History.* [Evanston]: Northwestern University, 1981.

Sedlak, Michael W., and Harold F. Williamson. *The Evolution of Management Education: A History of the Northwestern University J. L. Kellogg Graduate School of Management, 1908–1983.* Urbana: University of Illinois Press for Northwestern University, 1983.

Snyder, Alice W. *Inventing Medill: A History of the Medill School of Journalism, Northwestern University, 1921–1996.* Evanston: Northwestern University, 1996.

Ward, Estelle Frances. *The Story of Northwestern University.* New York: Dodd, Mead & Co., 1924.

Wilde, Arthur H., ed. *Northwestern University: A History, 1855–1905.* 4 vols. New York: The University Publishing Society, 1905.

Williamson, Harold F., and Payson S. Wild. *Northwestern University: A History, 1850–1975.* Evanston: Northwestern University, 1976.

Acknowledgments

A book such as this by necessity requires the contribution of many individuals in its creation. Special thanks are due to Northwestern University President Henry S. Bienen for his support of this project and of the sesquicentennial celebration.

In undertaking this project, we are very much aware of the work of University Archivist Patrick M. Quinn, who, for more than 25 years, has built and governed the archives. It is to this vast and impressive collection that we turned for the bulk of the research and illustrations that were used in this book. Kevin Leonard, Janet Olson, and Allen Streicker of the archives staff were unfailing in their commitment and enthusiasm for this project. Thanks also to their colleagues Matthew Cook of the Chicago Historical Society and Eden Juron Perlman of the Evanston Historical Society.

For two years the Northwestern sesquicentennial steering committee of Margo Brown, Susan Israel, John Margolis, Victor Rosenblum, Sheppard Shanley, Catherine Stembridge, Lisa Swanson, Jeremy Wilson, Patrick Quinn, and David Zarefsky has taken an active interest and provided important guidance in the content and design of this book.

Thanks also to the faculty members, some for their thoughtful interviews and others for their insightful observations, who contributed so much to the story: William Brazelton, the late Jerome Cohen, Leonard Evens, John Franks, Daniel Garrison, Hugo Gregory, Harrison Hayford, T. William Heyck, Kenneth Janda, Richard Leopold, Judith Levi, Laszlo Lorand, Melissa MacAuley, Raymond Mack, Emanuel Margoliash, John McLane, Dominic Missimi, Enrico Mugnaini, Dawn Clark Netsch, David Protess, David Rutherford, Frank Safford, Neena Schwartz, Clarence Ver Steeg, Andrew Wachtel, and James Webster.

Many others on the Northwestern campuses have assisted in research, locating, and in some cases providing illustrations, proofreading, and the myriad other important details that have made this book come to life: Kimberly Maselli and Nick Weir-Williams of Northwestern University Press; Elizabeth Crown, Marianne Goss, Stephanie Russell, and Patty Dowd Schmitz of the Department of University Relations; Bradford D. Hurlbut, Ken Kraft, and Jean W. Yale of the athletic department; Thom Duncan of the Kellogg Graduate School of Management; and Virginia Albaneso, Karen Campbell, Michael Connor, Steve Nafziger, and Tian Yin Qin, in the sesquicentennial office.

Trustees Lester Crown, Newton Minow, and Howard Trienens, and University staff and administration members David Easterbrook, Bruce Foster, Bonnie Humphrey, Bruce Kaiser, Chuck Loebbaka, Nancy Lyons, John Margolis, Marilyn McCoy, Joe Mroczkowski, Morteza Rahimi, Alice Snyder, Douglas Troutman, Ron Vanden Dorpel, Arnold Weber, and Jeremy Wilson all made contributions for which we are indebted.

In addition to the alumni already mentioned, we are grateful to Steven Albini, Shawn Armbrust, Larry Atkin, Robert J. Donahue, John R. Eshbach, Helen Sullivan Knight, Robert Leighton, Danielle Lodewyck, Rush Pearson, Robert J. Reichner, Jeffrey Rice, James D. Vail III, and Robert Yap for their respective roles in bringing this book to publication.

Finally, I would like to thank Alan K. Cubbage (MSJ '78, MSA '87), vice president for university relations, for his leadership and steadfast commitment to the sesquicentennial celebration.

Monica M. Metzler '86
Sesquicentennial Director

Aerial view of Northwestern's campus in 1907.

Index

Photo Credits

Note to the reader

Unless otherwise noted, all photographs, objects, and ephemera pictured in this book are from the Northwestern University Archives. Wherever possible photographs have been credited to the original photographers, regardless of the source of the photograph.

Copy photography and original photographs of three-dimensional objects by Professional Graphics, Rockford, Illinois.

Chapter 1

Pages 10 photo by Alexander Hesler; 12–13 (map) Chicago Historical Society ICHi 05654; 12 (Evans) Colorado Historical Society, (church) Chicago Historical Society ICHi 30638; 14 (background) Chicago Historical Society ICHi 14169; 15 (Lunt) photo by Chas. E. Smith; 16 (ad) Chicago Historical Society ICHi 30639; 18 courtesy of Albion College Archives; 22 (Foster) photo by Alexander Hesler; 26 (Noyes) photo by Chas. E. Smith; 28 photo by Alexander Hesler; 29 (background) Chicago Historical Society; 30 (couple) Evanston Historical Society, (Dempster house) Evanston Historical Society, (sleigh) Evanston Historical Society; 31 Evanston Historical Society; 32 (Round House) Evanston Historical Society; 33 Evanston Historical Society; 34 (aerial and University Hall) photos by Alexander Hesler.

Chapter 2

Pages 36 photo by Fowler; 40 photo by Alexander Hesler; 42–43 (background) photo by Alexander Hesler; 45 (background) photo by Fowler; 46 photo by Chas. E. Smith; 47 (Kennicott) photo by Eugene L. Ray; 54 *Harper's Weekly*, courtesy of Al Cubbage; 55 photo by Fowler; 60 (Class of 1880) photo by Alexander Hesler.

Chapter 3

Pages 62 photo by Fowler; 64 (Deering) photo by Smith's Photo Studio; 65 photo by Fowler; 70 (Landis) Graystone Studios; 73 (Woman's Medical School) photo by C. Tuegel; 76 photo by Fowler; 77 (music students) photo by Smith's Photo Studio, (Mandolin Club) photo by Chas. E. Smith; 79 photo by Chas. Aikin; 82 (Rogers) photo by Eugene L. Ray; 84 (tennis) *Syllabus* photo; 86 (Atchison) photo by Chas. Aikin, (Bartelme) *Townsfolk* magazine; 87 (Robinson) photo by C. A. Redington; 88 *Syllabus* photo.

Chapter 4

Pages 90 photo by Eugene L. Ray; 95 photo by Copelin & Son; 97 (football team) *Syllabus* photo; 101 (Wigmore) photo by Chas. E. Smith; 109 (Swift Hall) photo by Eugene L. Ray, (Heck Hall) photo by Evanston Photographic Service; 111 (Andersen) photo by Andrew Hurter; 114–15 photo by Fowler; 116 The Acinegraph Company, courtesy of Robert J. Reichner; 117 (Old College) S. H. Knox & Company, courtesy of Robert J. Reichner, (Heck Hall) C. R. Childs, courtesy of Robert J. Reichner, (Garrett) E. C. Kropp Company, courtesy of Robert J. Reichner.

Chapter 5

Pages 120–21 photo by Eugene L. Ray; 122 (gym) photo by F. P. Burke; 124 (Bauer) courtesy of Dorothy Bauer Erland, from *Northwestern Perspective*, (Breyer) photo by Eugene L. Ray, (Howell) photo by Eugene L. Ray, (Droegemueller) photo by Eugene L. Ray, (Robinson) courtesy of Betty Robinson Schwartz, from *Northwestern Perspective*; 125 (Kelly) courtesy of *Northwestern Perspective*; 126 (team) photo by J. D. Toloff; 130 (gate) photo by Capes Photo; 130–31 (background) photo by Chicago Architectural Photographing Company; 132–33 (background) photo by Capes Photo; 132 (Rogers) photo by Kaiden-Keystone Photos; 133 (Thorne Hall) photo by Capes Photo; 139 (Tau Delta Phi) photo by John D. Jones; 141 (construction and circulation desk) photos by Chicago Architectural Photographing Company; 144 (background) photo by John D. Jones; 145 photo by Eugene L. Ray; 147 Students Publishing Company; 148 (convention) photo by John D. Jones; 152 (Miller) Students Publishing Company, (1936 and 1941) photos by Paul Stone Raymor; 153 (1956, 1969, and 1960) photos by Evanston Photographic Service.

Chapter 6

Pages 154–55 Chicago Architectural Photographing Company; 157 (celebration) Students Publishing Company; 158 photos by Chicago Architectural Photographing Company; 160 Chicago Architectural Photographing Company; 161 (background) Chicago Architectural Photographing Company, (postcard) Lake County Museum, Curt Teich Postcard Archives; 164 (blood bank) photo by Kaufman and Fabry Company; 164–65 (Quonset huts) photo by Evanston Photographic Service; 165 (housing) The Steelcraft Mfg. Co., (cadets) U.S. Navy Official Photographs; 167 (classroom) photo by Evanston Photographic Service, (Wieboldt) photo by Carl Ullrich; 172–73 photos by Jim Bixby; 175 (voice and diction) photo by Hansel Mieth; 184 (team) courtesy of Santa Fe Railway; 185 (rally) photo by Ted Fredstrom.

Chapter 7

Pages 186–87 photo by Jackie Kalmes Photos; 191 (homecoming) photo by Evanston Photographic Service; 192–93 (background) photo by J. D. Toloff; 192 (lower) Students Publishing Company; 194–95 (background) photo by Jonathan Strauch; 194 (Delta Sigma Theta) photo by Evanston Photographic Service; 197 (coaches) photo by Evanston Photographic Service; 198 (McGaw exterior) photo by Chicago Architectural Photographing Company, (McGaw interior) Evanston Photographic Service; 202 (Allison) photo by Herb Comess; 203 (lower) photo by Boschke Photo; 205 (team) photo by Evanston Photographic Service; 211 photo by Vories Fisher; 215 (center) photo by Robert M. Lightfoot III, (lower right) Students Publishing Company, (lower left) photo by Evanston Photographic Service; 216 photo by Craig Weil; 218 (Jefferson) photo by Bob Hinshaw; 220 (protest) photo by Paul Rumage, Students Publishing Company; 221 (CIA) photo by Matt Eggemeyer; 224 (typing) photo by Robert M. Lightfoot III, (Medill class) photo by James Marchael, (Mikva) photo by Uldis Saule.

Chapter 8

Pages 226–27 courtesy of Perkins & Will; 229 photo by Uldis Saule; 233 photo by Mitchell Jordan; 234 (background) photo by Herb Comess; 236–37 (background) photo by Chromewerks; 236 photo by Jon Saunders; 237 (Pick-Staiger) © Diane Schmidt; 237 (Annenberg) photo by Dewey Hentges; 239 (Kellogg) © 2000 by Loren Santow, (Eisner) photo by Jim Ziv; 240–41 photo by Herb Comess; 242 (cross country) photo by Ralf-Finn Hestof, Students Publishing Company, (tennis) photo by Jonathan Daniel, NU Athletic Media Services, (field hockey) Students Publishing Company; 243 (swimming), NU Athletic Media Services, (volleyball) NU Athletic Media Services, (softball) NU Athletic Media Services; 244 photo by Bill Smith, courtesy of NU Athletic Media Services; 245 (Levy Mayer Hall) © Diane Schmidt; 246 (protest) photo by Rick Phillips, Students Publishing Company; 247 (frisbee) art by Craig Havighurst, (aerial) photo by David H. Schulman, Students Publishing Company, (sculpture) photo by Alex Garcia, Students Publishing Company; 248 (sundae) photo by Bonnie Eiffes, (WNUR) Students Publishing Company, (Special Olympics) Students Publishing Company; 249 (frisbee) photo by Lindsey Stephens, Students Publishing Company, (football) photo by Jonathan Kay, Students Publishing Company; 250 photo by Jim Ziv; 251 (background) photo by Matthew Savard, Students Publishing Company, (couple) Students Publishing Company, (resting) photo by Andrew Campbell for *Northwestern* magazine; 252 (baseball) NU Athletic Media Services, (tennis) photo by Scott Phillips, Students Publishing Company, (crew) Students Publishing Company; 253 photo by Paul Meredith, for *Northwestern* magazine; 254–55 (buttons) courtesy of Monica Metzler and Northwestern University Archives; 256 (background) photo by Chicago Architectural Photographing Company; 257 (sailing) photo by Jim Ziv; 258–59 (background and Schnur) photos by Jim Prisching, courtesy of NU Athletic Media Services, (aerial) NU Athletic Media Services; 260–61 (team, band, and Autry) photos by Jim Prisching, courtesy of NU Athletic Media Services, (Barnett) © Marissa Roth; 264 photo by Eugene Zakusilo for *Northwestern* magazine.

Page 274 courtesy of the Library of Congress, Prints and Photographs Divsion LC-USZ62-53414-DLC.